# Inside *El Barrio*

# Inside *El Barrio*

## A Bottom-up View of Neighborhood Life in Castro's Cuba

Henry Louis Taylor, Jr.

Kumarian Press
*An Imprint of Stylus Publishing*

*Inside El Barrio*

Published in 2009 in the United States of America by Kumarian Press, 22883 Quicksilver Drive, Sterling, VA 20166 USA.

The text of this book is set in 10/12 Palatino.

Editing and book design by Joan Weber Laflamme, jml ediset.
Proofread by Beth Richards.
Index by Robert Swanson.

Printed in the United States of America by Thomson-Shore, Inc. Text printed with vegetable oil-based ink.

∞ The paper used in this publication meets the minimum requirements of the American National Standard for Information Sciences—Permanence of Paper for printed Library Materials, ANSI Z39.48–1984

---

**Library of Congress Cataloging-in-Publication Data**

Taylor, Henry Louis.
 Inside el barrio : a bottom-up view of neighborhood life in Castro's Cuba / Henry Louis Taylor, Jr.
  p. cm.
 Includes bibliographical references and index.
 ISBN 978-1-56549-281-3 (pbk. : alk. paper) — ISBN 978-1-56549-282-0 (cloth : alk. paper)
 1. Havana (Cuba)—Social conditions. 2. Havana (Cuba)—Economic conditions. 3. Cities and towns—Cuba—Havana. 4. Neighborhoods—Cuba—Havana. 5. Havana (Cuba)—History. I. Title.
  HN210.H33T39 2009
  307.3'36208694209729123—dc22

                                                                    2008047211

*Para Omar Zulueta-Cardenas*
*Y*
*mis dos Amigas*

# Contents

# Illustrations

# Preface

On July 31, 2006, I was at a fiesta in Habana Este (East Havana) with a few of my Cuban friends. We were celebrating the completion of the research on *Inside El Barrio*. The research team, which was composed of the twenty *habaneros*, who conducted all of the 398 interviews, had finished its work earlier in the week. On that Monday night some team members, their *amigos*, and I had gathered to eat, drink, and celebrate Cuban style. As we were talking and laughing, our host burst into the room. "Fidel is sick, and Raul is in control of the country," she exclaimed. We rushed into the other room, gathered around the television, and listened to the brief announcement. We all sat in stunned silence. One young *Cubano* began to weep while others sat quietly, trying to grapple with the news we had just heard. Reflectively, someone muttered, to no one in particular, "Fidel has never given power like this to anyone." The world had changed, and a new era in the history of Cuban society had been born. This event also changed the purpose of *Inside El Barrio*. The book's goal now became to provide insight into the legacy of "Castro's Cuba" by examining everyday life and culture in Havana's neighborhoods.

My journey to this historic day started in the summer of 1999, when I first came to Cuba as the co-director, with Professor José Buscaglia, of a University at Buffalo (UB) Summer Study Abroad Program. The program ended in 2004 when President George W. Bush put a stop to summer study programs on the island. As a historian and urban planner who studies distressed urban neighborhoods in the United States and does practical work in them, I was interested in the Cuban approach to community development. Moreover, as an African American scholar, I wanted to learn more about Cuban society because its racial composition and history of slavery were similar to those of the United States. I wanted to know if the neighborhood effects in vulnerable neighborhoods in Cuba were the same as in the United States. From the beginning of my Cuban journey I intended to write a book about neighborhood life and culture. Therefore, when I arrived on the island in the summer of 1999, I had already formulated a strategy for studying Cuba and carefully documenting my experiences.

Five related events significantly influenced my thinking on Cuban society. First, the Cuban government allowed the UB summer program to stay at the *Convento Santa Clara* in *Habana Vieja.* By living in a neighborhood with ordinary *habaneros,* I was able to form friendships among neighborhood residents, mostly Afro-Cubans and mulattos. They treated me as an *amigo,* rather than a *turista,* and not only took me into their homes but also into their lives. Over the years we had many frank conversations, and these friends became my cultural guides through the intricacies, complexities, and contradictions of Cuban society.

One of the most important lessons I learned was that it takes time before most *habaneros* will befriend and then speak frankly with a newcomer. Without this "frankness," it is easy for a foreigner to be misled, misinterpret conversations, and/or form a false impression of everyday life and culture. For example, many *habaneros* employ both hyperbole and humor to grapple with their day-to-day realities. Thus, a *habanero* might say, "In Cuba, we never have enough to eat." This statement cannot be interpreted literally. What is really being said is: "We cannot afford to eat the things we really want. We want to eat steak and lobster the same as the tourists." A novice might believe that Cubans genuinely do not have enough to eat or that households suffer from chronic food shortages, which is not the case. Thus, in Cuba, it is very easy for the "real" meaning of a statement to be lost in "translation." The critical point here is that conversations in Cuba often require an elaborate distilling process to filter information and unearth the hidden meanings from stories. Early on, for example, I learned the importance of using a form of "data triangulation" in conversations and informal interviews. This technique involves asking the same questions to a wide range of people and cross-checking the accounts with other forms of data in order to authenticate and better interpret the true meaning. Also, I learned how to identify "Cuban metaphors" and then to probe more deeply to gain the genuine essence of what was being said.

Second, the summer course I designed consisted of two lecture classes, one taught by myself and the other by members of the Facutad Latinoamericana de Ciencias Sociales (FLACSO) at the Universidad de la Habana. We used field trips to augment the classroom lectures. My course, "Everyday Life and Culture in Havana," focused on providing students with an interpretive framework to view the impact of international tourism on neighborhood life and culture. The other course, "Revolutionary Cuba Today," taught by members of FLACSO, was based on four interactive themes: revolution and the construction of Cuban Society; community development and everyday life and culture; women, households, and the family; and social development and community participation. A Cuban specialist taught each of the segments.

FLACSO allowed us to visit every institution and organization we desired, including the Committees for the Defense of the Revolution, the Federation of Cuban Women, primary schools, family doctors' and nurses' offices, policlinics, urban agricultural farms, offices of elected officials (*consejos populares*), workshops for the integrated development of neighborhoods, and the like. These experiences, including sitting in on every lecture given by FLACSO, provided me with a great deal of insight into the organizational and institutional structure of neighborhoods. Moreover, over the five years of the program, we traveled, along with Dr. Buscaglia's students, to every part of the island from Pinar del Rio in the west to Santiago de Cuba in the east. Visiting small towns and large cities across the island gave me the opportunity to compare life in Havana with the rest of the country. This made it possible to appreciate both the similarities and the differences of the various regions. Moreover, endless conversations with students about their experiences and insights added even more texture to my understanding of the complexities of Cuban society.

Third, I became friends with Nehanda Isoke Abiodun, a member of the African American exile community in Havana, who had been forced to flee the United States during the civil rights era. My interaction with Nehanda was important for two reasons. First, as an African American living in Cuba, she had unique insight into black life in the United States and everyday life and culture in Cuba. Our conversations greatly expanded my understanding of neighborhood life and the Afro-Cuban experience. Second, because of this friendship, I was able to meet many black, white, and Latino scholars from the United States who were doing research on various aspects of Cuban life and culture. Discussions with these scholars enriched and broadened my viewpoints as well.

Fourth, over the years I made dozens of trips to Havana and traveled throughout the metropolitan region. I have literally visited every corner of the urban metropolis and spent time socializing with the locals, visiting households, going to discos and other entertainment centers, and getting a sense of similarities and differences in everyday life and culture across communities, as well as inside specific neighborhoods. I was able to enter many places that foreigners rarely, if ever, access. Because I could pass as a Cuban, my friends could take me anywhere, as long as I spoke minimally.

Finally, my own background and training allowed me to approach this study from an interdisciplinary perspective. I am an urban historian and urban planner, and a former clinical audiologist and medical school administrator. As an urban planner, I have done research on health, wellness, and neighborhood conditions in the United States. My current work in distressed U.S. neighborhoods cuts across a range of disciplines: education, health, disaster preparedness, and sociology, along with issues of social organization and the economic and physical development of neighborhoods. This academic and professional background, combined with immersion in the life of ordinary people in Havana, has given me considerable insight into the complex interrelationships among *habaneros*, their neighborhoods, and their government. Lastly, throughout this book, with the exception of my friend Omar, I used pseudonyms rather than the real names of the *Cubanos* who participated in or were interviewed in this study.

# Acknowledgments

No one writes a book without a lot of help and support from other people, and *Inside El Barrio* is no exception. The research for *Inside El Barrio* was supported by the University at Buffalo Center for Urban Studies as part of its quest to gain insight into the problems of developing distressed urban communities. The book rests on a foundation built on the contributions of four partners. Dr. Linda McGlynn, the technical and intellectual pillar of the project, has a Ph.D. from the School of Social Welfare at the University of Albany and has her own practice. McGlynn worked with me in the design and construction of the survey questionnaires. She also designed and supervised the development of the SPSS database and analyzed the data. Moreover, Dr. McGlynn edited the many drafts of this book. Her editorial responsibilities extended far beyond simple text editing. She forced me to clarify ideas and concepts and make the book readable. Her endless interrogations forced me to think more deeply and search for ways to unleash the explosive character of the narrative. She questioned the appropriateness of illustrations and encouraged me to find ones that were more suitable. It is no exaggeration when I say this book would not have been possible without her ideas, input, and thoughtful editing.

The work of Agustín Cebreco and Mariano Fernández provided the "on the ground" support that made this project possible. They assisted in organizing the network of *Cubanos* who interviewed their friends and neighbors. They believed in this project and worked tirelessly to make it happen.

The spiritual leader of the project was my beloved friend, Omar, who was lost at sea in search of his distorted notion of the American dream. Many people might refer to Omar as a *Jinetere* (street hustler), but he was not. Omar considered himself an entrepreneur who served as a tour guide for tourists and a broker for *habaneros*. He served as my cultural guide into the intricacies of Cuban society. He taught me the ways of the "street," and made his vast social network my network.

I also owe a special debt of gratitude to members of FLACSO for their support; they shared with me their knowledge of Cuban society and critiqued my book prospectus. Thanks are also due to Nehanda Isoke Abiodun, an African American living in Cuba, who shared with me her insights into Cuban and U.S. society and commented on earlier drafts of this book. Vicente Pérez, a *babalawo,* shared with me his knowledge of *Santería* and its role in the lives of *habaneros,* and allowed me to attend sacred ceremonies. I want to particularly thank the members of the research team whose interviews undergird this book. Lastly, I would like to thank all the many *habaneros* who shared their views of Cuban society with me.

Those in the United States who helped me significantly include my friend the late Walter Hill, a senior archivist/subject area specialist for African American History, Textual Reference Division, National Archives and Records Administration. Walter helped me with data collection at the National Archives. Jennifer Sepulveda, my graduate assistant, helped with the literary searches. Sandy Sheppard, also a graduate assistant, and Ph.D. candidate in the School of Social Work, developed the SPSS database and did the preliminary data analysis. I also want to thank Dr. Eugene Maguin, a research scientist and director of data analysis, in the UB School of Social Work, who helped to solve some of the complex data-analysis problems. Kevin Lopez, a graduate student, who also produced a film on Cuban tourism, *Entre Luz y Sol,* reviewed the Spanish version of the survey questionnaires for their understandability in a Cuban context. Nasser, a close friend, who is both a Muslim and *Saterían,* shared with me his knowledge of religion. Dr. Jin-Kyu Jung developed the GIS analytical framework used in the study, while Chauncey Carter, a graduate student in architecture, produced the maps. Dr. Sam Cole, a specialist in international tourism, shared with me his knowledge of tourism in developing countries. A special thank you is also due to Ms. Heddy Koznik, a worker in my building at UB. She always made sure my office was usable and the coffee pot was clean and turned off.

I want to thank particularly Professor José Buscaglia, who not only introduced me to the world of Cuba, but also shared with me his encyclopedic knowledge of the island. Dr. Sandy Flash supported my work in the UB Cuba Study Abroad Program. Frida Ferrer, program manager and assistant at the Center for Urban Studies managed my travels to the island and helped me with all aspects of the organization and administration of the project, and Jeffrey Kujawa, assistant director of the center, helped with the processing of the paperwork required for my numerous trips to Cuba. Finally, I want to thank my family—Aunt Thelma, Lorraine, Keeanga, Carol, Cinque, Jacques, Jasmine, Allanah, and little A.J.—for their ongoing support.

# Abbreviations and Acronyms

| | |
|---|---|
| ANAP | National Association of Small Farmers (Asociación Nacional de Agricultores Pequeños) |
| CDRs | Committees for the Defense of the Revolution (Comités para la Defensa de la Revolución) |
| CMEA | Council of Mutual Economic Assistance |
| CTC | Confederation of Cuban Workers (Confederación de Trabajadores de Cubano) |
| ELAM | Latin American School of Medicine (Escuela Latinoamericana de Medicina) |
| FEEM | Federation of Intermediate Level Students (Federación de Estudiantes de Enseñanza Media) |
| FEU | Federation of University Students (Federación de Estudiantes Universitarios) |
| FLACSO | Facutad Latinoamericana de Ciencias Sociales |
| FMC | Federation of Cuban Women (Federación de Mujeres Cubanas) |
| GDIC | Group for the Integral Development of the Capital (Grupo para el Desarrollo Integral de la Capital) |
| GIS | Geographic Information System |
| IFRC | International Federation of the Red Cross and Red Crescent Societies |
| INTUR | National Institute of the Tourism Industry (Instituto Nacional de la Industria Turísta) |
| NGO | nongovernmental organization |
| OPJM | Organization of Jose Martí Pioneers (Organización de Pioneros Jose Martí) |

| | |
|---|---|
| PNR | National Revolutionary Police Force (Policia Nacional Revolucionario) |
| PRC | Cuban Revolutionary Party (Partido Revolucionario Cubana) |
| UJC | Union of Young Communists |
| UNDP | United Nations Development Program |
| UNESCO | United Nations Educational, Scientific and Cultural Organization |

# Inside *El Barrio*

# PROLOGUE

In February 2008, Raul Castro assumed the reins as president of Cuba, ending the rule of *El Comandante* after almost five decades. After defying ten U.S. presidents for over forty-nine years, and becoming a legendary hero among third-world nations, the "bearded one" had finally stepped down, but only on his terms and only after he had successfully implemented a succession plan that ensured the old guard would be left firmly in power, thus ensuring his legacy. On reflection, the Age of Castro's Cuba actually came to an end nineteen months earlier, in the summer of 2006, when Fidel provisionally turned over power to his brother Raul. At that moment, as Fidel temporarily ceded authority, Raul moved forward with his plans to refashion society within the context of Cuban socialism. Thus, that fateful day in 2006 actually marked the beginning of the post-Castro era and the commencement of a new period in Cuban life, now under the guidance of Raul Castro.

*Inside El Barrio* seeks to gain insight into the legacy of Fidel Castro by bringing to light the importance of households, neighborhoods, and residential development in Havana between 1989 and 2006, the final and most complex period in the Age of Castro's Cuba. This book focuses on a study of Cuban households and neighborhoods during the era dubbed *El Período Especial* (the Special Period). The abrupt collapse of the Soviet Union and the East European Communist bloc in 1989 plunged Cuba into a catastrophic economic crisis, which spawned unprecedented hardship, magnified social tensions, and resulted in thousands of *Cubanos* fleeing the island. In July 1990, a somber Fidel Castro proclaimed that Cuba was in a Special Period in a time of peace and called upon the masses to be prepared for a sustained period of hard times.

*Inside El Barrio* aims to acquire deeper understanding of Cuban society by exploring what it means to live in a people-centered nation by examining the role of households and neighborhoods in mitigating hard times *and* helping residents to grapple with the complexities of urban life, particularly during *El Período Especial*. The book argues that because households are embedded in neighborhoods, and neighborhoods shape everyday life and culture, understanding the

1

interrelationship between the two is central to learning how *Cubanos* manage daily life. With the collapse of the Soviet Union and the re-emergence of international tourism, it is the stable, hyper-organized neighborhoods that have anchored Cuban society. Investigating how they operate will aid in understanding the sustainability of Castro's Cuba by showing how this society operates "on the ground," in vulnerable neighborhoods, where ordinary people live, work, play, and raise their families. The household and neighborhood experiences of Havana residents are not predicted to be identical to the experiences of those in other Cuban cities. However, because the ideological perspective of the leadership, the planning, and the types of organizational and institutional frameworks are all consistent throughout the island, many aspects of the Havana experience will mirror those found in other urban centers. Consequently, the Havana narrative can provide insight into neighborhood life and culture throughout the island.

## The Conceptual Framework

*Inside El Barrio* employs a conceptual framework informed by five interrelated themes. First, the book fashions a "bottom-up" understanding of city and neighborhood life by examining the outlook of ordinary people, especially Afro-Cubans and mulattos. The goal is to give voice to their perspective and to gain an understanding of the values and beliefs that inform their actions. While Cuba's ideology and official viewpoints are well known, very little is known about the views of the *clases populares*. Telling the story of people who have few written records, and who rarely make their public views known, is best accomplished using a case-study methodology. The idea is to create a small theater of investigation, based on an inquiry into neighborhood life, utilizing field work, participant observation, formal and informal interviews, and other approaches designed to interrogate the "unwritten" records.

Second, *Inside El Barrio* situates neighborhood life and culture within the broader context of metropolitan development. Neighborhoods do not exist independent of the metropolitan regions of which they are a part. Consequently, neighborhood development is directly affected by city building and metropolitan development, and this process is always informed by the ideological perspective of urban leaders. The nature of the built environment, the hierarchy of neighborhood, and the distribution of the population across geographic space are dictated by the ideological biases of the dominant social groups. The development of the city, therefore, is not driven by the "natural forces" of urbanism, but by the world view of its leaders and the political economy undergirding society. This interpretive framework suggests that the city-building and metropolitan-development processes differ in elite-centered and people-centered societies. By placing Cuban neighborhood development within this broader context, we will deepen our understanding of what it means to live in a people-centered socialist city.

Third, *Inside El Barrio* uses the neighborhood as a scheme of conceptualization for understanding and explaining everyday life and culture in Havana.[1] In this framework *neighborhood* is conceived as a "catalytic place" where an interactive relationship exists among people, the physical environment, social organizations, community institutions, and the government, rather than being the mere site of everyday life and culture. Thus, people act on the neighborhood place and the neighborhood place acts on people. This is why the "neighborhood effects" literature reasons that neighborhoods matter in the production of socioeconomic outcomes.[2] Based on a neighborhood's nature and character, it will either increase or decrease the risk of its residents to various social, economic, cultural, and health issues. This is why neighborhood matters in the city- and metropolitan-building process.

Fourth, this book uses a public policy framework to understand the choices and decisions made by the Cuban government in its quest to build the city and the nation. Ideology and problem definition dictate the type of policies that are formulated to resolve issues. The goal is to understand problems and solutions from a Cuban perspective by seeing how the government defined problems and then formulated the policies necessary to address them.

Fifth, and last, *Inside El Barrio* argues that an ideological duality has existed in Cuban society since the Ten Years' War, between 1868 and 1878. This duality emerged between the *clases económicas* (economic classes) and *clases populares* (popular classes) over the goals of the revolution and the type of society that should be built after the war. This ideological duality has persisted over time and continued to fuel the tensions between the *clases económicas* and the *clases populares* throughout the Republican and Revolutionary eras in Cuban history.

*Clases económicas* and *clases populares* were commonly used terms in nineteenth-century Cuba for the elites and popular sectors respectively. In this study the first term is employed to capture a broad range of elites (planters, property owners, merchants, business persons, bankers, railroad magnates, professionals, and some intellectuals). The popular classes include small farmers, peasants, blacks, mulattos, urban workers, students, and some intellectuals. Obviously, these are dynamic categories, and members in these categories change over time, but their relation to the economy and their basic ideological viewpoints remain essentially the same.

## Why Havana?

There are many reasons that can be used to justify a case study of Havana. It is the capital city and the largest and most important urban center in Cuba. After the 1959 Revolution, because of government focus on rural development, Havana experienced decades of under-investment in buildings and infrastructure. Following the abrupt collapse of the Soviet Union, however, the city became the centerpiece in a quest to use international tourism as the engine to drive economic development. Thus, Havana became the model of efforts to re-imagine and reinvent the city and the nation, with all the problems and contradictions inherent in such a transformation. It became the quintessential laboratory in the mission to use capitalism to save socialism. Havana is thus an ideal site for investigating how households, neighborhoods, and residential development affected the evolution of the city between 1989 and 2006, the final and most complex period in the Age of Castro's Cuba.

## Method and Data

Unpacking the rich, complex, and multilayered story of everyday life and culture in Havana's neighborhoods required an innovative research design that went beyond a single methodology.[3] Therefore, *Inside El Barrio* used a multi-methodological approach that incorporated ethnographic fieldwork, historiography, spatial analysis (geographic information system), oral interviews, survey research, and a synthesis of the secondary literature.

Research on this project extended over a seven-year period, from the summer of 1999 to December 2006, and moved through two distinct periods of investigation. During the first period, between 1999 and the summer of 2004, to gain insight into the complexity of street life and varied aspects of neighborhood life, culture, and institutional development, the participant-observation method of ethnographic fieldwork was employed along with digital photoanalysis and the informal interviewing of various heads of the Committees for the Defense of the Revolution (CDRs), the Federation of Cuban Women, and physicians at several family doctors' and nurses' clinics and policlinics.

These visits and informal interviews took place as part of the activities associated with a university study-abroad program. During this period data was gathered on the physical and social characteristics of neighborhoods, including the relationships among neighborhoods across the metropolis. In conducting informal interviews, open-ended questions were asked about various aspects of Cuban life and culture, including the operation and function of various organizations and institutions. All discussions and impressions were duly recorded, with the entire process being facilitated by the use of a digital recorder.

The digital photoanalysis was carried out in a systematic fashion, with some excursions taken to examine life and culture in various neighborhoods, while at other times photo sessions focused on discrete topics such as transportation, clothing, housing, architecture, tourist activities, and the like. Both still photographs and videos were utilized in these data-gathering activities. Later, a content analysis was made of all photos and videos.

The second period of research took place between the fall of 2004 and December 2006. During this period, the Geographic Information System (GIS) was used to study patterns of land use and the institutional development of neighborhoods, including the interrelationships among communities. A detailed spatial analysis was specifically made of the San Isidro neighborhood to study the dynamics of social and institutional processes operative at the neighborhood level. Traditional historical methods were also used to study manuscript collections at the U.S. Library of Congress and the U.S. National Archives. The goal was to understand the historic dimensions of U.S. policy toward Cuba and the U.S. rationale for intervening in Cuba's war against Spain. Lastly, during 2005 and 2006, surveys of 398 households in thirty neighborhoods across the metropolis were completed.

## The Survey Research Strategy

To gain insight into the perspective of *habaneros* on neighborhood life and culture, education, the family and doctor program, and disaster preparation, 398 surveys were distributed and completed using the snowball sampling technique to select the sample population.[4] The survey was conducted without any formal approval or authorization from the Cuban government. This was deliberate in order to reduce the risk of any form of censorship inhibiting the project or influencing either those interviewed or those doing the interviewing. Using relationships developed during the years of the university study-abroad program and building on these, a research team composed of twenty *habaneros* was organized; the team members subsequently conducted interviews with a variety of their neighbors, acquaintances, and friends. All of the researchers lived in the most vulnerable neighborhoods of the city, and most had only a high-school diploma or some technical training, though there was one lawyer and one schoolteacher on the research team. The level of neighborhood occupational diversity as well as the highly skilled work force, made it possible to assemble this unique type of research team.

Four of the interviewers were selected to serve as team captains. Their responsibility was to recruit other researchers and to train and oversee their work. They, in turn, recruited people they knew and trusted. These individuals were then trained and several proxy interviews were held to ensure their mastery of proper interviewing techniques. The team captains, in turn, trained the interviewers operating under their direction. Using this approach, 398 interviews were conducted in thirty Havana neighborhoods. The interviews were with household heads, and the sample was biased toward the most vulnerable neighborhoods in the city. This was purposeful as well in order to obtain the perspectives of those who lived in the city's most troubled communities, based on the assumption that one can gain insight into a city's soul by examining the experiences of those "farthest down" in the metropolis. Finally, both the confidentiality and anonymity of all involved, both interviewers and interviewees, were guaranteed, with participants being assured that no identifying information would be made available to anyone.

At the operational level, the Spanish translation of the questionnaires was double checked to ensure comprehension in the Cuban context. After the initial translation of the surveys, Kevin Lopez, a University of Buffalo Latino graduate student familiar with "Cuban Spanish" again checked the Spanish translation and wording of the questionnaires. Once in Havana, Cuban team captains also checked the translations and wording of the questionnaires. At each benchmark in the survey process, questionnaires were reviewed with the team captains. Questions and responses were continually evaluated to check for any answers or other evidence that would indicate interviewee misunderstandings or which might impinge on the validity or reliability of the responses. The team captains also recorded and discussed anecdotal information about the surveys, adding any concerns or questions the respondents offered in addition to the set questions.

All the interviewers were compensated for their participation in the project. Rather than pay them based on a fee-per-interview basis, a set fee was paid for their time. This was done to remove the pressure to complete interviews, possibly in a rushed manner, in order to be reimbursed. Only those people who expressed a commitment to the project were selected to participate as interviewers, and transactions were based on the Cuban principles of trust and reciprocity. The approach was quite successful, with the team completing 398 interviews. The interviewers had a range of ideological perspectives. Some were highly supportive of the government, others were not, and still others were not concerned about politics at all. Nonetheless, they all believed that the project was important and wanted to be a part of an effort that would allow the voices of ordinary people to be heard.

SPSS was utilized to manage and analyze the survey data. Sandy Sheppard was responsible for building the extensive database from the surveys, operating under the direction of the author and Dr. Linda McGlynn, who has extensive experience using the SPSS statistical package. The data analysis was carried out by the associate who supervised the construction of the database. Dr. Eugene Maguin was called on whenever we encountered complex data-analysis problems.

## Overview of the Chapters

*Inside El Barrio* consists of five chapters and an epilogue. The first chapter provides a prologue to the 1959 Revolution and explores three interrelated themes. First, it discusses the evolution of an ideological duality between the *clases económicas* and the *clases populares* as *Cubanos* struggled for their independence against Spain. Second, it outlines the process by which the U.S. military government incorporated the *clases económicas* into a governing system based on an alliance between the Cuban government and the U.S. business community. Last, the chapter argues that the Cuban revolution, launched in 1868, was never really finished because U.S. intervention thwarted its goals.

Chapter 2 outlines the *rebelde's* quest to remake the capitalist city in the image of the *clases populares*. It shows the central role played by ideology in the city building and metropolitan development process by outlining the *rebelde's* desire to transform the elite-centered city into a popular-centered one. Chapter 3 shifts to a focus on neighborhood and community development. It examines the philosophical foundation of Cuba's unique approach to community development and the forces that gave birth to the hyper-stable and hyper-organized neighborhoods that anchored Cuban society. It concludes with an analysis of residents' perceptions of primary education, the family doctor and nurse program, and disaster preparedness.

Chapter 4 is a case study of the San Isidro neighborhood in Habana Vieja. By examining the interplay among primary schools, the family doctor and nurse programs, the *consejos populares* and other institutions within a neighborhood context, this chapter illustrates how the operation of neighborhood life and culture lowers residents' risks to a host of socioeconomic problems, as well as helping them survive the city during hard times. Chapter 5 takes a close look at how *habaneros* made ends meet during the complexities of *El Período Especial*. It places this struggle within the context of the reemergence of international tourism and development of "consumerism" among *habaneros*. The Epilogue offers a reflection on the findings of the study and comments on the current situation facing Cuba today.

# 1

# THE UNFINISHED REVOLUTION

Ideological Dualism
and Establishing Ties of Singular Intimacy

The relentless late-nineteenth-century struggles for national liberation formed and fashioned much of the indomitable spirit of the Cuban people. Between 1868 and 1898 *Cubanos* fought against Spain in the Ten Years' War (1868–78), the Little War (1879–80), and the War of Independence (1895–98). Although active fighting stopped after the Little War ended in 1880, José Martí, Antonio Maceo, and other leaders of the insurgency continued to work tirelessly, preparing for the 1895 War of Independence. Then, in April 1898, the United States intervened and transformed that war into the Spanish-Cuban-American War. Thus, a continuous state of conflict existed in Cuba for more than thirty years. The Spaniards thought the greatness of their nation hinged on retaining Cuba as the crown jewel of their colonial empire, while *Cubanos* viewed the revolution in terms of *independencia o muerte* (independence or death). This intransigence caused the insurgency to become one of the bloodiest and most destructive revolutions in the Americas. When the years of warfare finally ended in 1898, the economy and country lay in ruins.

## Emergence of the Ideological Duality within Cuba Libre

At the onset of the struggle, an ideological duality emerged between the *clases económicas* and the *clases populares* based on differences over the goals of the revolution and the type of society that should exist in the post-independence era. The views of the *clases económicas* and the *clases populares* did not remain static but continued to evolve and develop over time. As the ideological differences crystallized, they transformed the Cuban struggle for independence into

9

a revolution characterized by a double consciousness—a duality featuring two warring souls vying for supremacy, two conflicting notions of revolution and freedom, two different views of the place of blacks and mulattos in Cuban society, and two irreconcilable visions of the type of society that *Cubanos* should build after independence.

The ideological split began to surface during the Ten Years' War. Before 1868, white fear of black rebellion was the basis of the *creole* elites' rapprochement with Spain. The Haitian Revolution (1791–1804) had demonstrated that slave rebellions could readily evolve into struggles for national liberation. Cuban planters worried that a war of independence against Spain might turn into a race war and result in the eventual establishment of a black republic. At the same time, the upheaval and subsequent devastation of the Haitian sugar industry had enabled Cuba to dominate the world's sugar market. Thus, planters continued to expand the sugar industry dramatically, and by mid-century Cuba was the world's leading producer of sugar.

This expansion necessitated the importation of thousands of slaves, thus transforming the island's population. By 1850 the enslaved and free people of color constituted the majority of the inhabitants of Cuba. The elites believed that Afro-Cubans, if not watched closely, would seek revenge by killing white men, raping white women, and creating havoc across Cuba and the entire Caribbean. This fear reinforced conservatism and caused the *clases económicas* to handle virtually all grievances against Spain within the existing colonial framework.

During the 1860s the tension between Spain and Cuba continued to grow and produced a radical element that was no longer primarily concerned with the likelihood of Cuba becoming another Haiti. These planter rebels had concluded that a successful revolution needed to incorporate not only the rich and literate, but also the "ignorant, the peasant, the cigar maker, (and) the freedman." This broad movement also had to include the slaves whose "numbers" were necessary to defeat the Spanish.[1]

Among the radical elites was Carlos Manual de Céspedes, a planter from the eastern province of Oriente, where the effects of the economic crisis were harshest and the contrast with the prosperous western region starkest. In this region landowners had less capital with which to develop their plantations, had smaller land holdings, and continued to rely primarily on animal power. The fragile nature of the eastern plantation system meant that aggressive forms of taxation and economic downturns had a much greater impact (see Map 1–1).

With this context in mind, on October 10, 1868, an angry Céspedes assembled the slaves on his small sugar plantation at Yara Village and freed them. Calling the now former slaves "citizens," he exhorted them to join with him and other planters in an insurrection to liberate Cuba from Spain. This was the *El Grito de Yara* (The Shout at Yara) that not only marked the beginning of the Ten Years' War, but also represented the clarion call that led to the establishment of a multiracial army to carry out the revolution against Spain.

The moment Céspedes invited slaves and free blacks along with white peasants, small farmers, and urban workers to join the insurrection, he opened up a Pandora's box that allowed conflicting beliefs about the revolution and the future of Cuba to emerge and crystalize into a true ideological duality. Despite the intensity of these differences, they did not shatter the unity within Cuba Libre. The ultimate goal of liberating Cuba from Spain was more important to *Cubanos* than any differences that existed in how this was to be accomplished.

**Map 1–1.    Cuba in 1899**

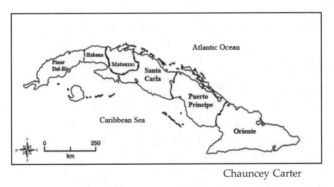

Chauncey Carter

## The Duality Part One: The *Clases Económicas*

The *clases económicas* wanted a revolution in order to oust Spain and establish an independent society based on a close relationship with the United States, one that might eventually even include annexation. Regardless, after independence was achieved, most planters believed that Cuba needed to develop intimate ties with the United States. Plantation society was a hierarchical social system composed of the *latifundia* (large sugar estate) and subordinate social classes, and the elites wanted to sustain that way of life by establishing a republic that gave them power and control over the *clases populares*. To achieve this goal, they needed the United States to provide markets for Cuban sugar and tobacco and to buttress their authority.

To the *clases económicas*, freeing slaves to participate in the insurrection had nothing to do with racial equality. To these elites, Afro-Cubans were cannon fodder for the revolution and unreliable allies who might turn Cuba Libre into a war to establish a black republic. Concurrently, the elites did not trust blacks and mulattos because they believed Afro-Cubans had their own racialized, political agenda. Consequently, throughout the struggle with Spain, the elites tried to control Afro-Cubans and limit their influence and power in the insurgency. For example, at critical junctures they refused to provide blacks and mulattos with needed guns and ammunition.

During the Ten Years' War, because they were afraid of alienating powerful members of the planter class, the elites kept the Liberation Army and black *mambises* (Cuban guerrilla fighters) from invading the central and western provinces, strongholds of the sugar plantation system.

At the same time, to U.S. officials they portrayed blacks and mulattos as docile, obedient, and faithful to whites, with a subservient destiny in independent Cuba. For example, Bartolomé Masó, president of the Cuban provisional government in 1897, said:

> Our Negroes . . . are most uneducated laborers, quite unfitted [sic] for holding positions. They will have the citizen rights, as given in the United States, and with sufficient employment will give no trouble. The population of Cuba is composed of one-third colored, either mulatto or Negro. Yet, some gravely predict Cuba's future as a second Hayti [sic] or Liberia—a Negro republic. This idea is manifestly absurd. Cuba is much underpopulated, and one of our first measures will be to induce a restricted immigration of those likely to assist in developing our immense resources. Our Negroes will work as before in the cane fields, and I see no reason to anticipate trouble from them. We have no colored officials in this government, and very few of our officers are black, *though the slaves we freed by the last war are fighting faithfully in this.* (emphasis added)[2]

### The Duality Part Two: Beliefs of the *Clases Populares*

The *clases populares*, especially Afro-Cubans, had a different vision of the revolution and their destiny in an independent Cuba. Although these groups left few written records, if we take their actions, community narratives, institutional and community-building activities as a guide, we can gain insight into their views of the revolution and the type of society they hoped to build after independence. The members of the *clases populares* had no false consciousness. They knew where to draw the line between equality and fair treatment, injustice, and exploitation. Those Afro-Cubans who joined the insurgency were not fighting to develop a more paternalistic slave system or to replace the Spanish ruling elite with a propertied *creole* elite. Rather, a dream of racial equality and social justice fueled their participation in the multiracial Cuban Liberation Army *(el Ejército Liberación)*. In this sense, despite its many imperfections, the Liberation Army represented a prototype of the society they hoped to build. Within the army Cubans of color occupied positions of prominence, prestige, and power; they made up an estimated 40 percent of the senior commissioned ranks.

The emergence of powerful black and mulatto military leaders, such as Antonio Maceo and his brother José, Flor Crombet, Guillermón Moncada, Agustín Cebreco, Quintín Banderas, and Jesús Rabi demonstrated that Afro-Cubans could rise to positions of power within the military based on merit and ability. According to Bernabé Boza, Máximo Gómez's chief of staff, "Here nobody cares about the color of a man, but about his talents and his self-respect."[3] The Afro-Cuban general Agustín Cebreco echoed the theme: "Here we are putting the principles of democracy into practice, because the hazards of war purify and unify, and will enrich our people who despite everything tend to the better."

Likewise, white peasants and small-farm owners also longed for a republic based on equality and socioeconomic justice. Their world changed dramatically after 1879 when a worldwide industrial revolution combined with the rise of the beet-sugar industry to trigger a reorganization and modernization of the Cuban sugar industry. This process created great hardship for peasants and small farmers. To survive in the highly competitive nineteenth-century world sugar market, Cuban sugar producers had to reach two interrelated goals. First, they had to increase the output of sugar as well as significantly lower its price. The producers achieved this goal by developing the large-scale central factory system of production *(centrales)* and by expanding the cultivation of sugar through the expropriation of *hacienda comunera* (communal lands) along with the holdings of peasants and small farmers. This process of land concentration allowed the planters to achieve their second goal in assembling a cheap labor force. The cane cutters usually worked for only three or four months a year. They had to fend for themselves the other seven or eight months. In addition, the typical *centrales* of the 1890s controlled many aspects of the workers' lives, including the general store where the laborers bought supplies, the hotels, houses, barracks, either permanent or temporary, the barbershop, the butcher, the drugstore, and sometimes even the gaming house or brothel. The destruction of the foundation of subsistence agriculture combined with displacement to transform peasants and small farmers into wage earners forced to labor on the *latifundia*.

This radical transformation of the countryside resulted in a social environment that fused the goals and aspirations of the rural popular classes, both Afro-Cubans and white. By turning many small farmers and peasants into agricultural workers, by forcing others to become "social" bandits, and by turning still others into beggars and vagrants trying to survive in urban areas, the elites unwittingly created a common set of experiences that strengthened the bonds of racial and class unity among the *clases populares*. According to Louis A. Pérez, what developed in Cuba was a type of outlawry similar to that which Eric Hobsbawm has described as social banditry—lawlessness as social protest. Social bandits gained support from farmers and peasants— many of whom were driven from their lands by the planters' expansion of their sugar *latifundias*. In this evolving social world, as Rebecca Scott points out in her study of the sugar district of Cienfuegos, many forms of cross-racial interaction occurred in the work place, public spaces, and in the expanding integrated residential settlements that reinforced these fraternal bonds.

Like their rural counterparts, the action of urban workers suggests that their views on equality and justice fed an ideology that countered the social ideals of the *clases económicas*. The radicalization of the labor movement, the establishment of mutual-aid societies, schools, cultural and recreational centers, workers associations and unions, and the growing popularity of consumer and producer cooperatives among the working class reflected this counter ideology. For example, in January 1879, approximately two hundred cigar workers formed the first cooperative in Cuba, La Reguladorea, which established a popular lodging and eating house in downtown Havana. Artisans in the western provinces also established food co-ops, cigar and cigarette producer co-ops, as well as co-ops to build homes for their members.

These activities suggest that the popular classes had a moral vision of society based on justice and the socioeconomic principles of reciprocity and the equitable distribution of wealth. According to James C. Scott, these same principles served as the foundation of socioeconomic justice among Southeast Asian peasants. Scott defines reciprocity as the equitable distribution of goods and services based on a fair exchange for labor and services, while equitable wealth distribution refers to the right of community members to a standard of living consistent with the strength of the local economy. On the other hand, exploitation and injustice existed if society distributed wealth too unevenly and if some individuals or groups benefited unfairly from the efforts of others.[4]

Historian Aline Helg argues that the socioeconomic principles outlined by James C. Scott were applicable to urban and rural Afro-Cubans, along with white peasants, small farmers, agricultural laborers, and white urban workers. Their way of life, based on *La hacienda comunera*, subsistence farming, cooperatives, and mutual-aid societies, reflected a moral vision based on reciprocity and the equitable distribution of wealth. This moral vision of society was reflected in expressions such as "pedimos lo que nos toca por razón" (we demand what we rightly deserve) and "merecemos justicia . . . como justa remuneración de [nuestros] sacrificios por la independencia y la libertad de Cuba" (we deserve justice . . . as a just reward for [our] sacrifices for the independence and freedom of Cuba).

Lastly, white members of the *clases populares* did not share the *clases económicas'* racial antipathy to Afro-Cubans. An example of this is the Afro-Cuban support of the establishment of all-white Abakuás in the 1830s. For whites to become members of this secret organization they had to adopt and practice African cultural elements preserved by the Abakuá. The struggles of Afro-Cuban peasants, small farmers, and agricultural workers strengthened the bonds of racial and class unity among the rural popular classes, while the activities of Afro-Cubans in the urban trades combined with their daily interactions with white workers to produce racial and class unity within the late-nineteenth-century labor movement.

James W. Steele, a U.S. traveler in Cuba in 1880, commented on the nature of race relations in a Havana working-class neighborhood: "I do not mean to say there is no social distinction against him. He lives and has his pleasures apart, but he is not shunned, hated, driven from enjoyment of public resorts and occupations because he is black. *Nor is the man who chooses to associate with him, as many do more or less*, abandoned, shunned and forsaken on that account." (emphasis added)[5] Historian Philip A. Howard suggests that Steel's observations reflected the desires of working-class whites and blacks for economic advancement and political and social equality with the dominant white classes of the island. This does not mean that racism did not exist among the popular classes. Rather, it is to argue that their racial views differed significantly from those of the *clases económicas* and that the former supported the idea of building a society based on racial and socioeconomic justice while the latter did not.

Both Martí and Céspedes believed that the insurgency needed to build a multiracial coalition to defeat the Spanish, the difference being that Martí elaborated a powerful ideology that advocated racial fraternity. The Ten Years' War, he believed, had transformed Cuba into a land where struggle erased racial distinctions, leaving only Cubans. In *Our America* Martí challenged the validity of racial concepts by asserting, "There is no racial hatred, because there are no races." He believed that race was a tool invented by the elites to justify expansion and empire and to divide the anticolonial movement. Martí argued that racial bigotry was a "sin against humanity"; thus he made racial equality the foundation of Cuba Libre. Martí's credo of racial unity found receptivity among the popular classes, but it never resonated among the elites. They accepted the doctrine *una republic cordial, con todos y para todas* (a cordial republic with all and for all) for pragmatic reasons, but they never embraced the ideal of an independent Cuba built on racial and socioeconomic justice.

## Tension and Conflict within Cuba Libre

While the ideological duality did not destroy Cuba Libre, its impact was detrimental. The differing ideologies continually vied with each other for supremacy within the revolution. Between the Ten Years' War and the Cuban War of Independence in 1895, profound changes in property relations and production modes, along with fluctuations in social groups, commercial ties, and political loyalties combined with market failures and the inadequacy of colonial reforms initiated after the Pact of Zanjón to generate hardship and turmoil throughout Cuba. As discontent spread, the social composition of the liberation movement shifted and conditions were ultimately fashioned that made it possible for the ideological perspective of the *clases populares* to gain sway in Cuba Libre.

During the 1880s the interplay of diminishing markets, falling prices, rising taxes, and increased operating costs forced many sugar planters and ancillary businesses into bankruptcy. By the mid-1880s, Cuba was in a depression. In the first three months of 1884, financial losses from business failures totaled approximately seven million dollars. Historically, cigar production had provided employment for thousands of agricultural and urban workers, especially in the two western provinces of Havana and Pinar del Rio. By the early 1890s the decline of cigar exports caused thirty-five thousand cigar makers to lose their jobs, with the remainder reduced to part-time work. Conditions in the Cuban countryside were even more desperate. The abolition of slavery in 1886 further complicated the situation by adding thousands of new workers to the labor force during a time when *latifundismo* (land concentration) was turning thousands of farmers and peasants into agricultural wage earners, vagrants, beggars, and social bandits.

This deteriorating socioeconomic environment caused many *Cubanos*, black and white, to seek emigration as a solution to their economic problems. Thousands from across the race and class divide fled to Europe, Latin America, and the United States. Many of the workers immigrating to the United States settled in Key West, Tampa, Ocala, and Jacksonville and found jobs in the newly expanding cigar factories. By the 1890s the transformation of Cuban society caused the popular classes to believe that their socioeconomic problems stemmed as much from the economic activities of the creole elites as from the injustices of Spanish colonialism.

This caused the goal of political separation from Spain to mutate into an independence movement based on populism and the radical reconstruction of the prevailing social order. This vision of Cuba Libre was ambiguous and imprecise. The popular classes spoke in terms of hopes, dreams, and aspirations rather than of programs, institutions, and governing structures. Nonetheless, on the eve of the Cuban War of Independence, the social, economic, political, and racial discontent of the popular classes had spawned a powerful movement for socioeconomic change.

In this context of transition, change, and turmoil, José Martí rose to become the most influential exponent of Cuban independence. To defeat the Spanish, Martí believed that Cuba Libre needed to establish a revolutionary party that would give the movement ideological substance along with an organizational structure and institutional framework. Toward this end he established the Cuban Revolutionary Party (PRC) in 1892 and developed a program based on socioeconomic justice and racial equality and the ideals of reciprocity and equitable distribution of wealth. To gain support among the popular classes, Martí focused on labor issues while condemning social injustice and racism. At the same time, his argument that labor reform could circumvent class struggle cemented his relationship with the *clases económicas* as well.

Most important, Martí believed the United States posed a greater threat to Cuban independence than Spain. He was forceful and blunt in his warnings. In an unfinished letter, written just before his death on May 19, 1895, Martí wrote: "It is my duty . . . to prevent, through the independence of Cuba, the USA from spreading over the West Indies and falling with added weight upon other lands of Our America. All I have done up to now and shall do hereafter is to that end. . . . I know the Monster, because I have lived in its lair—and my weapon is only the slingshot of David."

## The Cuban War of Independence: 1895–1898

The *clases populares* dominated Cuba Libre when Cuba launched its War of Independence in February 1895, and José Martí and Antonio Maceo were the watchdogs of their ideological perspective. Martí made the ideological views of the popular classes the dominant force in Cuba Libre, while Maceo was the ideology's guardian on the ground, where the *clases económicas* constantly threatened it. After their deaths in 1895 and 1896, the elites seized control over Cuba Libre. To strengthen their power over the revolution, the elites initiated a purification campaign to purge the Liberation Army of its leaders from the popular classes, especially Afro-Cubans. Although bravery and military achievements still led to promotions in combat units, the new demand for education accelerated the removal of blacks, mulattos, and other members of the *clases populares* from the army's officer corps.

A similar process took place in the provisional government. The new assembly of representatives, elected in October 1897, did not have a single Afro-Cuban member. Instead, it consisted of "men of refinement," many of whom were graduates of colleges in the United States. The administrative leaders of the provisional government were all white as well. Bartolomé Masó replaced Cisneros as president. Máximo Gómez was reelected general-in-chief, while Antonio Maceo's position of lieutenant general went to Calixto García. Tomás Estada Palma remained the Cuban diplomatic representative delegate in the United States.

The War of Independence lost some momentum after Maceo's death but regained it by the end of 1897. The agony of battle, disease, and malnutrition combined with tropical heat to sap the will of the Spanish army to fight. Faced with defeat, the new liberal ministry of Práxedes Mateo Sagasta, in a last-ditch effort to save the colony and end the war, initiated a series of colonial reforms to appease the *Cubanos*, including the granting of home rule. This plan failed. Spain miscalculated the Cuban people's desire for independence, and the appeasement scheme emboldened, rather than pacified, the Cubanos.

The leaders of Cuba Libre indeed perceived the appeasement effort as a sign of weakness. They rejected the Spanish offer of home rule and reaffirmed their credo of *independecia o muerto* (independence or death). In December 1897, Estrada Palma informed the U.S. State Department that colonial reforms were not an acceptable basis for the cessation of hostilities. "As the representative of the Cubans in arms, and under their instructions, it is my duty to announce that nothing short of absolute independence will be accepted by us as the basis of peace. . . . We will never lay down our arms until we have freed ourselves from the sovereignty of Spain." Buoyant Cubans felt that the defeat of Spain was imminent. In January 1898 a confident Máximo Gómez reported from the field that "the enemy is crushed and in complete retreat from here, and the time which favored their operations passes without them doing anything."

## The United States Intervention and Occupation

Officials in the United States followed events in Cuba with growing dread and alarm. In late 1897, Secretary of State John Sherman said, "Spain will lose Cuba. That seems to me to be certain." The success of the rebellion created a crisis for the McKinley administration. For decades, U.S. opposition to Cuban independence influenced policy formulation on the island. From the time of Thomas Jefferson's first administration in 1801, the United States mused over the possibility of possessing Cuba.[6] It said the island, situated as it was at the entrance to the Gulf of Mexico and the Caribbean basin, could serve as a bulwark of defense in U.S. hands.

Commercially, the island's location made it literally an extension of the southern United States plantation and agricultural region, and a place of potentially lucrative investment and trade (see Map 1–2). Thus, geopolitical and economic interests tied the United States to Cuba. For these reasons the United States wanted to integrate the island into the North American union, and until this could be achieved, the goal was to keep Cuba from falling under the sway of any foreign power other than Spain.

The United States embedded its Cuba policy within the framework of the Monroe Doctrine, according to which the United States proclaimed that European powers could no longer colonize or interfere with the affairs of nations in the Western hemisphere. Implicit in this policy was the expectation that colonies in the Americas would fall under the influence of the United States when they severed ties with the mother country. The theory of political gravity, formulated by John Quincy Adams, formed the basis for this "ripe fruit" (*la fruta madura*) policy. Adams argued that there were laws of political gravity as well as laws of physical gravity. Just as ripe fruit blown from a tree cannot help but fall to the ground, so too will Cuba gravitate toward the United States when Spain loses its grip on the island.[7] The impending success of the Cuban revolution now threatened everything. Unless the United States could find a way to intervene and take control of the war, as well as the later peace process, Cuba might be lost forever.

Accomplishing this task would not be a simple one. Although the McKinley administration did not favor Cuban independence, many U.S. citizens and members of Congress did. During 1895, when Grover Cleveland was still president, the Cuban delegation to the United States (the Junta, as people called them) waged a highly successful campaign to win broad-based support for U.S. recognition of Cuban belligerency rights. This issue was important because recognition of belligerency rights meant that the United States viewed Cuba as a de facto state waging a legal war against Spain. According to international law, a legal war exists only if the conflict is between two political bodies or states, even if one is a de facto nation. To meet fully the test of de facto statehood, the state must have a provisional government with an army, which observes the basic rules of "civilized" warfare, operating under its leadership.

**Map 1–2:    Cuba in Relationship to North America and the Caribbean Basin**

The Junta believed that recognition of belligerency rights was a matter of great strategic importance. Minimally, it meant that the United States viewed the combatants as members of a *de facto* state, "entitled to all the privileges of honorable warfare and capable of fulfilling neutral obligations." Such recognition, the Junta believed, would facilitate the securing of loans and the purchasing of guns and ammunition, all of which would be needed to hasten Spain's military defeat.

The Junta's promotional campaign was highly successful. In 1896 the U.S. Senate and the House of Representatives passed resolutions affirming Cuba's right to independence. Grover Cleveland vehemently opposed the resolutions. While reaffirming his support of Spanish sovereignty over Cuba, he stressed that the interests of the United States differed from and took precedence over the interests of both Cuba and Spain. The president argued that Cuba was not a *de facto* state and not ready for self-government.[8]

Then, for the first time, Cleveland issued a stern warning to Spain. The war was getting out of hand. Now, it was threatening U.S. interests. The Spanish needed to understand that under no circumstances would the United States stand by and watch Cuba reduced to "utter ruin." Therefore, Spain must end this struggle or suffer the consequences. William McKinley adopted this policy when he took office in 1897. During the first year of his administration, the crisis worsened. In December the Cubans rejected the Spanish peace compromise that included the right to home rule.

The insurgents' rejection of the peace offering made it clear that Spain was losing control of the island. Combined with *Cubanos'* successes on the battlefield, congressional supporters of Cuba Libre were much encouraged. On January 19, 1898, in the House of Representatives, Ferdinand Brucker of Michigan proposed a resolution supporting Cuban belligerency; however, the McKinley administration succeeded in keeping Congress from voting on the resolution. Despite the executive's attempts to thwart progress toward Cuban independence, the House and Senate continued to debate the issue passionately.

Congressional debates notwithstanding, time was running out for McKinley. It was late spring, and the Spanish army was weakening and growing increasingly desperate. Meanwhile, a confident Cuban army patiently waited for the rainy season, and summer, when the intense tropical heat would become its greatest ally. When that moment arrived, the Cubans planned to launch their final offensive. Most observers, inside both the United States and Cuba, believed the Spanish would be defeated before the end of September 1898. Consequently, if McKinley could not settle the conflict during the spring, then Cuba might be lost forever. Deeply concerned, the president worked tirelessly to find a solution "by which Spain can part with Cuba without loss of self-respect and with certainty of American control."

This, however, did not come to pass. The Cubans wanted absolute and complete independence, nothing less. By early spring McKinley had only two options: accept Cuban independence or intervene in the conflict. Cuban independence was not an option for the president. This left intervention as the only viable choice, and on April 11, 1898, in a message to Congress, McKinley outlined a "neutral" intervention strategy. This line of action made no mention of recognizing the Cuban provisional government or the right to independence. Intervening in the war as a "neutral" gave the United States not only the power to lead the war against Spain, but also the ability to control the peace process and establish a "stable" Cuban government after the war.

Simply put, "neutral" intervention meant the United States would not only usurp the role of the Cuban army as liberators but would also assume the power "to secure in the island the establishment of a stable government, capable of maintaining order and observing its international obligations, insuring peace and tranquility and the security of its citizens as well as our own, and to use the military and naval forces of the United States as may be necessary for these purposes."[9]

The Cuban delegation denounced McKinley's proposal. Horatio S. Rubens, the Junta's chief legal counsel in New York, released a statement warning the U.S. government that Cuba would treat any intervention that recognized neither the provisional government nor the Liberation Army as a declaration of war. Rubens asserted that if the United States did "seek to extend its authority over the government of Cuba and the army of liberation, we would resist with force of arms as bitterly and tenaciously as we have fought the armies of Spain."[10]

McKinley's decision to intervene in the war, combined with the opposition of the Cubans, forced congressional supporters of Cuba Libre to alter their strategy. The question of recognizing belligerency rights was now a moot issue. Pro-independence congressional representatives now tried to shape the language in the joint resolution that outlined the parameters of the war against Spain. Their main objective was to incorporate recognition of the Cuban provisional government and the island's right to independence in this document. This, they felt, would protect Cuba from annexation or colonization. The Senate passed the amendment, 42 to 35, on April 19, 1898, and the House concurred the same day, 311 to 6. President McKinley signed the joint resolution on April 20, 1898, and the ultimatum was forwarded to Spain. Thus, after a bitter debate, Congress finally compromised and agreed to forgo its demand for recognition of Cuban independence in exchange for an amendment that would keep the United States from turning the island into a U.S. colony.[11]

Senator Henry M. Teller of Colorado, with input from Senators David Turpie of Indiana and Joseph B. Foraker of Ohio, proposed what would become Article 4, which came to be known as the Teller Amendment. It proclaimed, in essence, "that the United States hereby disclaims any disposition or intention to exercise sovereignty, juris-diction, or control over said island except for pacification thereof, and asserts its determination, when that is accomplished, to leave the gov-ernment and control of the island to its people."

The Teller Amendment allayed Cuban suspicions of possible an-nexation or recolonization by the United States and persuaded the Cubans that any U.S. intervention would be consistent with their goal to establish an independent Cuba. With the roadblocks to war removed, the McKinley administration moved forward with its in-tervention strategy. On May 1, 1898, ten days after the signing of the joint resolution, the Spanish-Cuban-American War began. Less than three months later, on August 12, the "splendid little war" ended.

## Establishing Ties of Singular Intimacy

U.S. intervention in the Cuban War of Independence gave the United States authority to control both the war and the peace pro-cess. The Treaty of Paris, signed by Spain and the United States on December 10, 1898, in Paris, France, gave the United States the right to occupy Cuba with a temporary military government for the pur-pose of stabilizing the island, establishing an independent republic, and formulating a treaty to determine the future relationship between the two countries. This occupation lasted from January 1, 1899, to May 20, 1902.

Although the joint resolution and the Treaty of Paris gave the United States power to establish a "stable" government in Cuba, by pledg-ing that the United States would leave the island as soon as the paci-fication process was complete, the Teller Amendment protected Cuba from colonization. Congress also passed the Foraker Amendment as a rider to the Army Appropriations Bill in February 1899 to further protect the island from exploitation by U.S. business interests. This amendment prohibited the U.S. military from granting franchises or concessions for railroads, streetcar lines, or electric lights to U.S. busi-nesses during the military occupation. Although the Teller and Foraker amendments did prevent the United States from annexing or colo-nizing Cuba, they did not stop the government from transforming the island into a dependent republic.

## The Military Government

The task of transforming Cuba from a Spanish colony into a de-pendency of the United States became the responsibility of the U.S.

Military Government, which took control of the island on January 1, 1899. The McKinley administration constructed a policy framework to guide the activities of the Military Government during the occupancy. Although no blueprint existed, the president knew exactly what he wanted to accomplish before the United States transferred sovereignty to Cuba. McKinley told Major General John R. Brooke, in a December 22, 1898, confidential letter, that the United States would remain in Cuba until "the people have established a firm and stable government."[12] During his 1899 message to Congress, McKinley clarified what he actually meant by a stable government:

> This nation has assumed before the world a grave responsibility for the future good government in Cuba. . . . The new Cuba yet to arise from the ashes of the past needs to be bound to us by ties of singular intimacy and strength if its enduring welfare is to be assured. Whether these ties shall be organic or conventional, the destinies of Cuba are in some rightful form and manner irrevocably linked with our own.[13]

General Leonard Wood, who replaced Brooke as military governor of Cuba on December 13, 1899, further developed McKinley's definition of a "stable" government.[14] He defined "ties of singular intimacy" and "stability" wholly in terms of "business confidence" in Cuba. "When people ask me what we mean by a stable government in Cuba," Wood clarified in 1900, "I tell them when money can be borrowed at a reasonable rate of interest and when capital is willing to invest in the island, a condition of stability will have been reached."[15]

Wood was talking about investments by U.S. business interests, not entrepreneurs from European countries. Thus, by "stable" government, the McKinley administration meant restructuring Cuban society so that it was economically compatible to that of the United States. This meant infusing Cuba with notions of "liberal developmentalism" and forming a governance structure imbued with laws and policies that facilitated U.S. investment, trade, and economic development. In addition, reconstructing Cuban society along these economic lines meant constructing a physical environment that facilitated business development, immigration, and settlement by U.S. entrepreneurs, professionals, and workers.

Underpinning liberal developmentalism was the belief that the U.S. market-based economic system was superior to other economic systems. From this perspective, nations should desire to replicate the U.S. approach and develop democratic governments that support it. Thus, the notions of building a stable government with ties of singular intimacy to the United States meant turning Cuba into a "republic modeled closely upon the lines of our great Anglo-Saxon republic."[16]

## Finding Cuban Collaborators

The belief that *Cubanos* were inferior people incapable of self-government informed Wood's approach to developing a stable government in Cuba. "We are dealing with a race that has steadily been going down for a hundred years, and into which we have to infuse new life, new principles, and new methods of doing things," Wood wrote to McKinley shortly after taking office.[17] Nonetheless, Wood knew he would have to locate *Cubanos* who were willing to become collaborators with the United States in order to succeed in turning Cuba into a U.S. dependency (by *collaborator* I mean those *Cubanos* who were willing to subordinate Cuban national interests to the interests of the United States for their own personal gain). Wood believed that he could find such collaborators among the "better class" of Cubans. However, before achieving this goal, the military governor would first have to devitalize the *independentista* ideal and disempower the *clases populares*.

*Independentista*, the passionate desire for freedom among the popular classes, represented the most formidable challenge to U.S. hegemony. Therefore, the United States had to weaken the independence movement, which involved first disbanding the Liberation Army and then neutralizing the potential political power of the *clases populares*, especially Afro-Cubans. After the war, General-in-Chief Máximo Gómez told his commanders to maintain the army until further notice. Although the socioeconomic conditions of the rebel veterans grew increasingly desperate, Gómez was unwilling to disband the army until there was a clarification of the military status of the North Americans.

Tensions between the National Assembly and the United States deepened as the Military Government took formal control over the island. Meanwhile, in central Cuba, illness, malnutrition, and death from starvation had become common throughout the insurgent camps, and an increasingly despondent and alienated Gómez lacked the resources to relieve the distress. These conditions also led to a deterioration of his relationship with the Cuban National Assembly. In late December 1898, frustrated with the failure of the National Assembly to get relief for the army, Gómez appealed directly to Washington for assistance, and the McKinley administration responded quickly. It hoped to weaken oppositional forces inside Cuba by working with Gómez to disband the Liberation Army. Robert Percival Porter,

McKinley's special commissioner to Cuba, became the administration's chief negotiator. He assured the general that the United States would help mitigate the conditions of his troops and that they would leave the island once the pacification campaign was complete. Convinced by Porter, Gómez accepted three million dollars to help his soldiers return to civilian life and to facilitate the dissolution of the Liberation Army.[18]

Gómez's acceptance of the money without prior authorization from the National Assembly triggered a crisis within the Cuban insurgent leadership. The National Assembly rebuked the general and then ousted him for insubordination. The *clases populares* responded angrily by holding rallies, mass demonstrations, and public processions that protested Gómez's expulsion. The constant attacks and erosion of popular support led to the National Assembly's demise. In early March it dissolved, leaving the McKinley administration with a dramatic victory. The North Americans effort to coopt Gómez led not only to the disbanding of the rebel army, but also to the downfall of the National Assembly.

Weakening the potential political power of the *clases populares* represented the second step in the effort to devitalize *independentista*. Wood believed helping the "better classes" gain political power was key to institutionalizing U.S. influence on the island. This group, like the North Americans, opposed Cuban independence and believed the island's future lay in establishing close socioeconomic ties with the United States. "The men whom I had hoped to see take leadership," said Wood in December 1900, "have been forced into the background by the absolutely irresponsible and unreliable element. . . . The class to whom we must look for stable government in Cuba are not as yet sufficiently well represented to give us that security and confidence which we desire."[19]

Against this backdrop, the politics and passion of the popular classes were great concerns to both Wood and to the McKinley administration. The "ignorant masses, unruly rabble and trouble makers—the element absolutely without any conception of its responsibilities or duties as citizens," General Wood warned, are "the only people who are howling for [independence]." Limiting suffrage was one way to decrease their influence. Unless curtailed, Wood argued, this "unruly rabble" would use the ballot box to thwart U.S. power and hegemony. Liberal suffrage "would be fatal to the interests of Cuba and would destroy the standing and influence among all thinking people in the island," Wood reiterated in a February 1900 letter to Elihu Root. Wood also warned Root that unlimited suffrage would seriously undermine the economic development of Cuba: "I believe that if it were known to be a fact that we were going to give universal suffrage it would stop investments and advancement in the island to the extent which would be disastrous in its results."[20]

The McKinley administration decided to pursue a policy of "limited suffrage" to thwart the popular classes' aspirations. Paradoxically, Wood, Root, and McKinley planned to use "democracy" to maintain control over the popular classes. By restricting the right to vote, Root said they could keep the "mass of ignorant and incompetent" *Cubanos* from participating in the establishment of the republic. At the same time, limited suffrage would help them promote the "conservative and thoughtful control of Cuba by Cubans" and avoid the perpetual revolutions characteristic of Central America and the West Indies.

In early 1900 the United States undertook a census of the island to assist in developing the guidelines for limited suffrage. The final provisions required voters to be able to read and write or to own real or personal property worth $250. The results were telling. By Root's calculations, two-thirds of all adult Cuban males were excluded from the franchise. Suffrage restrictions reduced the electorate to approximately 105,000 males, 5 percent of the total population. To avoid alienating most army veterans, who did not qualify based on these requirements, Wood formulated a "soldier clause" that allowed all veterans to vote. Even so, the suffrage requirements had a devastating impact on Afro-Cubans. According to the 1900 census, about 74 percent of Afro-Cuban males (compared to 47 percent of white males) could not read, which meant that they could not vote.[21] Most significant, limited suffrage muted the voice of Afro-Cubans in the municipal elections, where the selection of representatives to the constitutional convention took place (see Table 1–1).

**Table 1–1.** **Afro-Cubans as a Percentage of the Population of Municipalities**

| Municipality | Number | % Afro-Cuban |
|---|---|---|
| Havana | 425,000 | 25 |
| City of Havana | 236,000 | 27 |
| Mantanzas | 203,000 | 24 |
| Pinar del Rio | 173,000 | 38 |
| Puerto Principe | 88,000 | 18 |
| Santa Clara | 357,000 | 30 |
| Sanitago | 327,000 | 45 |
| Cuba | 1,573,00 | 32 |

War Department, Report on the Census of Cuba, 1899
Government Printing Office, 1900

After the National Assembly dissolved, the Liberation Army disbanded, politically neutralizing the *clases populares*. Leonard Wood moved forward with the plan to collaborate with the "better classes," who were natural allies of the North Americans. Most had traveled to or studied in the United States. They celebrated U.S. capitalism, and their racial views mirrored the views of the North Americans. Moreover, most elites believed their survival now depended on having a positive relationship with the United States. The wars with Spain devastated the Cuban economy and left many elites in ruin and without access to the capital needed to revive their damaged estates or to pay off loans. Therefore, they needed to secure jobs and opportunities for economic advance from the North Americans. Simultaneously, after the war, thousands of Cuban expatriates began returning to the island in search of positions in the rapidly expanding bureaucracy. Many of these exiles were U.S. citizens with bilingual skills and insights into both Cuban and U.S. culture, which made them invaluable to the United States.

## Creating the Governance Structure: Connecting Cuban Elites and U.S. Businesses

The United States did not plan to use the elites simply as political surrogates or puppets in a dependent republic. Rather, they wanted to incorporate them into a governing system based on an alliance between the Cuban government and the U.S. business community. Business and economic development would be the "ties of singular intimacy" that would bind Cuba to the United States. The U.S. goal was not only the political ascendancy of the "better classes," but also their incorporation into U.S. business firms operating in Cuba. The resulting relationship would merge the interests of Cuban elites with U.S. business interests and the U.S. government. Such an interactive relationship would spawn a governing regime capable of influencing and promulgating laws and public policies favorable to U.S. business investment and trade inside Cuba. To make this happen, U.S. corporations used economic rewards to incentivize cooperation among bureaucrats and the Cuban government.

In this study the concept *governance regime* refers to an alliance among politicians, bureaucrats, policymakers, and an array of businesspersons concerned with trade, investment, and other issues that promote economic development. In Cuba, the alliance was concerned primarily with the development of a political agenda, including the promulgation of laws and policies that favor U.S. economic and cultural penetration of Cuba. Although the precise makeup and the character of this business-state governance alliance varied over time, it remained a central feature of Cuban political life from 1903 to the 1959 Revolution.

Leonard Wood, thus, expanded his definition of a stable government to include positive, interactive relationships between the Cuban government and U.S. business interests. He based his goal of establishing ties of singular intimacy between Cuba and the United States on the use of direct U.S. investments, along with the utilization of U.S. business networks, to bind together the Cuban government and U.S. business community.[22] Wood believed that such ties would lead to Cuban stability and prosperity and allow the country to grow along the lines of a modern corporate state. However, before Wood could reach this goal, he and his entrepreneurial cohorts had to solve two problems. First, he had to circumvent the Foraker Amendment, so that U.S. companies could invest in Cuba. Second, once in Cuba, U.S. companies needed to develop a system of incorporating Cuban elites into their ranks and of imbuing them with U.S. corporate culture.[23]

## The Cuba Company

A close examination of the activities of the Cuba Company provides insight into how Wood and U.S. business interests created a Cuban governing regime based on interlocking relationships with U.S. corporations. The Cuba Company was not only the largest single investor in Cuba during the first two decades of the twentieth century, but it also became a model of the type of business-government alliance that would shape the Cuban governance system.

When the military occupation began, the Cuban economy needed to be reconstructed and redeveloped. U.S. entrepreneurs viewed Cuba as an ideal site for investment. The *clases económicas* lacked the capital to develop the island's resources, land was inexpensive, and a largely jobless and impoverished population constituted a cheap source of labor. The public-service sector also offered great opportunities. The need for streetlights in Havana and other cities; the pressure to repair and build aqueducts and sewage systems; the desire for improved transportation; the need for schoolbooks, desks, pencils, and the like— all these represented lucrative opportunities for potential investments.

The uncertainty of Cuba's postwar political environment did not concern U.S. entrepreneurs. No matter what destiny held for the island, business leaders believed that Cuba would remain attached to

the United States, and this optimism was sufficient for them. The eastern provinces, where the revolution had originated, looked particularly tempting. Less developed than the western half of the country,
the provinces of Camagüey and Oriente had abundant resources, a
good portion of which were yet to be exploited. These were territo-
ries filled with vegetation, dense forests, and virgin soil. Oriente, in
particular, had rich mineral deposits, which started attracting U.S.
metallurgical companies in the 1890s. The landownership structure
still reflected a communal and subsistence-based society. The boundaries of many of the large estates were inexact, and the property rights
of the occupants were tied to complicated formulas. All of this made
legal enforcement of land claims difficult, and these circumstances
encouraged and greatly facilitated the acquisition of Cuban lands by
U.S. investors.

Concurrently, Leonard Wood believed that the undeveloped nature of the eastern provinces thwarted his ability to gain political and
military control of Cuba and represented a barrier to the island's economic development. He thought that the construction of a railway
across the island would solve this problem by opening up the eastern
provinces and stimulating economic development throughout the
entire country. William H. Carlson, special commissioner of railroads
for the island, in a 1900 report to Wood wrote that the establishment
of a central railroad that penetrated the eastern provinces would be

> the greatest and grandest enterprise which is before the people
> of Cuba today, and it will do more good for the people and the
> material interests of the island than any other enterprise which
> is now being carried on in Cuba. In addition to helping to bring
> about a better railroad service, lower rates, and quick transpor-
> tation, it will develop a region of virgin land of the greatest rich-
> ness, which is now covered by extensive forests of valuable
> hardwood. These lands will be transformed into plantations,
> orange groves, and happy homes of industrious people who
> will settle along its route.[24]

Robert Percival Porter, whom McKinley sent to Cuba to report on
its industrial, commercial, and financial conditions, echoed these
views:

> No revolution could have existed in Cuba if such a railroad had
> been completed by the former government, and nothing will so
> rapidly tend to the revival of commercial and general business
> as the facility for quick passage from one end of the Island to
> the other. . . . All political turbulence will be quieted thereby

and prevented in the future. The entire country will be open to commerce; lands now of practically no value, and unproductive, will be worked; the seaport towns will become active and commerce between the island and the United States will soon be restored to the former figures.[25]

Porter went on to say that such a railway would stimulate economic development by creating links to shipping ports on both coasts, and he believed, along with Wood, that building a central railroad was one of the Military Government's most urgent tasks. This is where William Van Horne, the U.S. railroad builder, enters the story. His interests ran parallel to those of Wood and Porter. As president of the Canadian Pacific Railroad, Van Horne had constructed the world's longest and most expensive railroad. Like Wood, Carlson, and Porter, he believed the building of a central railroad line that traversed the island was key to Cuba's economic development. Toward this end, he wanted to build a 350-mile railroad that would extend from the end of the United Railways of Havana at Santa Clara to Santiago, the eastern port of Cuba. Before moving forward with this project, Van Horne discussed the idea with President McKinley, who promised to help in any way possible. With that guarantee, Van Horne founded the Cuba Company on April 25, 1900, in Jersey City, New Jersey.

The Foraker Amendment, which prohibited the Military Government from granting any franchises or concessions as long as the island was occupied, was the biggest obstacle now facing Wood and Van Horne. As the highest ranking U.S. authority in Cuba, Wood was responsible for enforcing the Foraker Amendment. Although an ardent supporter of the railroad project, he wanted to move with caution because of the complexities involved in circumventing the amendment. To this end he sought the counsel of Elihu Root, who was a corporate lawyer prior to becoming secretary of war.

In a letter of December 22, 1900, Wood wrote:

I do not think that it is contrary to the letter or spirit of the Foraker resolution since the State is not making any concessions. . . . I think, nevertheless, that this business deserves to be thought through and definitely concluded. If there are objections it is better to have them now than later. . . . I think that the matter is of great importance to the island and I would like to finish the work if at all possible.

While Wood was consulting with Root, Van Horne and his lawyers developed a stratagem base on "revocable licenses." These would be licenses that did not provide the recipient with any permanent rights and could be revoked at any time. For example, when the new government of Cuba was inaugurated, it would have the power to revoke the permit. Consequently, the "revocable license," because it did not provide the holder with interminable rights, in actuality did not violate the Foraker Amendment. That is, Wood and Van Horne believed that providing the Cuba Company with a revocable license would enable them to build a railroad traversing the island because the license was not a permanent franchise or concession.

Not only did this loophole allow Wood and Van Horne to circumvent the Foraker Amendment, but Wood became so fond of this proposition that he expanded its use to include virtually all businesses wanting to establish operations in Cuba. Through its use he ultimately granted hundreds of franchises, permits, and other concessions to mining companies, sugar mills, and real-estate firms, particularly in Camagüey and Oriente. Wood also used revocable permits to carry out massive infrastructure and other public-works projects.[26]

## Building the Business-Government Alliance

Successfully circumventing the Foraker Amendment meant that Van Horne could move forward with the central railroad project. Crucial to his corporate model was the incorporation of *Cubanos* into the business by using a "collaboration" stratagem based on hiring and retaining them at all levels of the company, especially in the ranks of middle management (engineers, accountants, and corporate lawyers) and executives. Van Horne believed that for the company to be successful, it needed elites with knowledge and understanding of Cuban culture, as well as contacts and connections with other members of the *clases económicas*.

To strengthen the attachment of these elites to the company, as well as to give them a stake in its growth and development, Van Horne provided them with opportunities to own stock in subsidiaries. Stock ownership also gave the corporation a cadre of Cubans who could argue on its behalf in nationalist terms. Within this scheme, Van Horne not only employed Cubans in the firm, but also hired them as consultants and advisers to work on problems and issues confronting the company. This strategy of employing elite Cubans, as well as hiring them as consultants, facilitated the corporation's ability to build an informal business network based on relationships with elite Cubans, including politicians, government bureaucrats, professionals, and businesspersons.

Van Horne believed the building of this informal network was key to developing a profitable and influential corporation in Cuba. The underlying principle was to establish lasting relationships between elite *Cubanos* and the Cuba Company based on mutual interests, economic gain, and unquestioned loyalty. The fundamental goal was for the corporation to replace *patria* as the focal point of allegiance and commitment among elite *Cubanos*. Van Horne wanted these elites to view the growth and development of the Cuba Company as central to the growth and development of Cuban society, as well as their personal pathway to individual success and prosperity. This would enable elites to rationalize easily the placement of the corporation's interests above those of Cuba as a whole. Thus, Wood's strategy for establishing a "stable" government in Cuba nicely complemented Van Horne's strategy for building the Cuba Company.

Wood believed that empowering the "better classes" was a critical component in the goal of creating a stable government in Cuba. The strategic plan was to prepare Cubans for self-government through participation in municipal elections, governmental administration under U.S. supervision, and the holding of a constitutional convention to set up Cuba's government and to frame its future relations with the U.S. government.

Wood pursued a twofold strategy to promote the political ascendancy of the "better classes" and to shape the outcomes of the constitutional convention. First, he appointed prominent Cubans, recommended to him by other members of the *clases económicas*, to important governmental and administrative posts throughout the country. Whenever possible, these appointees were U.S.-educated *Cubanos* who desired close relations with the United States. Wood outlined this approach while still governor of the Santiago Province:

> The policy in all appointments has been to gather together the most prominent and reliable men, present to them the situation, explain what appointments I wish to make, and then to call on them for recommendations, impressing on them the fact that a failure to recommend good men will result in a loss of confidence on my part, and be disastrous in the end to their cause.[27]

Using this approach, Wood named José Ramón Villalón, an U.S.-educated engineer, as secretary of public works, and Enrique José Varona, who had been exiled in New York, as secretary of education. Other prominent Cubans were appointed to key posts within the insular government, which handled civil affairs in Cuba, including the administration of provincial and municipal governments. Second,

Wood worked tirelessly to get the "better classes" elected to public office in municipal government and as delegates to the Constitutional Convention.

Wood believed the election of elites to the Constitutional Convention was extremely important because this body would play a decisive role in shaping the Cuban republic and its future relations with the United States. In a pre-election report to McKinley, he mused, "I have seen most of the prominent men, using every effort to have them send the best and ablest men to the Constitutional Convention without consideration to political parties. Some of the men nominated are excellent, others are bad. I hope, however, that the latter will be defeated."

The Wood and Van Horne stratagems continued to work in tandem. The placement of prominent Cubans in positions of power facilitated the passage and promulgation of laws and policies that helped the Cuba Company circumvent the Foraker Amendment. Cuban lawyers provided the expertise and insight into Spanish law and Cuban jurisprudence, while U.S. lawyers provided the U.S. railroad law perspective. Wood also worked with Van Horne to generate Cuban legislation that not only facilitated the development of the Cuba Company, but also allowed the railroad company to circumvent the revocable-license restraint. For example, Wood allowed the railroad giant to reframe Cuba's railroad legislation. After developing a draft modeled on Canada's railroad policy, which was reviewed by experts from the U.S. Interstate Commerce Commission, Wood and his associates drafted the railroad law for Cuba. Significantly, Chapter 11, Section 3, of the General Railroad Provision made it possible for the Cuba Company to secure an "irrevocable permit," which took effect when U.S. occupation ended.

Given the importance of the Constitutional Convention in shaping Cuba's future, Van Horne wanted to ensure that advocates for the company's interests were present at the convention. The company arranged with Horatio Rubens, a former counsel to the Cuban Revolutionary Party in New York, to serve as its attorney and representative at the convention. In addition, Van Horne secretly hired Rafael Manduley and Gonzalo de Quesada, two wealthy Cuban lawyers, to serve as delegates and further protect the Cuba Company's interests at the Constitutional Convention.

Despite all of this activity, Van Horne was not worried about his company's future in Cuba. He knew that the United States was attempting to impose the Platt Amendment, which would govern future Cuban-U.S. relations. Article 4 of this amendment was made to order for the Cuba Company. It mandated: "That all acts of the United States in Cuba during its military occupation thereof are ratified and validated, and all lawful rights acquired thereunder shall be maintained and protected." The Platt Amendment, by making it impossible for the Cuban republic to rescind or overturn any decision made by the Military Government, secured the future of the Cuba Company.

This meant that the new republic could now no longer void any of the so-called revocable permits issued by the Military Government during the occupation. Wood and Van Horne had cleverly used the revocable-permit concept to bypass the Foraker Amendment, and then used the Platt Amendment to circumvent the constraints imposed by the revocable permits. Simply put, Wood and Van Horne maneuvered around the barriers imposed by Congress to protect Cuba from economic exploitation to validate and solidify U.S. business interests. This deception did not go unnoticed by the advocates of Cuba Libre. José Lacret Morlot, a general in the Liberation Army as well as a delegate to the Constitutional Convention, declared in an insightful letter to the editor of the influential Havana daily *La Lucha*, "The companies that are not legitimate will be legitimized by the Platt Amendment, which tramples on legality."

However, the enduring relationship between the Cuba Company and its associates made its business network particularly effective. In Cuba, the elites migrated back and forth between public and private life. Over time, this meant that the Cuba Company always had friends in positions of power and influence to assist the corporation. For example, José Miguel Gómez, the provincial governor and a businessman who had close contacts with the company during its early years, became president of Cuba in 1909. Later, after returning to private life, he became a sugar-cane supplier to the Cuba Company's mills. Mario G. Menocal, a sugar-mill manager with a close relationship with the Cuba Company, became president of Cuba in 1913. A vice-president of the Cuba Company, Domingo A. Gáldos, later became a senator, while José Tarafa, a major shareholder, officer, and director of the Cuba Company, also became a senator.

The experiences of the Cuba Company were duplicated by other U.S. corporations operating in Cuba. While the specific strategies of each firm varied, the most successful ones built vibrant informal business networks that used Cuban elites to link their corporations to both the government and the Cuban professional class. In this environment the U.S. business firm replaced *patria* as the focal point of the elites' loyalty and allegiance. Together, these varied business networks produced a tangled web of relationships based on an alliance between U.S. business interests and the Cuban government. This alliance formed a governance regime that influenced the promulgation of laws and the shaping and implementation of policies favorable to

U.S. corporations. This governing regime made it possible for U.S. businesses to assume a leading role in transforming and developing Cuban society.

Through their domination of the economy, U.S. business interests and government reduced Cuba to dependency on the United States. Between 1896 and 1914, U.S. business investments grew from $50 million to $215 million, and U.S. business became the primary source of jobs and opportunities on the island. By 1925, the United States completely dominated the Cuban economy, especially the sugar industry, where the United States owned 41 percent of all mills and controlled 60 percent of the harvest, which totaled $750 million.

At this juncture, while Wood had succeeded in establishing a stable government in Cuba, he was deeply concerned about the sustainability of this government. He feared that the *clases económicas* would not be able to retain power once the United States dissolved the Military Government. Although greatly weakened, the idea of Cuba Libre and the forces of *independentista* were still strong. Within this context Wood and Elihu Root believed the United States needed a fail-safe device to protect U.S. interests and keep the "better classes" in power. Again, the Platt Amendment served as that device.

Enacted into law by the Congress in February, it was the final component needed to protect U.S. interests after the occupation ended. The Platt Amendment limited Cuba's capacity to function as an independent republic by restricting the island's ability to enter treaty relations with other nations, by imposing debt restrictions, and by prohibiting the cession of national territory to any foreign power except the United States. In essence, the amendment made Cuba a nonfactor in the international arena and restricted its reciprocal relations almost exclusively to the United States. Most significant, the Platt Amendment made permanent any actions taken by the Military Government during the occupation and gave the United States "the right to intervene for the preservation of Cuban independence."

## The Unfinished Revolution

The fragility of the "better classes" notwithstanding, the United States was able to achieve hegemony over Cuban society because of the creation of strong links between the Cuban elites and the U.S. business interests during the military occupation. The resulting governance regime facilitated U.S. investment in the island and the continued development of laws and policies that favored investment and trade by the U.S. business community. Yet, Cuba never became the model Anglo-Saxon republic Wood envisioned. The North Americans were never able to imbue Cuba with the core values and beliefs of a modern capitalist state. The *clases económicas* did not grasp fully the liberal development ideal, nor did they succeed in creating an institutional framework or a social and cultural order that supported a modern corporate state.

Two structural issues lay at the center of the problem. First, as U.S. business interests gained control over the Cuban economy, they virtually eliminated their Cuban competition. Reduced primarily to middle-management positions and to the margins of business development, politics became one of the few places where Cuban elites enjoyed a competitive edge over the North Americans. In a Cuban society dominated by U.S. capital, the government became the primary means through which most *Cubanos* could acquire wealth and power. As a result, bribery and corruption became characteristic features of the new republic.

Second, the policies enacted by the U.S. Military Government turned the Cuban economy into a monoculture dominated by the sugar industry. The land reforms instituted by Wood made it possible for U.S. corporations to seize huge tracts of land, which they used for sugar production. Sugar-centered development, in turn, established the fundamental logic of Cuban politics and society. *Sin azucar, no hay país* (without sugar, there is no nation), as José Manuel Casanova of the Sugar Mill Owners Association frequently said, became the nation's credo. The centrality of sugar production reinforced a vicious cycle: without sugar, there was no Cuba, and there was no sugar without the U.S. market. Trade reciprocity—preferential tariff treatment for Cuban sugar in the United States in exchange for reduced customs duties on U.S. exports to Cuba—reinforced the monoculture and prevented economic diversification by favoring sugar at the expense of developing other products.

Sugar production, in turn, spawned economic exploitation. The sugar industry depended on seasonal labor and controlled the most fertile land. Sugar production required both high levels of structural unemployment and the concentration of land, which undermined the subsistence and small farming economy. During the non-growing season, thousands of sugar workers huddled in urban centers, struggling to make ends meet. The domination of Cuban society by the sugar industry also reinforced dependency on the United States, curtailed economic growth, restrained standards of living, institutionalized economic exploitation, and thwarted the struggle for racial and socioeconomic justice.

On May 20, 1902, the United States recognized Cuban independence and transferred power to the newly elected president, Tomás Estrada Palma. "As president of the Republic of Cuba," Estrada Palma said, "I hereby receive the Government of the Island of Cuba which you transfer to me in compliance with the orders communicated to you by the President of the United States and take note that by this act the military occupation of Cuba ceases." A coalescence of interests between nascent U.S. imperialism and the hopes and aspirations of the *clases económicas* made this day possible. Yet, the Platt Amendment cast its shadow across the island. It not only gave the United States the right to intervene with military force should events on the island seem dangerous to U.S. interests, but also the right to lease land for a naval base on Cuban soil. Such a military base would provide the North Americans with a permanent location on Cuban territory.

The Platt Amendment combined with the creation of a "collaborative" relationship between the Cuban "better classes" and U.S. business interests facilated the transition of the island from a Spanish colony to a dependency of the United States. In this sense, the establishment of the Cuban Republic in 1902 represented a triumph of the *clases económicas* over the *clases populares.* This triumph, however, did not put an end to the struggle between the popular classes and the economic classes, and their North American allies. The struggles spawned by the ideological divide within Cuba Libre would persist over time.

This was the case because the revolution launched by *El Grito de Yara* was unfinished. Building a society based on the principles of reciprocity, the equitable distribution of wealth, and socioeconomic justice remained a dream deferred. Consequently, these ideals would continue to fuel the twentieth-century struggles against dependency and U.S. hegemony, just as they forged the tenor of the nineteenth-century struggle for independence from Spain.

# 2

# THIS TIME THE REVOLUTION
# IS FOR REAL

"This time the revolution is for real!" proclaimed Fidel Castro upon entering Santiago de Cuba on January 1, 1959. Marching through the towns and villages, from Santiago to Havana, Fidel called upon Cuba to purify itself and prosper. Crowds roared "Viva," applauded, and flung bouquets when they were finally able to catch a glimpse of Castro and his *barbudos* (bearded ones). "This time the revolution is for real" meant that Fidel and the *rebeldes* intended to finish the revolution started by their forebears in 1868. They would fulfill the *mambises'* dream of building a society based on the principles of reciprocity, the equitable distribution of wealth, and racial and socioeconomic justice.

Building such a society would not be easy. An exuberant Fidel repeatedly cautioned the crowds: "This is going to be a year of work. We had a quieter life in the hills than we are going to have from now on. Now we are going to *purify* this country" (emphasis added).[1] This meant that the *rebeldes* intended to remake Cuba in the image of the popular classes. In his 1953 defense before the Batista government's magistrate, later published as *History Will Absolve Me*, Fidel Castro outlined his program for a reconstructed Cuban society: "The problem of land tenure, the problem of industrialization, the problem of housing, the problem of unemployment, the problem of education and the problem of health care; we have here six concrete points to which our efforts will be directed, with resolve."

The revolution imbued Cuban society with a new logic, and the interests of the popular classes were now at the center of national development. Thus, at the core of the *rebeldes* program was the goal of improving the living standard and quality of life for all *Cubanos*, especially peasants, the unemployed, seasonal sugar and domestic workers, and those laboring in the informal sector. In this quest to create a new society, Castro not only wanted to reconstruct the physical and social environment but also to create a new culture to inform everyday life; while the *rebeldes* had a general program in mind, they did not possess a blueprint to frame this endeavor. Thus, re-creating society in the image of the popular classes would require intelligence, creativity, determination, and patience.[2]

When the Revolution triumphed on January 1, 1959, Havana was a "capitalist" city that dominated an underdeveloped island. The typical features of underdevelopment characterized Cuba: unemployment, weak industrialization, a deficient infrastructure, low technology, and poor educational and health indicators. All of these characteristics were evident in Cuba's towns and cities as well as in the capital city of Havana. The most striking feature of Cuba at this time was the bipolar geographic schism that existed between rural and urban development. As a consequence, the *rebeldes* initially placed their greatest emphasis on rural development, and this was the context within which efforts to remake the city in the image of the popular classes took place.

## Rebuilding the City in the Image of the Popular Classes

When the *rebeldes* seized power, they inherited urban centers with a capitalist-built environment that reflected the architecture, property development, land-use structure, and spatial organization of Colonial (1512–1897) and Republican (1898–1958) elite societies. This urban-built form had evolved through almost 450 years of capitalist development and encompassed the totality of the physical environment, including roads, factories, office buildings, retail stores, houses, cultural and recreational institutions, educational centers, and healthcare facilities, as well as their spatial patterning and location in geographic space.

The city-building process refers to the course of action used to develop urban areas, including city planning and design, construction, and placement and patterning of structures and places within geographic space. It also includes the formulation of a legal framework that defines property ownership, establishes the regulations that guide real estate transactions, and determines the land-use framework that shapes urban development. Paul L. Knox, R. Richard Wohl and Anselm L. Strauss, Denise L. Lawrence and Setha M. Low, and others say the built environment also possesses a symbolic dimension that transmits social messages, which express the ideology, power relationships, attitudes, values, and beliefs of the dominant social group.[3] Thus, during the Republican era, the buildings, parks, boulevards, and neighborhoods, along with their urban design and spatial patterning within the metropolis, communicated social messages that legitimated the power and authority of the *criollo* elites and their U.S. supporters. This thesis posits that the built environment is a "partisan" settlement that produces a physical environment that replicates the prevailing socioeconomic order.

The urbanists David Harvey and Richard E. Foglesong agree. Harvey argues, for example, that the capitalist-built environment is a mirror and mold of elite society and that the elite-centered city-building process produces a physical environment that reflects the system of race and class stratification and unequal distribution of wealth characteristic of elite, market-based societies.[4] Foglesong goes on to say that in elite societies, a "for-profit" market system of land-ownership places city building under the control of land speculators, commercial property developers, homebuilders, and related architectural and urban planning firms.[5] The ability of the private sector to control city building and urban progress leads to the construction of a built environment that is characterized by uneven neighborhood development and class and race stratification. Thus, for Castro and the *rebeldes* to achieve the lofty goals of the Revolution, they had to change radically this building process and to resymbolize the city.

## Building the Elite-Centered City

The Havana of January 1959 was an expansive metropolis of approximately 1.27 million people in the city proper, with another 1.36 million residing in the outlying areas. This large city, covering about 186 square miles, dominated the island. When the revolution triumphed, 21 percent of the island's population, or one out of every five Cubans, lived in Havana. Not only was it six times the size of Santiago de Cuba, the nation's second largest city, but it was also the capital city, a major port, and the commercial center of Cuba.

Between 1519 and 1958, an elite-centered city-building process had shaped the development of Havana. During the Colonial period, 1519 through 1897, Havana expanded primarily within the confines of the walled city.

During the first half of the nineteenth century, the booming economy triggered significant population growth and development in Havana. The Cuban wars of independence (1868–78, 1879–80, and 1895–98), however, brought this dynamic period of city building and urban development to a halt. The wars devastated the Cuban economy, and the resulting poverty and hardship retarded population growth and development. For example, between 1827 and 1862, Havana's population increased by 102 percent, from 90,023 to 190,332. However, in the thirty-year period between 1869 and 1899, the population grew by only 42,000 residents, from 211,696 to 253,418 (19 percent), and this increase is possibly due to an influx of transients who were not included in the previous census.

Throughout this period a depressed economy, limited governmental resources, and precarious living conditions combined with deficient roads and a poor infrastructure to thwart the city-building process.[6] The *criollo* elite and Spanish merchants tried to launch new city building projects, but these efforts did not significantly offset the economic difficulties and thereby frustrated city building and further urban progress. The outbreak of war in 1895 worsened urban conditions and ended the Colonial era of city building.

## The Elite-Centered Republican City (1898–1958)

When the United States gained control of Cuba in 1898, although the wars of independence had impeded city building, the North Americans still found a city with a significant level of urban infrastructure and physical development. Metropolitan Havana at that time consisted of three distinct areas. The "central core" formed one district and consisted of Habana Vieja, Centro Habana, and portions of El Vedado and Cerro. "Suburban" Havana formed the second district. This area consisted of Miramar and Mariano to the west of the Almendares River and Víbora, Luyanó, and Santos Suárez to the south. The outlying towns and villages, including Guanabacoa, Regla, and Santiago de las Vegas, formed the third district. However, poor roads and arterial connections kept the outlying region from being linked effectively to the rest of the city.[7]

The goal of Leonard Wood, U.S. military governor, was to remake and transform Havana into a modern corporate city that would be the island's economic and governance center. Toward this end, during the military occupation, between 1898 and 1901, he launched an aggressive city-building program that eventually turned Havana into an expansive, elite-centered urban metropolis. The for-profit land and housing market and economic development informed a city-building and urban-development process led by U.S. builders, architects, engineering firms, urban planners, bankers, and law firms. This was a dynamic period of city building in the United States, and Havana became an urban laboratory where U.S. city builders used new ideas on urban development to shape the city.

Turning Havana into a modern corporate center first required the building of an infrastructure capable of supporting the city's growth and development. Toward this end, during the occupation, the U.S. program completed the construction of networks of water mains, natural gas and sewage lines, electric streetlights, telegraph and telephone lines, and established garbage collection. Significantly, it expanded street paving and replaced the horse-drawn trams with electric streetcars.

This emerging transportation network made possible the city's geographical expansion, as well as the development of modern forms of land use and property development. For example, the electric streetcar system tied the southern suburban communities of Jesús del Monte, Lawton, Luyanó, and Santos Suárez and the western suburban communities of Vedado, Miramar, Buena Vista, La Playa, and Mariano to the central core (Habana Vieja and Centro Habana). The widening of the Malecón (the avenue along the sea wall) and the bridging of the Almendares River in the mid-1920s combined with the electric streetcar to facilitate the development of elite neighborhoods in Miramar and other western suburbs.

In the late 1940s and 1950s the construction of tunnels under the Almendares River and Havana Bay reinforced this pattern by accelerating the development of Miramar and the western suburbs. Concurrently, the tunnel under Havana Bay hastened the development of Havana's eastern region.[8] Thus, the transportation network formed an urban scaffold that framed and directed the city's growth and development (see Table 2–1).

Table 2–1.    Population Growth of Havana and Cuba, 1899–1958

| Year | Havana | Cuba | % Havana |
|------|--------|------|----------|
| 1899 | 253,418 | 1,572,797 | 15.0 |
| 1907 | 302,526 | 2,048,980 | 14.8 |
| 1919 | 363,506 | 2,889,004 | 12.6 |
| 1931 | 728,500 | 3,962,344 | 18.4 |
| 1943 | 946,000 | 4,778,583 | 19.8 |
| 1955 | 1,223,900 | 5,829,029 | 21.0 |
| 1958 | 1,361,600 | 6,548,300 | 20.9 |

Scarpaci, Segre, and Coyula, *Havana*, 120.
Note: Population data for Havana in the 1931, 1943, and 1953 censuses refer to the former municipalities of the present City of Havana and have been adjusted to reflect the present city.

By 1958 Havana's modern corporate city consisted of a central core (Habana Vieja and Centro Habana), a secondary administrative/educational/entertainment node, and a hierarchical residential settlement. The central core functioned as the metro's government, administration, commercial, retail, social, and tourist area, which was centered in the spatial margin separating Habana Vieja and Centro Habana. The secondary node, with governmental, education, social, and tourism functions, emerged in Vedado between 1930 and 1958 in the Plaza Cívica and La Rampa areas.

## Residential Development, Housing, and Neighborhoods

Havana's urban morphology also consisted of a hierarchical residential structure in which the population was distributed across neighborhoods that differed significantly in terms of housing quality and physical conditions. Housing and neighborhoods reflect the soul and social conscience of a city. While monuments and great architecture define the outstanding cultural elements of a society, it is the communities found within them that reveal the metro's true values, beliefs, and attitudes.

During the Republican era residential segregation and spatial exclusivity became characteristic features of the elite-centered city. Havana's for-profit land and housing market led to a model of residential development that mimicked the classic pattern, which stratified neighborhoods based on housing cost and type and spawned the segregation of people by race and class. This pattern of residential segregation took form as the city expanded outward. When elites abandoned their housing in Habana Vieja and Centro Habana, working-class and low-income groups gradually replaced them.

Over time, Habana Vieja and adjacent industrial neighborhoods became home to the working class, those with low incomes, the seasonally unemployed, and immigrant workers who lived mostly in *solares, cuarterías, ciudadelas, pasajes,* and *accesorias. Solares* and *cuarterías* were dilapidated rooming houses that resulted from the transformation of the old baroque, neoclassical, and eclectic mansions of Habana Vieja, Centro Habana, Cerro, and El Vedado. A *ciudadela* is a house composed of one or two stories of rooms alongside an interior courtyard and is a variant of the tenement building, while an *accesoria* consists of one-bedroom apartments on the lower floor of a building that can be accessed directly from the street.

Concurrently, those workers with the lowest incomes moved into shantytowns composed of makeshift shacks that formed along the city's edge, in the southern and southwestern sections. The most infamous of these shantytowns were Las Yaguas, Llega y Pon, and La Cueva del Humo. As late as 1950, almost half of Havana's housing stock was in bad condition, and 6 percent of the population lived in shantytowns. These poor and marginal communities lacked the basic elements of infrastructure, and the few known governmental attempts to provide decent housing for workers did not make any sustainable impact.[9]

Simultaneously, urban planners and developers embedded elite neighborhoods in Vedado, Miramar, and other western neighborhoods in a "garden city" environment characterized by lush vegetation, parks, gardens, and homes designed by professional architects. In these exclusive neighborhoods the wishes of the elites, along with the entrepreneurial spirit of developers, influenced neighborhood planning and design. Access to land was controlled through land and building costs, and the routine practice was to reserve the best settings for the rich, thus leaving less favored areas and industrial surroundings to the poor and the working classes.

By 1958 the capitalist city-building process had produced a residential environment demarcated by distinct differences in housing quality and neighborhood conditions. Havana's morphology of residential space bore the stamp of class. The wealthy and upper middle classes lived in Vedado, Miramar, and other western neighborhoods, while the middle classes dominated southern suburbs like Víbora and Lawton. Workers dominated neighborhoods in Jesús Marie, Centro Habana, Habana Vieja, Habana Este, and in the outlying towns and villages. Still other workers clustered in shantytowns scattered along the city's edge.

Race joined with class in shaping Havana's residential land-use pattern. However, in Havana, unlike in U.S. urban centers, racial residential segregation took place only in the neighborhoods of the elites. In these communities the color line was impermeable, even for educated and professional Afro-Cubans. According to Afro-Cuban journalist Gustavo Urrutia, "decent" black families had difficulty gaining access to skyscrapers and modern apartment buildings.[10] When Afro-Cubans attempted to rent an apartment in an exclusive neighborhood, property owners often told them the unit was rented.

A different story unfolded in working-class neighborhoods. In these communities Afro-Cubans did not encounter housing discrimination. Here, the color line was porous. Not only did blacks and whites live together, but they consistently interacted with one another in everyday life. Some whites even adopted dance, music, and religious practices symbolic of Afro-Cuban culture and also broke the color line by developing interracial relationships, both platonic and romantic. Reality at this level frequently led foreign observers to highlight that race did not affect social relations on the island.

Racial affinity notwithstanding, the concentration of Afro-Cubans in the lowest paying, least attractive jobs in the city's occupational structure meant they had to find lodging in the least desirable neighborhoods within working-class communities. Therefore, although Afro-Cubans did not encounter racial barriers in working-class communities, low incomes forced them to live in the worst housing and neighborhood conditions. Consequently, they were over-represented in *solares* and *ciudadelas*, and in shantytowns. There is no evidence to suggest that housing discrimination operated in working-class neighborhoods in Havana in the same manner that it did in working-class neighborhoods in the United States.

Regardless of race relations, housing was still a serious problem for all workers in Havana. For example, as late as 1951 between forty thousand to fifty thousand *habaneros* lived in shantytowns, while another estimated 200,000 people resided in *solares* and *ciudadelas*. This meant that about one-third of the city's population had to tolerate very poor conditions. Thus, in Havana's elite-centered city, the elites—both *criollos* and North Americans—lived in residential worlds that differed dramatically from the *clases populares*, especially Afro-Cubans.

## The Monumental City

During the Republican era the elites embedded Havana in a symbolic environment that conveyed messages about their socioeconomic values and beliefs and reinforced their ideology and relationship of power over the popular classes. Consequently, from the U.S. military occupation onward, successive governmental administrations in Havana sought to construct a monumental city that imbued the landscape with narratives celebrating the superiority of capitalism, glorifying bourgeois wealth and power, and legitimizing U.S. dominance and the hierarchal social order.

It took many years to construct the monumental city. The process involved several master plans, including those by Enrique Montoulieu (1922), Pedro Martínez Inclán (1925), Jean-Claude Nicolás Forestier (1926), Eduardo Cañas Abril (1951), and Paul Lester Wiener and others (1958), and employed numerous architects and builders, who produced buildings that reflected diverse architectural styles. Within this framework, both informing and integrating their activities, was the singular goal of creating monuments that communicated the beliefs, ideology, and culture of the ruling elite.[11]

These city builders—government officials, urban planners, landscapers, architects, engineers, and builders—understood that city building was an activity that reflected the politics of an urban area, its way of life, and the future its leaders sought to realize. Operating within this context—the synthesizing work of French landscape architecture—Jean-Claude Nicolás Forestier, along with others, blended this eclectic collection of monuments together in a symbolic setting that imbued Havana with the governing regime's ideology.[12]

Some signs and symbols were more important than others in representing the social order of the governing regime. Thus, an urban monumental typology evolved that consisted of four hierarchical tiers. The first was the symbolic core, which was located primarily in the spatial margin separating Habana Vieja and Centro Habana, and then extending from the Prado to the Almendares River, along the Malecón, Havana's seaside promenade. The secondary tier consisted of a series of monuments scattered throughout the city, including the luxurious country club in Mariano, Plaza Cívica, the Columbus Military Base, and the Havana Hilton, built in 1958. The exclusive residential enclaves of the elites formed the third symbolic tier, while the places and spaces occupied by the popular classes denoted the fourth and final tier.

## The Symbolic Landscape

The elites established the symbolic core in the spatial margin separating Habana Vieja and Centro Habana (see Map 2–1). The core became a boundary that separated the "old city" from the "new city" and symbolized the severance of Cuba from its colonial past. To create this radical fissure in the spatial margin, planners used a different type of urban design and constructed buildings made spectacular by their architectural design and scale as well as their placement in a green setting dominated by parks, gardens, memorials, and a tree-lined promenade.

The mixture of palatial residences, governmental buildings, social clubs, casinos, retail outlets, theaters, hotels, tobacco factories, and parks made the symbolic core a hub of governance and social, cultural, and elite recreational activities, as well as a center of tourism. This diverse grouping of structures, particularly with the tobacco factories situated so close to the working-class neighborhoods, made this urban setting unique in Latin America. Moreover, this positioning of

**Map 2–1.    The Symbolic Core**

Havana, Cuba

The Symbolic Core

buildings and public spaces so close to the residential quarters of the working class bolstered the core's symbolic power. Because of its proximity to the popular classes, this hub provided the *clases populares* with a daily reminder of their place in the social order—and the omnipotence of the United States and the *clases económicas.*

The buildings, parks, and memorials in the symbolic core form a narrative about the elites' culture and way of life. For example, the Palacio Presidencial (1920) and the Capitolio (1929) represented the governing power and authority of the *criollo* elite and their U.S. collaborators. The Palacio is the symbolic equivalent of the White House in the United States, while the Capitolio was the seat of governmental power on the island. The eclectic facade of the Palacio radiated power and dominance, while the Capitolio, in its resemblance to the

U.S. Capitol, represented U.S. authority and influence. The capitol's dome dominated the Havana skyline and constantly reminded *habaneros* of the North Americans' presence (see Photo 2–1).

Other symbols celebrated the wealth, high culture, and the pleasure-seeking lifestyle of the elites and highlighted the cosmopolitan character of the city they created. For example, the Centro de Dependientes (Clerks Center) (1907), the Centro Gallego (Galician Center) (1915), and the Centro Asturiano (Asturian Center) (1927) were social clubs and mutual-aid societies that reflected and legitimized the opulence of the elites. The location of upscale hotels (Inglaterra, Plaza, Telégrafo, and Sevilla Biltmore), theaters, casinos, and the elegant homes of the elites along the Prado highlighted the cosmopolitan character of the city.

**Photo 2–1.    Capitolio (far right) and Other Buildings and Parks that Formed the Symbolic Core**

The elites then sought to legitimize their rule by claiming the heroes of the struggle for independence as their own, believing that this would justify both U.S. domination and the rule of the *clases económicas*. This was achieved through the strategic placement throughout the city of memorials to the nineteenth-century war heroes José Martí, Maximo Gómez, Antonio Maceo, and Calixto García. This symbolization of the built environment was acutely powerful. The monument of José Martí, leader of the 1895 War of Independence, was situated in the shadow of the Capitolio. Standing tall in Parque Central, with the Capitolio and Centro Gallego forming a backdrop, José Martí, as if lecturing to the masses, seems to be saying, "I support this elitist regime and all that it stands for."

The memorial to the commander-in-chief of the Revolutionary Army, Maximo Gómez, fronted the Palacio Presidencial in a garden-like setting located on the Malecón. This location presented Gómez as the saintly guardian of all Cuban presidents, past and present. At the same time the memorial axis of Gómez, Antonio Maceo, and Calixto García, strategically placed along the seaside promenade, transformed these war heroes into the spiritual protectors of the elite-centered city and nation. The monuments of Gómez and García look outward toward the Florida Straits, while the memorial to Maceo faces inward. Thus, symbolically, Gómez and García protect the nation against external enemies while Maceo shields it from enemies within. From this vantage point on the boundary of Habana Vieja, the core casts its symbolic shadow across the entire metropolis. From the memorial to the Maine and the Hotel Nacional, to the exclusive residential enclaves of the elites in Miramar, and then to the brothels and dilapidated housing of Habana Vieja, the symbolic city reinforced the omnipotence and cultural superiority of the governing regime.

### Dismantling Elite-centered Republic City (1958–2006)

In *History Will Absolve Me* Fidel Castro outlined his vision for Cuban society. Although his treatise provided a framework for the radical restructuring of Cuban society, it did not offer specific guidelines for transforming this vision into a reality. In Asian and European socialist cities, leaders had dismantled the for-profit land-and-housing market, but these urban places had city-building practices and racial and ethno-cultural histories that differed significantly from those in Cuba.[13] Their experiences provided ideas but not a prototype directly applicable to the Cuban experience. Meanwhile, in the Americas, market-centered development informed city building. In this regard the Havana of January 1959 bore the stamp of U.S. market-centered urban development more than any other metropolis in Latin America.

Collectively, these factors greatly complicated the task of transforming Havana into a people-centered metropolis. At the same time, the popularity of the Revolution facilitated the process. The Cuban Revolution was hugely popular, and the vast majority of people wanted radical change. Therefore, the *rebeldes* could proceed uncompromisingly in their quest to transform Cuba and remake the city. The *rebeldes* placed the popular classes at the center of their developmental strategy and used standard of living and quality of life, rather than profit making, as their guide to action.

At the onset of the Revolution, the *rebeldes* placed rural over urban development, especially in the case of Havana. Castro believed transforming the countryside was essential to the re-creation of Cuba as a people-centered society. The goal was to bridge the drastic differences between life in the capital city and the rest of the country. The disparity between the urban and rural standards of living in 1959, particularly the widespread poverty and deplorable living conditions found in the countryside, anchored this perspective.[14] Focus on the country-side, however, did not mean the *rebeldes* forgot about Havana and other urban centers. They were deeply concerned about their capital city, especially the race and class segregation; the increase in tene-ments, slums, and shantytowns; and the exorbitant rents charged for apartments and houses. Thus, despite limited resources, the regime moved forward with its bold plan to remake both the city and the country in the image of the *clases populares*.

## The Popular-centered City-building Process

To reinvent the urban metropolis, the *rebeldes* used social develop-ment to inform urban development. This rationale was outlined in the Preamble to the October 1960 Urban Reform Law, which critiqued the urban land market system:

The universal problem that is the housing crisis is particularly acute in underdeveloped countries such as ours [where there has been] intervention of speculative factors so that the lack of industrial development appropriate to our necessities and pos-sibilities led to the investment of private capital in the building of revenue producing buildings on urban lands, an investment pattern based on excessive profit, and with total disregard for the social function of property.[15]

The Preamble stressed the essential role played by "social func-tion" in city building and the necessity of using economic develop-ment to drive social development. The "social function" concept was based on the premise that neighborhoods were not only places but social organizations that could produce positive social outcomes if they functioned properly. A strong neighborhood had attributes that increased the social welfare and quality of life among its residents, including good housing and access to food, education, and medical care. The underlying principle was that building strong neighborhoods not only involves improving the physical environment but also build-ing resilient organizations and placing institutions in them that facili-tate their ability to function as a social unit.

In their approach to neighborhood development the *rebeldes* also sought to establish a minimum standard of living beneath which no resident should fall. Therefore, rather than build "safety nets" for people who might encounter hard times or target the poor for special programs, the *rebeldes* declared social welfare a "human right" and established universal policies designed to benefit the entire population. In this way there was no social stigma attached to those receiving help from the government. At the same time, when shortages existed, or during difficult economic periods, the government monitored the most vulnerable and at-risk populations, and they received help first.[16]

The *rebeldes* also believed that economic development should finance the social functions of the nation. The goal was not to generate private wealth, but rather to acquire the resources needed to secure and sustain social development:

> The revolution has postulated that the economic development of our country, the increase in production, the equitable distribution of wealth, the definitive elimination of archaic privileges that continued to leave our means of progress in the hands of foreign monopoly, and the definitive bases for economic development, which can provide solutions which originated in the social scheme did not rest on firm economic development.[17]

To codify their approach to city building, the *rebeldes* reconstructed a legal framework intent on removing the for-profit land-and-housing market from the city-building process and established new policies to guide urban development. Between 1959 and 1963 the regime passed a series of urban laws that eliminated the multiple ownership of property and forced owners to sell undeveloped land to the government at a price fixed by the regime. These codes practically eliminated land speculation. These laws, combined with the government's proclamation that it was responsible for the production and distribution of housing, eliminated the for-profit housing market. Later updates to the Urban Reform Law enshrined these codes and further developed the principles undergirding them.[18]

## The Housing Crisis and the City-building Process

The government considered the housing crisis, both in rural and urban areas, one of the country's most serious problems. Because of the interrelationship between housing and neighborhoods, the focus on the housing crisis became inseparable from the neighborhood development strategy. The *rebeldes* could not remake the city in the image of the popular classes without improving their housing conditions and developing the neighborhoods in which they lived. For this reason, housing and neighborhood development became the focal point of the popular-centered city-building process.

The first step in reorienting the city-building process was to outline the philosophical foundation upon which to develop the approach to housing and neighborhood improvement. In the Preamble to the Urban Reform Law, the government declared that housing was not a commodity but a basic human right. Therefore, every family was entitled to a decent dwelling unit, and it was the responsibility of the government to make this happen. The ultimate goal was to provide *Cubanos* with free lodging. To "secure" housing and to reduce its cost, within the first three months of the revolution the government stopped evictions, reduced rents 30 percent to 50 percent, and drastically reduced telephone and electricity rates. Later, the government mandated that rents could not exceed 10 percent of a family's income.

To improve the living conditions of residents at the bottom of the economic order, the regime embarked on an aggressive campaign to demolish the largest and worst of the shantytowns, including Llega y Pon, Las Yaguas, and La Cueva del Humo as well as the notorious tenement called Carreño, located near La Rampa. The residents in these locales built replacement houses through the Self-Help and Mutual Aid Programme. The remaining shantytowns were renamed *barrios insalubres* (unhealthy neighborhoods) to emphasize that the issue was the quality of the housing, not the economic status of the residents.

A second wave of shantytown clearance and replacement occurred in the late 1960s and early 1970s as part of the creation of the Havana Green Belt. Concurrently, the government collaborated with residents in the remaining *barrios insalubres* to improve their neighborhoods. The *rebeldes* located schools and health clinics in these communities and made the residents rent-free leaseholders. They also established transportation links between the *barrios insalubres* and other parts of the metropolis. The conditions improved so much in these settlements that the term *shantytown* no longer accurately described them.

Shantytowns and overcrowding were symptomatic of a severe housing shortage. To increase the supply of good housing, the government resolved to build thousands of new units. Between 1959 and 1993, for example, about 1.3 million new housing units were constructed. The main goal of the *rebeldes*, however, was to turn homeownership into an engine to drive community development.[19] They believed homeownership would fortify and stabilize neighborhoods by:

- strengthening the attachment between people and the places in which they lived;

- motivating residents to maintain and upgrade their homes;
- facilitating development of the social function of neighborhoods; and
- increasing social capital and neighborhood cohesiveness.

Therefore, instead of pursuing a public-housing strategy that created a renter class, the *rebeldes* pursued a strategy of turning most *Cubanos* into homeowners. The 1960 Urban Reform Law established two basic tenure forms: homeownership and long-term leaseholding in government-owned units. The 1984 and 1988 Housing Laws transformed most leaseholders of units built or distributed by the government into homeowners. The government also legalized the ambiguous ownership status of thousands of builder-owners. In 1958, about 75 percent of Cubans rented the dwelling units in which they lived. By the late 1990s, more than 85 percent of Cuban households contained homeowners, who paid little or nothing for their units except maintenance, repairs, and utilities. Thus, the government transformed Cuba from a land of renters into a country that had the highest rate of homeownership in the Americas and one of the highest in the world.[20] When one adds the rent-free lease householders to the homeowners list, Cuba emerges as a nation with one of the highest, if not the highest, rates of housing security in the world. People not only are assured of having a home, but they have the promise that no one will take this home away from them.

## *Permutas* and Neighborhood Stability

Homeownership and the lease-free rent system had the effect of "freezing" people in residential space. The emergence of the new housing tenure system meant that where one lived before the revolution determined where one lived after the revolution. While there were exceptions to this rule, the majority of *Cubanos* remained "in place" after the Revolution. Because the government functioned as a broker in most real-estate transactions, it was difficult for people to move from one home to another. This limited residential mobility had the unintended result of increasing neighborhood stability. Due to the complexities involved in buying and selling housing, many Cubans favored housing exchanges (*permutas*). *Permutas* were possible because home loans were viewed as personal loans, not mortgages. Therefore, houses could not be used as collateral, and the loans that residents had accompanied them wherever they went. This lending system simplified housing exchanges with the main challenge being to find someone willing to make a trade.

The case of Maria Lopez-Maceo exemplifies this process. Maria Lopez-Maceo lived with her daughter in the Santos Suárez neighborhood. Her apartment consisted of two bedrooms, a kitchen, a bath, and a balcony. Lopez-Maceo, however, did not like the community. It was too quiet and dark at night (there were few streetlights). She wanted to live in a more exciting place, and so she decided she would try to move. Maria Lopez-Maceo found someone willing to exchange a much smaller unit in Habana Vieja for her larger home in Santos Suárez. In some instances when the exchange of housing units is unequal, the person with the larger unit will demand cash to make the exchange even. Typically, this is an under-the-table agreement that does not involve the government. However, Lopez-Maceo did not request additional cash.

Lopez-Maceo's new apartment had only one room, a kitchen, and a small bath. In the absence of building-code enforcement, the high ceiling in her apartment made it possible to build an additional room by lowering the ceiling and turning the space between the old and the new ceiling into a loft *(barbacoa)*. This is a common practice in Havana. The crowded living conditions notwithstanding, Lopez-Maceo loves her new neighborhood. Many people, like Maria Lopez-Maceo, are able to find others willing to exchange homes, even when significant differences exist between the two structures.

## Community Participation and City Building

In 1959 Fidel Castro outlined the challenges facing the Cuban people and exclaimed: "You must all be heroes in this time of peace. The Cuban people are intelligent enough to do what they have to do." Fidel meant that the masses would have to become an integral part of the nation-building process if the *rebeldes* were to realize their goal of remaking society in the image of the popular classes. The 1961 Literacy Campaign set the tone for the Revolution, when the regime mobilized thousands of *Cubanos to* join the campaign to eliminate illiteracy in the country.

In 1971 Fidel Castro himself established the microbrigade movement as a strategy for supplementing the home-building activities of the government. According to this plan employees would be given release time from work to build homes, while those remaining behind in the workplace would keep production at its normal output. The microbrigade team would distribute housing to the members, as well as to other employees, based on need and merit. Over time, the microbrigades became social brigades, as the government's growing emphasis on neighborhood linked them to the community-development process. In this capacity the brigades worked closely with neighbor-hood residents to construct child-care centers, schools for the handi-capped, health clinics, neighborhood doctors' homes and offices, and other social facilities.

The neighborhood-development strategy led to the incorporation of other organizations and groups into the city-building process. In 1988, for example, the regime formed the Comprehensive Workshops for Neighborhood Change. These workshops are composed of inter-disciplinary teams of architects, sociologists, engineers, and social workers who develop strategies to deal with issues related to hous-ing, economic development, and other aspects of community and so-cial improvement. Within this framework the Committees for the Defense of the Revolution (Comités para la Defensa de la Revolución, CDRs) anchored these city-building activities at the neighborhood level.

The CDRs, established in 1960 to expose counterrevolutionary ac-tivities at the neighborhood level, created an organizational infrastruc-ture that supported neighborhood development. A CDR exists on every block and possesses the capability to mobilize residents around any issue. This mobilizing capacity is possible because of the CDR's intimate knowledge of the neighborhood and its residents. Every resi-dent in a neighborhood must register with the local CDR, even if he or she chooses not to be a member. The activities of the CDR comple-ment the work of other neighborhood-based organizations, and its coordinating and mobilizing capability helps to explain how the re-gime is able to achieve high levels of community participation.

## Ending Neighborhood and Spatial Exclusivity

Breaking down the barriers of neighborhood and spatial exclusiv-ity was another goal of the popular-centered city-building process. The almost complete abandonment of exclusive neighborhoods by their owners facilitated this process. Thousands of elites fled the is-land after the *rebeldes* seized power. The government confiscated their deserted houses and converted many into schools and dormitories for thousands of children on scholarships; they also became homes for government officials, dignitaries, foreign experts, and diplomats. The government turned other houses into museums, embassies, and facilities with various social functions. Former employees, who some-times took over a mansion after the owners left, occupied still others. The government also set aside land in the western part of the city for the establishment of biomedical research centers and medical educa-tion. These activities dramatically changed the class character of the western suburbs and turned Havana into an inclusive city.

Efforts toward inclusion, however, were not perfect. The housing tenure system, which virtually froze people in neighborhood space, caused many of the residential patterns that originated in the Republican era to persist. This meant that the physical condition and quality of life in some neighborhoods were better than in others, but these differences were no longer embedded in ideology and reproduced by the city-building process. Thus, although the ecological or structural features of the new popular-centered urban metropolis resembled aspects of the old elite-centered city, the content and substance of the new metropolis differed significantly.

## On Becoming a People-centered Urban Metropolis

The people-centered approach to city building brought about substantive changes in Havana. The emphasis on the social function of the metropolis combined with a dismantling of the urban land market to fashion an urban environment that differed significantly from the elite-centered city. Low-density communities became a characteristic feature of most Havana neighborhoods, and work continued simultaneously to improve the urban infrastructure, expand green spaces, create new cultural and recreational centers, and open up all waterfronts and beaches to the public. These activities transformed Havana into a truly inclusive city.

The absence of a capitalist consumer market led to the decline of retail activities in the city, especially in Centro Habana, along Neptuno, Calzada De Galiano, and other historically commercial streets. These streets still bustled with life; however, retail shops and stores marketing upscale brand-name products and settings designed to increase consumers' likelihood to purchase no longer existed. Rather, stores sold basic goods and generic merchandise, devoid of fancy displays enticing customers.

Public spaces, including streets such as the Prado and the Malecón, became animated, lively places, which people used for varied activities: playing dominos and chess, volleyball and stickball, rollerblading, talking with friends and lovers, exercising, or just meditating. For example, children often play soccer or hold karate classes on the grounds of the Capitolio; farmers' markets are occasionally held on the Paseo del Prado, and artists sell their paintings and young people rollerblade there, as well; while on the side streets, people repair cars, socialize, listen to music, and play an assortment of street games (see Photo 2–2). Along the Prado many of the social clubs and fancy homes of the elites have been turned into facilities with social functions, such as schools, libraries, theaters, dance studios, and so on.

Photo 2–2.    Social Life on the Prado

Meanwhile, the Malecón became the most popular space in the city (see Photo 2–3). In the summer *habaneros* turn the rocky shoreline into a beach, while year round they sit along the wall, talking, drinking rum, fishing, or just enjoying the cool breeze. In the people-centered city these public spaces become extensions of the living space, a community commons where intimate encounters occur and people engage in a wide assortment of interactive activities.

Photo 2–3.    The Malecón as a Beach

Despite efforts to strengthen the social function of the city and solve the housing problems, Havana nonetheless became a crumbling urban center. Limited resources, exacerbated by chronic shortages of paint and building materials, meant that the regime could not simultaneously develop the rural areas and sustain the development of Havana. This led to the city's dramatic decline. In 1994, for example, about 614 buildings simply collapsed, and another 375 had to be demolished.[21] When he first saw Havana in 1988, James A. Michener cried out: "What a shock! My God! This city needs ten million dollars' worth of white paint! For the houses and business places in that part of town were so decrepit in appearance that anyone who loved cities would have to protest; it was entire streets, almost whole districts; proof that a beautiful city was wearing away was inescapable."[22]

## The Resymbolization Process

The transformation of Havana from an elite-centered city into a people-centered city also required a resymbolization of the urban metropolis. Between 1898 and 1959 the elites and their U.S. collaborators built a city that painted the urban landscape with their ideological viewpoint and that normalized a hierarchal social order that placed the popular classes at the bottom. The *rebeldes* could not truly realize the goals of the Revolution without resymbolizing this urban setting.

This resymbolization process involved the reuse of buildings, public spaces, and lands, with an emphasis on the symbolic core. The first step was the transformation of public spaces. Parque Central, for example, became a people's park that provides a serene setting where *habaneros* can quietly sit, people watch, and talk with friends. An *esquina caliente* (hot corner) developed where baseball fans regularly gather, just to the south of the Jose Martí statue, to debate about the sport. The park also serves as a political forum, where the government holds rallies in the shadow of the monument to José Martí. Likewise, the once elite Paseo del Prado is a now an informal gathering place, a site where children play, people talk, walk, read the newspaper, or negotiate housing exchanges.

Second, the resymbolization process involved the reuse of buildings and residences in the area. For example, the Capitolio became a library, and El Centro Gallego, the Galician social club, became the Gran Teatro, the national theater of Cuba. The theater offers a variety of National Ballet and Opera performances that are reasonably priced and accessible to all the Cuban people. The Centro Asturiano, the Asturian social club, was first turned into the postrevolutionary People's Supreme Court and later the Museo Nacional de Bellas Artes (National Museum of the Arts). El Centro Dependiente (a grandiose social club that can accommodate five thosuand couples), located along the Prado, became a library and the national ballet school, while many other elegant residences of the elites were turned into homes for the popular classes. Tourist hotels and restaurants remain concentrated in this area, but the social function and class character of the core has changed significantly. A new story has emerged from this resymbolized landscape. It is a narrative about the social function of the city, an animated public space created by and for the masses.

The most significant resymbolization project involved recreating the Palacio Presidencial as the Museo de la Revolución (see Photo 2–4). As the symbolic equivalent of the White House in the United States, the Palacio anchored the city's symbolic core and originally represented the power and authority of the Cuban elites as well as validating U.S. domination of the island. In the transformation process the *rebeldes* placed a tank used to repel the 1963 Bay of Pigs invasion in front of the Palacio, while in the rear, in the former palace gardens, they established the Granma Memorial. This memorial preserves the yacht that brought Fidel, Che Guevara, Camilo Cienfuegos, Raúl Castro, and others from Mexico to Cuba on December 2, 1956. Shortly after landing, the Batista Army attacked and killed most of the Granma collaborators. About two dozen rebels escaped, regrouped, and went on to lead the Revolution to triumph. The memorial also contains another revolutionary icon, the bullet-riddled "Fast Delivery" truck used in the student commandos' assault on the Palacio in 1957.

**Photo 2–4.    A Resymbolized Palacio Presidencial**

The transformation of the Palacio into the Museo epitomizes the triumph of the *clases populares* over the *clases económicas* and their U.S. allies, as well as the powerful and unstoppable character of the revolutionary movement. This transformation created a domino effect that altered the iconic meaning of monuments throughout the remainder of the symbolic core. When the Republican leaders erected a statue of General-in-Chief Maximo Gómez in front of the Palacio, along the Malecón, they created a symbol that transformed the *clases económicas* into war heroes and legitimized their rule and U.S. domination. Moreover, the placement of the monuments to Gómez, Maceo, and Calixto García along the Malecón turned these heroes of the independence wars into the symbolic guardians of the Republican state.

The resymbolization process changed this social message. By turning the Palacio into the Museo, the *rebeldes* tied the Gómez, Maceo, and García statues to the popular classes and the triumph of the Revolution in 1959. In this resymbolized setting, Gomez and Garcia, whose statues look out toward the Florida Straits, now protect Cuba from its external enemies, the North Americans and the elite Cuban exiles living in the United States, while Maceo, whose statue looks inward, guards the island against its internal enemies, those *Cubanos* who seek to destroy revolutionary solidarity and collaborate with the enemy. Throughout the urban metropolis the symbolism was altered to tell the Revolution's story. From the transformation of the Plaza Cívica to the Plaza de la Revolución, the conversion of the Columbia Military Base into the Ciudad Libertad (a complex of primary and secondary schools), to changing the name of the Havana Hilton to the Habana Libre, the resymbolized urban metropolis reflected the new ideology, values, and beliefs of the *rebeldes*.

## The Special Period: International Tourism and the City-building Process

Nothing lasts forever, and Cuba's Golden Age came to an abrupt halt in 1989, when the Soviet Union and the East European Socialist bloc collapsed. This, followed by the dissolution of the Council of Mutual Economic Assistance (CMEA), a trading bloc among socialist countries, plunged the island into a deep economic crisis. Then, to make matters worse, the United States intensified its economic embargo, making it even harder for Cuba to acquire food, technology, and investment capital from abroad. As the Cuban crisis deepened, food shortages spawned malnutrition, power outages occurred frequently, the absence of consumer goods and products created frustration, and

Cuba's renowned education and health-care systems suffered. The lack of oil and gasoline generated transportation woes: people had trouble getting to work, factories closed, and farm produce often did not make it to market. Unemployment, along with hopelessness and despair, increased.

As the situation deteriorated, reporters from around the world descended on Havana to witness the anticipated fall of Castro's Cuba. The idea of Cuba's imminent collapse was based on the syllogism that the Revolution was nothing more than an epiphenomenon of Soviet expansionism. Therefore, according to the domino theory, the implosion of the Soviet Project and the fall of the European Socialist bloc meant that the disintegration of the Castro regime would soon follow. Argentinean reporter Andre Oppenheimer outlined this theme in his nearly five-hundred-page apocalyptic book *Castro's Final Hours: The Secret Story behind the Coming Downfall of Communist Cuba.* Caught in the grips of this unprecedented economic disaster, in July 1990 a somber Fidel Castro told the Cuban people their country was in a Special Period in the Time of Peace *(Período Especial en Tiempo de Paz).* This national emergency, occurring in peacetime, represented as serious a threat to national survival as war against a powerful enemy, he posited. Therefore, *Cubanos* must cast away their illusions and prepare for struggle during these hard times.

With few options, the regime pursued an aggressive policy based on reinserting the Cuban economy into the world market, making international tourism the principal component of the new economic strategy, developing joint ventures with foreign companies, and permitting more than one hundred private-sector self-employment jobs to operate. Then, to secure the hard currency needed to offset limited credit and to operate more effectively in the world market, in 1993 the regime legalized the U.S. dollar and allowed families to receive remittances from abroad. Remittances provided Cuban families with an unprecedented source of unearned income and became an invaluable source of revenue for the state. By 1997, for example, the amount of remittances sent to Cuba was estimated at more than US$700 million annually. These economic development policies led to a modification in city building and urban development and dramatically altered Havana's urban landscape.

## Remaking Havana as a Tourist City

In this crisis setting, although the *rebeldes* emphasized economic development, they did not minimize the importance of social development. Rather, the goal was to blend economic and social development in a manner that made possible the building of a strong economy, while simultaneously bolstering the city's social function. Nonetheless, in the Special Period the people-centered city-building process emphasized economic development—but in a manner that reinforced the social goals of the revolution. International tourism became the engine that drove economic advancement. Cubans used to say "Sin azúcar, no hay país" (without sugar, there is no country); now they say "Sin turismo, no hay país" (without tourism, there is no country). Against a backdrop of economic catastrophe, the prime objectives of city building was (1) remaking Havana as a tourist city; (2) creating retail facilities to "capture" the U.S. dollars from both tourists and *Cubanos;* and (3) strengthening community participation and the social function of neighborhoods.

This approach proceeded in unpredictable, multifaceted, and sometimes contradictory ways. Turning Havana into a tourist city was a tricky proposition. Urban tourism is a unique industry in which cities become commodities and sites of consumption for travelers. Thus, to convert a city into an international tourist destination, not only must a tourism niche be identified and developed, but also a sophisticated tourist infrastructure must be developed to support the industry. Colonial architecture provided Havana with a unique niche in the highly competitive Caribbean tourist industry, and this led to the development of urban-heritage tourism as the economy's principal component. Spanning about five hundred years, Havana has the finest assemblage of colonial architecture and fortifications in the Americas, and this colonial-built environment became the city's most important tourism asset. Urban-heritage tourism anchored the new tourist economy, and the restoration and renovation of historic buildings and places drove its development.[23]

Converting Havana into a world-class tourist city was a complex undertaking that involved two interrelated processes. First, with its treasure chest of colonial architecture and fortifications, the restoration of Habana Vieja, the Old City, became the focal point of the city's tourism strategy. Designated a World Heritage Site by UNESCO in 1982, Habana Vieja was a living museum with a diverse landscape of narrow streets and plazas featuring Spanish, Moorish, Greek, and Roman architectural styles. It was also a densely populated area that contained numerous dilapidated structures and a largely Afro-Cuban population. Thus, the task of transforming Habana Vieja into the city's prime tourist site involved historic preservation and renovation, as well as community development.

The Castro regime gave responsibility for achieving this goal to Eusebio Leal, historian of the city, and a former participant in the Revolution. During the 1970s Leal argued that the architectural gems of Habana Vieja were part of the nation's cultural heritage that needed to be preserved and celebrated, not merely an assemblage of artifacts of past bourgeoisie wealth and glory. He put forward a restoration strategy based on the premise that international tourism could function as a vehicle for generating revenues to (1) restore the cultural artifacts of Habana Vieja; (2) turn the community into a good place to live; and (3) provide the state with needed resources.

The goal was to transform Habana Vieja into a living community that accommodated both tourists and *habaneros*. This meant designing the Old City as an authentic place with historic buildings, monuments, fortifications, museums, and other facilities that met the needs, desires, and expectations of tourists, while simultaneously restoring the area as a functional community with stores, family doctor and nurse offices, schools, and other social facilities. Under the direction of Leal the northern core of Habana Vieja became a prime tourist site and was transformed into a dreamscape—an authentic, historical place restored so that it met the needs, wants, and expectations of tourists. This meant turning historic buildings into hotels, bars, restaurants, entertainment places, museums, art galleries, shops, and stores, and making the place safe.

To achieve these goals, the regime established an unprecedented economic development organization. In 1993, Law 143 turned the Office of the Historian of the City into an NGO with governmental powers and authority, including the powers to plan, finance, oversee restoration, and guide the overall development of Habana Vieja, including levying taxes and establishing relations with national and foreign entities. Under Leal's leadership, heritage tourism in Habana Vieja became the foundation of urban tourism in Havana and a magnet that drew thousands of visitors to the city.

The second key to converting Havana into a tourist city required the development of a sophisticated infrastructure to support the industry. Although Habana Vieja represents only a small part of the city, its conversion into the city's prime tourist destination triggered related historic restoration, renovations, and new construction across the city, especially in Vedado and Miramar. Urban tourism is a highly competitive industry in which thousands of visitors are invited to the city have fun and enjoy leisure time. To accommodate these visitors, the city must construct an infrastructure consisting of exquisite hotels, fine restaurants, exotic entertainment venues, fancy retail boutiques, along with banking facilities, communications networks, conference centers, and an efficient transit system.[24]

Within this framework the city built new hotels and rehabilitated existing ones. Between 1990 and 2000, the number of hotel rooms in Cuba, keeping pace with arrivals, doubled from 18,565 to 37,178. In

Havana alone the total number of rooms increased from 4,682 rooms in 1988 to 12,002 rooms in 2002. During the 1990s the quality of hotels in Cuba was typically lower than that of competing Caribbean destinations. In 1998, only 7.1 percent of the hotels in Cuba had a five-star rating, 30 percent had four-stars, and 66 percent were either two or three stars. Thus, with the expansion of tourism, Cuba was under constant pressure to increase the quality as well as the quantity of available rooms. By mid-2000, Cuban officials predicted 64 percent of their rooms would be in the four- and five-star categories.

In contrast to affluent visitors, other tourists, especially young travelers and those on a limited budget, prefer to stay in more modest places located in parts of the city that bring them into contact with ordinary *Cubanos*. To fill this market niche, the *rebeldes* turned to the self-employment sector. After 1993 the government allowed *Cubanos* to rent rooms in their homes to tourists. Between 1998 and 2002 the number of *casas particulares* increased from 1,537 to 4,980 across the island, while in Havana they increased from 2,284 to 2,730. This self-employment option led to the reuse of many dwelling units. Many *Cubanos* turned homeownership into an opportunity to make extra money by renting rooms out to visitors. Thus, the homes of an indeterminate number of *habaneros* became part-time bed-and-breakfast facilities.

The development of the tourist infrastructure spread beyond Habana Vieja as a growing number of hotels, retail outlets, and office complexes developed in other parts of the city. Miramar became the preferred location for working and living among foreign investors, executives moving to Havana, students, and conventioneers. The infusion of commercial activities into this once-elite residential neighborhood changed its complexion. For example, in a 1996 land-use survey in Miramar, urbanist Joseph L. Scarpaci found that growing numbers of Cuban and foreign commercial establishments based on tourism and the import-export sector—including advertising, telecommunications, hard-currency changing retailers, banks, and the headquarters for joint-venture firms—were locating in this community, many in facilities previously with social functions. Cuban and joint-venture firms, for example, turned the large homes, which once held students who came from the provinces to study in the capital or migrants who moved to the city from the eastern provinces, into office space, sales rooms, dining areas, and apartments for foreigners.[25]

Reinforcing this pattern of city building and urban development was self-employment, legalization of the dollar, and the ability of families to receive remittances from abroad. After 1993, the creation of small, neighborhood-based entrepreneurship changed street life and the urban fabric across Havana. For example, the transportation crisis led to a huge increase in use of bicycles. In 1990 *habaneros* used their bicycles for recreation and sport. The crisis changed this. Between 1990 and 1995 the number of bicycles in Havana increased from about seventy thousand to one million as biking became an important form of intra-urban transportation. Moreover, through self-employment many *Cubanos* turned vintage U.S. automobile into taxis. Meanwhile, the increased use of bicycles, bici-taxis, automobiles, and other motorized vehicles also led to a rise in bicycle- and auto-repair shops and parking lots.

This unique assemblage of vehicles rambling along Havana streets created a surreal atmosphere that contributed to the exotic character of neighborhood life. Adding to the transformation of the streetscape was the appearance of an assortment of street vendors who performed shoe and watch repair, recycled cigarette lighters, and sold flowers and peanuts. One began to notice the presence of signs announcing the existence of an indeterminate number of homes serving as *paladares* (restaurants) and *casas particulares* (rooms to rent). These signs provided additional evidence of the changing nature of the built environment to accommodate the tourist economy. These and other forms of self-employment required state licensing and operated under strict regulations, including high taxes. Even so, self-employment flourished as the market for nongovernmental services grew.

The influx of tourists and foreign investors combined with the legalization of the dollar and the allowance of remittances to trigger the reemergence of a vibrant retail sector in Havana, primarily in Habana Vieja, especially along Obispo, in the La Rampa area, around the Universidad de la Habana and in Miramar. These retail activities included the development of a vibrant souvenir sector, which sold sculptures, paintings, *criollo* clothing, rum, tobacco, cigarettes, and other memorabilia.

A lively retail sector that sold goods and services primarily to *Cubanos*, although tourists could shop at these establishments as well, also surfaced. As previously mentioned, following the collapse of the Soviet Union, Cuba needed hard currency to operate in the world market. The regime created a retail sector to "capture" these dollars. The most important retail establishment was the dollar store or *mercado* (market). These small stores carried out transactions only in dollars or *convertibles*. To make them attractive to consumers, they had greater diversity and carried higher quality goods than did *pesos* stores or *bodegas* (corner stores). Typically, *mercados* carried foods and beverages, including beer and rum, and some *mercados* also carried a small quantity of appliances, electronics, and apparel. *Mercados* became an omnipresent feature of Havana's changing urban fabric; they were found along commercial corridors, in every neighborhood, along the beachfronts, and throughout the tourist districts.

Augmenting the *mercados* was the emergence of a "market-style" retail sector among *Cubanos* (see Photo 2–5)). The older retail sector processed transactions only in *pesos* and sold mostly recycled clothes, inexpensive apparel, and new and used appliances. The store environment was drab and colorless, with no chic in-store or window displays to encourage buying. The new retail sector differed significantly and mimicked the design of retail shops in market-based consumer societies. These establishments created store environments and window displays that encouraged consumer buying and sold brand-name and upscale clothing, along with high-end appliances and electronics.

**Photo 2–5.   Display Window on Neptuno near the Prado**

The Manzana de Gómez building at the intersection of Zuelueta and Neptuno, across from Parque Central, the Harris Brothers Company building on Bernaza, situated on the western edge of Habana Vieja, and La Época department store at the intersection of Calzada de Galiano and Neptuno in Centro Habana, all provide examples of this new form of retailing. In addition, in 2004, San Rafael, between Prado and Calzada De Galiano, was turned into a commercial district that catered to *habaneros*. The district not only included retail shops and stores, but also entertainment venues, restaurants, bars, and *mercados*.

Most interesting, these new retail shops appear to be designed as much for entertainment as for shopping. People appear to be window shopping and socializing as much as, or more than, they are making purchases. For example, the San Rafael commercial district is a popular gathering place where people hang out but do little actual shopping, except for minor transactions in the *mercados*, eateries, and bars situated along the street. The La Época department store even has a bar in the store basement where folks relax over a *cerveza* (beer) or glass of rum. Though most *Cubanos* cannot afford the merchandise in these retail shops, the availability of an assortment of apparel, appliances, and electronics does tend to weaken trade in the black market, while at the same time allowing the government symbolically to increase the availability of consumer goods. Still, the black market for clothing continues to flourish. In the *Casa de Ropas* (clothing house), some *habaneros* sold designer clothes, including shoes to *Cubanos* who could afford them.

## New Forms of Elitism and Exclusivity and Other Contradictions

Tourism, in any third-world country, is a problematic industry because the very presence of tourists highlights the disparities in wealth and power between their nation and the host country. Tourists, independent of their will or intent, illustrate the inequalities that exist between people of the First World and the Third World, and their close, face-to-face contact can continually remind residents of their poverty in relation to that of the tourist. These problems are greatly magnified in a people-centered society like Cuba, which eschews individualism and Western-style consumer culture. Within this context Cuban tourism spawned a new form of elitism and spatial exclusivity in Havana. Annually, the tourist industry invites to the city thousands of visitors with money to spend on study, work, sports, or leisure. To accommodate these visitors, the government has established more exclusive places such as nightclubs, restaurants, shops, and hotels, including some with private beaches.

Unwittingly, the tourist facilities became new icons of wealth and power, which celebrate the high status of foreign visitors and praise the culture and success of market capitalism. For example, tourists do not view hotels simply as places to sleep; rather, they view them as sanctuaries that provide them unique and pleasurable experiences. Thus, when touring people want lodging in an upscale hotel, they want an environment that provides them with an exotic experience, and they want restaurants imbued with a sense of originality and local culture.

Tourism, on a positive note, did spark an economic recovery and provided the resources needed to fund social development programs, including those related to health, education, and recreation. Concurrently, international tourism turned Havana into a tourist city. This transformation necessitated the development of a physical environment to accommodate the tourist economic sector. Ironically, this city-building process imbued the urban landscape with new symbols of elitism and glorification of the market economy.

## Keeping the Focus on Neighborhoods and Social Development

When the *rebeldes* seized power in 1959, Havana was one of the most prosperous cities in Latin America. However, the misdistribution of wealth and an elite-centered process of city building and urban development forced the popular classes to live on the economic margins. Many resided in bad housing, situated in neighborhoods characterized by inadequate schools and poor health care with few opportunities for socioeconomic advancement. The *rebeldes* intended to address these urban issues, as well as the deplorable living conditions found in small towns and rural areas. Social development and improving the quality of life among the *clases populares* became the centerpiece of their city-building and nation-building activities. Within this context the *rebeldes* believed the purpose of economic development was to generate the resources needed to bolster the social function of urban and rural areas. Thus, they believed the secret to remaking society in the image of the popular classes was to build an economy capable of supporting a high level of social development. However, the U.S. economic embargo, which closed markets and limited resources, threatened the regime's ability to achieve the lofty goals of the Revolution.

This forced Cuba to forge an alliance with the Socialist bloc. Buoyed by generous subsidies and trade agreements with the Soviet Union and the CMEA, the *rebeldes* launched an aggressive program to re-make the city and nation in the image of the popular classes. Based on the philosophy of putting people first, the regime ended land specu-lation and dismantled the for-profit land and housing market. They turned Cuba into a nation of homeowners; eliminated shantytowns; trained teachers and doctors; built schools, hospitals, and clinics; made health care universally accessible; and bolstered the living standard and quality of life among the popular classes. In many respects this period represented a Golden Age of the Revolution.

The collapse of the Soviet Union and the dissolution of the CMEA ended this period of prosperity and achievement. Survival became the regime's top priority, and it responded by placing the emphasis on economic development while simultaneously attempting to sus-tain the gains made in social development. City building and urban development changed but did not lose their prime focus on social development. Nonetheless, in order to survive the catastrophic eco-nomic crisis Cuba had to reinvent itself. No other options existed. This meant pursuing an economic strategy that included market ele-ments and initiating other reforms designed to make Cuba competi-tive in the world market. The most significant reforms involved emphasizing tourism and legalizing self-employment, the U.S. dol-lar, and the ability of residents to receive remittances from abroad.

These economic reforms brought about a sea change in Cuban life and culture as Cuba created a mixed economy, acquired new interna-tional allies, and fostered a different set of attitudes about economic development. Self-employment and access to the dollar started to restructure social relations among the popular classes, socioeconomic divisions began to appear, racism flared its ugly head, and a new popular culture emerged as frustration and dissatisfaction deepened. Most important, tourism meant the re-creation of the physical envi-ronment to accommodate international visitors and other elements of the new economy.

While city building and urban development did spawn symbols of elitism and generated contradictions, they did not lose their popu-lar-centered focus. The city-building strategy had to adjust to operat-ing in an environment infinitely more complex and treacherous than that of the period from 1959 to 1988. Still, the regime's emphasis on economic development and building the tourist city did not cause the government to abandon social development. On the contrary, as the crisis deepened, the regime increased its reliance on the resiliency, initiative, and creativity of the popular classes. The goal was to bol-ster the organization of neighborhoods, strengthen their social func-tion, expand participatory democracy, and fortify the neighborhood links to the government.

# 3

# INSIDE *EL BARRIO*

Neighborhoods matter greatly in the social development of communities. "Neighborhood effects" research demonstrates that neighborhoods can contribute to negative social outcomes, such as crime, violence, drug abuse, poor schooling, obesity, and other health problems. Equally important is the capacity of neighborhoods to lower risk by providing the resources needed to support a healthy life and culture.[1] Thus, neighborhoods can either contribute to the increased vulnerability of their residents or bolster their resiliency, enhancing both physical and social well-being. Put another way, neighborhoods are never simply neutral sites where everyday life and culture unfold. Rather, they are catalytic places where interactive relationships exist among people, the physical environment, social organizations, and the institutional infrastructure, which includes the relationship between government and the neighborhood. Most important, neighborhoods do not just evolve in a spontaneous manner, independent of conscious thought or action. Rather, they are the products of deliberate policy outcomes, whether that policy is stated or unstated.

## *El Barrio* and City Building in Havana

The development of *el barrio* reflected the *rebeldes'* effort to build a society based on the principles of reciprocity, the equitable distribution of wealth, and racial and socioeconomic justice. Because no blueprint existed, they learned how to create people-centered neighborhoods through the process of building them. This method required patience, flexibility, the blending of idealism with pragmatism, and the ability to learn from mistakes. This approach turned Cuban neighborhoods into stable, well-organized communities that helped *Cubanos* survive the collapse of the Soviet Union by mitigating the most harmful effects of the socioeconomic crisis. Consequently, the disintegration of the CMEA and the East European Communist

71

Bloc produced an economic catastrophe, hard times, frustration, anger, and social unrest, but it did not produce demands for regime change and the resurrection of capitalism. An examination of everyday life and culture inside *el barrio* will provide critical insight into the reasons why these did not happen.

## The Philosophical Foundation

The metamorphosis of Cuban neighborhoods resulted from Castro's goal of building communities that supported resiliency, reciprocity, solidarity, and good health among residents. During the 1980s the *rebeldes* intensified their quest to strengthen *el barrio*. In 1987, for example, the government established the Group for the Integral Development of the Capital (Grupo para el Desarrollo Integral de la Capital—GDIC). This interdisciplinary organization advanced a new model of neighborhood development based on the social function of communities.[2] Undergirding the model is the belief that residents are bio-psycho-social beings who have an interactive relationship with their neighborhood. Accordingly, the health and social well-being of people is related to the conditions of life found in the communities where they live. This viewpoint fused together the notions of neighborhood and social development and placed them at the core of the community development process.

Within this context the GDIC believed that community development should be a community driven process in which residents worked in partnership with professionals to develop their neighborhoods. Toward this end, in the most troubled communities, the GDIC established Los Talleres de Transformacion Integral del Barrio (workshops for integrated neighborhood transformation), interdisciplinary teams consisting of architects, sociologists, social workers, engineers, and residents that focused on the social, physical, and economic development of communities.

The development of social capital anchors this approach. Social capital refers to a network of formal and informal relations based on trust, solidarity, reciprocity, and normative standards of behavior informed by collective values, beliefs, and attitudes, along with the resources, skills, and capabilities found among individuals, households, and institutions in neighborhoods. This conceptualization suggests that social capital can exist at the individual, household, and/or neighborhood level. In this sense social capital is a dynamic force; its ability to equip people to solve problems, to create normative standards of behavior, to mitigate hard times, to make progressive neighborhood change, and to structure a nurturing, supportive, and sustainable social environment determines its overall value.[3]

## Neighborhood Distinctiveness

During the 1980s, before the collapse of the Soviet Union, the *rebeldes* realized that the urban metropolis was too large and the needs of each community too unique to address through a "one size fits all" method of problem solving (see Map 3–1). Metropolitan Havana is a rambling city composed of interlocking neighborhoods that are remarkably diverse in terms of housing types, community design, physical characteristics, and physical conditions.[4]

**Map 3–1. Municipalities of Havana, Cuba**

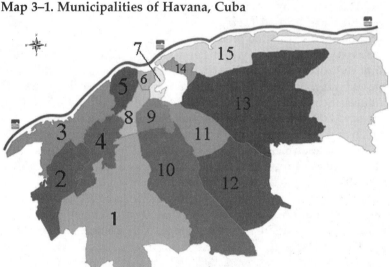

1-Boyeros; 2-La Lisa; 3-Playa; 4-Mariano; 5-Plaza de la Revolucion; 6-Centro Habana; 7-La Habana Vieja; 8-Cerro; 9-Diez de Octubre; 10-Arroyo Naranjo; 11-San Miguel del Padron; 12-Cotorro; 13-Guanabacoa; 14-Regla; 15-Habana del Este

In Havana's central core, for example, we find the high density, animated neighborhoods of Habana Vieja, Centro Habana, and Vedado. The city's architectural treasures are mostly concentrated in these areas. Dwelling units, which are one, two and three stories, along with occasional high-rise apartment buildings, dominate the residential landscape. The buildings, including the single-family dwellings, are literally attached to one another and communicate directly with the street. Because of age and neglect, many structures in the core neighborhoods are in poor condition, and there is a lack of open, green space. Yet, at the same time, the colonial-built environment combines with the congested, lively streetscapes to create an environment reminiscent of an eighteenth- or nineteenth-century city. The imagery of these neighborhoods brands Havana and imbues the city with its distinctive character.

Just to the south of the central core are communities such as Lawton, Vibora, and Cerro. These neighborhoods comprise mostly detached, single-family dwelling units with an intermixture of two-story buildings. These are low-density neighborhoods with more open space and greenery, and many of the detached dwelling units are designed with decorative columns for the front porches. In the late nineteenth century these dwellings served as summer homes for the elites, but today housing and infrastructure conditions in many of these neighborhoods are quite poor.

Across the Havana Bay, in the eastern part of the city, the architectural style of housing and the rhythm of daily life differ greatly from the core neighborhoods. The eastern part of the city includes the old industrial communities of Regla and Casablanca, with their modest one- and two-story dwellings, as well as neighborhoods like Alamar, which are characterized by the uninspired, monotonous, Soviet-type multistory apartment buildings constructed in a super-block style. Many of these eastern communities developed after the Revolution and reflect the government's efforts to build high-quality, low-cost housing units. Although many of these dwellings are esthetically challenged, overall housing conditions here are superior to those units found in the older areas, such as Regla, Casablanca, Habana Vieja and Centro Habana.

A contrast to the newer eastern Havana neighborhoods is the picturesque Cojimer, a community made famous as the home of Ernest Hemingway. Although a quaint oceanside neighborhood, Cojimer also contains diverse housing that ranges from Soviet-style high rises to nineteenth-century single-family dwellings to seaside cottages. Although situated in a semi-rural setting, eastern neighborhoods are nevertheless animated and cosmopolitan. One reason is that many of the residents originally migrated from Habana Vieja and Centro Habana and brought with them the vibrancy of urban life in the central core.

To the west are found communities such as Miramar and La Playa. This is the most cosmopolitan part of the city, and it projects an air of confidence, sophistication, and worldliness. Western neighborhoods were mostly built during the Republican era, and the streetscapes are reminiscent of the city-beautiful movement in the United States. These neighborhoods range from the old bourgeois communities of Cubanacan and Siboney to the beautiful oceanside neighborhood of Santa Fe, with its one-story, detached cottages. Added to the mosaic of dwelling units are the numerous modern high-rise apartment buildings and luxury hotels.

Offering a dramatic contrast to the western neighborhoods are the outlying neighborhoods, such as Trebol, Wajay, Cacahaul, and Santiago de la Vegas. These communities, which are situated on the city's southern and western fringe, have a small town and rural flavor with their tiny shacks, wandering farm animals, and urban/rural way of life. For example, one might find horses grazing in a field or eating leaves from a tree while, at sunset, a farmer may be herding goats homeward along the main street. These communities seem to be part of another world, yet they are only a short drive or train ride from the central core.

A wide range of housing and neighborhood types are found in these semi-rural communities, including detached single-story and two-story buildings, and high-rise apartments built by the residents themselves. The dwellings are mostly modest structures, often constructed with concrete blocks. The single-family housing units are typically built with flat roofs so that families can add rooms when they secure additional resources. Scattered in the midst of the fringe neighborhoods are a number of *barrios insalubres*. These settlements are usually hidden from view, across the railroad tracks or in some other obscure location within the community. Most of these communities have dirt roads, and housing conditions are very poor. This extraordinary diversity in neighborhoods explains why the *rebeldes* abandoned the idea of a top-down neighborhood development strategy. However, the *rebeldes* did not view the issues of top-down and bottom-up development as an either/or question. Rather, they sought to create an interactive top-down and bottom-up approach to neighborhood development based on a combination of centralized and decentralized decision making.

## Homeownership and Housing Security as the Foundation of Community Development

The *rebeldes* made homeownership and housing security the foundation of their approach to neighborhood development. They viewed housing as a human right rather than as a commodity to be bought and sold on the open market. Consequently, during the first days of the Revolution, the *rebeldes* took measures to develop neighborhoods based on the security of housing tenure. For example, they stopped evictions, reduced most rents by 30 percent to 50 percent, and aided potential homeowners by a Vacant Lot Law designed to stimulate construction and eliminate land speculation. The law established two basic tenure forms: homeownership and long-term leaseholding in government-owned units. Individuals could not own more than one permanent and one vacation home and the law prohibited all private renting. In this new setting most tenants became homeowners, amortizing the price of units with their rents.[5]

There are no mortgages or land or property taxes. Financing for purchasing units or materials for repairing houses is considered a loan, not a mortgage, and therefore dwellings are not used as collateral. Non-payment of rent or loans is addressed by garnishing wages or bank accounts, not through eviction. By the late 1990s, more than 85 percent of Cuban families were homeowners, paying little or nothing for their units aside from maintenance, repairs, and utilities. An additional number of *Cubanos* lived in rent-free dwellings, which were usually in poor condition. This method of housing distribution gave Cubans the most secure housing system in the Americas.

## Neighborhood Stability

An unintended consequence of the *rebeldes'* housing strategy was the creation of highly stable neighborhoods where people aged in place. Because housing was administratively allocated and distributed by the government, rather than sold on the open market, it was difficult for *Cubanos* to move from one housing unit to another. This connected many *Cubanos* to the same house and neighborhood for an extended period. Stability, in turn, generated a strong attachment to place and gave residents a direct stake in the development of both their housing units and the communities in which they were embedded. Thus, the Revolution "froze" people in place, and the hyper-stability that resulted formed the context in which Cuban neighborhoods evolved and social capital was accumulated.

## Household Structure and Composition

While the housing distribution system produced highly stable neighborhoods, a severe housing shortage, especially in Havana, shaped the structure and composition of households.[6] Most *habaneros* live in extended or nuclear family households, composed of both married and unmarried couples. In Cuba, like the rest of the Caribbean and Central America, there is a high rate of couples living together in consensual unions rather than marriage. In 1995, for example, 42.2 percent of Cuban household heads were married and 24.6 percent of household heads were in consensual unions. A handful of *Cubanos* live in what Mario Coyula, the Cuban urbanist, calls "composites," which are households that include at least one person unrelated to the household head. Only a handful of Cubans live alone, and there are even fewer households consisting of just mother and child. In Cuba, unlike the United States, single mothers tend to live with their parents and/or other relatives.

Culturally, Cuban households are close knit with a tradition of responsibility and caring for family members. For example, José Banderas is a forty-four-year-old retired worker who had a debilitating stroke that left him confined to a wheelchair. He lives in an eight-person household with his wife, three sisters, his mother and father (an eighty year old with Alzheimer's disease), and his wife's mother. His sisters assist with the care of José and his father. They view this as part of their responsibility as family members and could not imagine not having them in a caring home environment. Extended families that contain and nurture vulnerable groups, such as handicapped persons, elders, and unmarried women with children, lower the risks for its members of socioeconomic and health problems. These household configurations strengthen the social function of communities and reinforce neighborhood stability.

## Occupational Diversity

The occupational diversity of Cuban neighborhoods also bolsters the social function of neighborhoods and reflects the stability generated by the housing distribution system. When the incomes of residents improve, they typically remain in the same neighborhood rather than move to a new location. This is a social asset that imbues the community with a strong culture of work. Even in the most vulnerable neighborhoods, most households have one or two members who are either in the labor force or have retired. Because most households have multiple workers, even during periods when unemployment is high there is usually someone in the household working. Moreover, many households also have members who moonlight in either the formal or informal economy. The culture of work combines with neighborhood stability to produce communities with a broad mixture of occupational types. For example, a typical neighborhood might contain medical doctors, nurses, seamstresses, mechanics, dancers, security guards, telephone operators, janitors, schoolteachers, gardeners, accountants, bartenders, taxi drivers, computer operators, electricians, carpenters, prostitutes, hustlers, and more.

The level of educational attainment among residents makes neighborhoods even stronger. The *rebeldes* made education one of the foundations of the Revolution, and the literacy campaigns of the 1960s virtually wiped out illiteracy. Education is free at all levels, and 98 percent of Havana's children aged six to fourteen were attending school in 2000. Most *Cubanos* have a high-school education, and many have gone on to technical school or college. The multiracial and cross-occupational character of neighborhoods combined with the high levels of educational achievement provide most neighborhoods with residents who have the skills and abilities to drive the community-development process.

## Racial Diversity

The Revolution stabilized people in residential space. The racial diversity of neighborhoods, then, is a reflection of the pre-revolutionary residential pattern in which Afro-Cubans and working-class whites lived in the same communities. It is worth noting that race is a very tricky social concept in Cuba. Throughout the nineteenth century Cuba had a two-tiered racial classification system, which perpetuated the notion of a *raza de color* (race of color) or *clase de color* (class of color). No distinctions were made between mulattos and blacks, and *Cubanos* referred to both *pardos* (mulattos) and *morenos* (blacks) as *Negros* (blacks). Although similar to the racial system in the United States, the Cuban system differed in one significant respect: "visible" African ancestry, not the "one drop of black blood rule," separated whites from blacks and blacks from mulattos.[7]

In this regard, the Castro regime uses the term *skin color* rather than *race* in the census and other demographic studies to designate racial and ethnic differences. In practice, however, a combination of hair texture and skin color appears to be the critical determinant in the current culture determining who is white, black, or mulatto. For example, Omar Cardenas, a dark-skinned *habanero* with curly, European-type hair, describes himself as mulatto, a self-designation confirmed by his identification card. Ana Maria, a dark-skinned woman also with curly, European-type hair, describes herself as a mulatto, as well. At the same time, Roberto, who is lighter than both Omar and

Ana Maria, has kinky, African-type hair and considers himself black, a self-determination also confirmed by his identification card. Hair texture appears to be as important, if not more important, than skin color in determining racial classification. Concurrently, *Cubanos* consider light-skinned *habaneros* with kinky, African-type hair as mulattos. However, based on field observations, many *habaneros* who consider themselves mulattos would be classified as black in the United States.

These definitions notwithstanding, Havana neighborhoods are racially very diverse, even the communities with the worst housing conditions and the most vulnerable population groups. Most significant, this study as well as Coyula and Hamberg's study "Understanding Slums," indicates that whites compose the majority of the population in the city's most vulnerable neighborhoods. Afro-Cubans, black and mulatto, are not isolated from whites in these localities. The fact that people from across the color divide live together, especially in neighborhoods confronting serious challenges, has mitigated racial conflict, reinforced solidarity, and bolstered social capital.

## *El Barrio* as an Urban Village

The hyper-stability of neighborhoods created an intimate, face-to-face environment that generated a village-like urban atmosphere where trust and solidarity undergirded community life. Because people lived in the same neighborhood for many years, they forged a collective spirit based on bonds of friendship, trust, and reciprocity. The physical organization and structure of *el barrio* reinforced the village-like character of Cuban neighborhoods. For example, many Cubanos live in multistory apartment buildings. The strength of community is especially strong in these apartment buildings because of the potency of the cooperative and reciprocal nature of relationships. This happens because neighbors must work together to solve mutual problems such as water shortages, excessive noise, elevators that do not work, and similar maintenance issues. Likewise, in communities like Habana Vieja, Centro Habana, and Vedado, the maze of interlocking passageways and courtyards, which characterize the internal structure of these areas, literally creates a "neighborhood within a neighborhood." Again, within this shared space people regularly interact and work together to make their living environment thrive. Necessity and shared residential space, then, formed the foundation for trust, solidarity, and reciprocity upon which Cuban neighborhood life is based.

## Neighborhood Organization, Community Participation, and Participatory Democracy

Unlike elite-centered societies, in Cuba community development was based on a collaborative relationship between government and neighborhood residents, and civic society operated primarily within the governance structure.[8] The development of such communities required the accomplishment of three objectives. The first was the establishment of a network of mass organizations that incorporated most of the population; the second, the development of neighborhood institutions with interactive relationships with residents and neighborhood-based mass organizations; and last, the establishment of interactive links between neighborhoods and the government.[9] Toward this end, at the beginning of the Revolution the *rebeldes* sorted the population into a series of mass organizations based upon residence, age, gender, and occupation, and then they structured these groups along horizontal and vertical lines. The key groups were the following:

1. Comités de Defensa de la Revolución (Committees for the Defense of the Revolution—CDRs)
2. Federación de Mujeres Cubanas (Federation of Cuban Women—FMC)
3. Asociación Nacional de Agricultores Pequeños (National Association of Small Farmers—ANAP)
4. Confederación de Trabajadores de Cubano (Confederation of Cuban Workers—CTC)
5. Federación de Estudiantes Universitarios (Federation of University Students—FEU)
6. Federación de Estudiantes de Enseñanza Media (Federation of Intermediate Level Students—FEEM)
7. Organización de Pioneros José Martí (Organization of José Martí Pioneers—OPJM)

These organizations reflected the "interests" of different groups within the society, functioned both as mutual-aid societies and self-help organizations, and created a culture of civic engagement. Their purpose was to facilitate the participation of all *Cubanos* in the nation's most important social, political, economic, and defense decisions. To create interactive linkages between the organizations and the government, the *rebeldes* designated all mass organizations to be official components of the government. These organizations overlaid the neighborhood place and reinforced the ethics of solidarity, cooperation, reciprocity, and participation in neighborhood life and culture.

At the neighborhood level the most important organization is the CDR. When originally formed in September 1960, the organization's goal was to maintain internal vigilance against counterrevolutionary activities, but it morphed over time into the single most important neighborhood organization in Cuba. The CDR is the social glue that holds Cuban neighborhoods together and the engine that drives neighborhood life.[10]

The CDR is a voluntary organization with a membership of about 80 million; it covers over 80 percent of the population fourteen years of age and older. Every city block and large apartment building has a CDR, and officers are democratically elected at annual elections. Most CDRs have a president, secretary, and treasurer, and the membership appoints coordinators of six different work areas: neighborhood watch, public health, youth, recycling, finance, and volunteer work. Because they live in the same neighborhood and interact on a daily basis, members know one another. If residents are not satisfied with an officer, they have the power to remove him or her.[11]

Every person must register with the CDR in his or her block and the organization maintains records on all residents, including a person's friends, visitors, family members, work history, day-to-day activities, and participation in neighborhood life. In order to change residence, a person must secure permission from the CDR so that the family food identification card can be transferred to the new address. Repairing or remodeling a house requires a certificate from the CDR to request the necessary building materials. Volunteer work projects are organized under the auspices of the CDR, and the CDRs monitor systems for distributing neighborhood goods and services as well as transmits complaints and suggestions to the municipal assemblies.

The CDR is also a valuable "reference" source for residents, which allows the organization to play a significant role in the lives of most *habaneros*. For example, those seeking admission to the university, medical school, or a job must get a letter of recommendation from the CDR. The "best" students are considered the ones who have both good grades and a history of involvement in neighborhood life and culture. For this same reason, if a person gets into trouble and the police want to know if he or she is a good neighbor, a positive statement from the CDR could be very helpful.

The CDR has evolved into an organization that drives neighborhood development. It is concerned with most aspects of neighborhood life, including mobilizing residents around various issues, maintaining neighborhood safety and security, and other aspects of neighborhood life and culture. For example, the CDR organizes mass discussions of major legislation and organizes community-health campaigns, such as blood donations, immunization and sanitation drives, pollution control, prenatal care, and health education. The CDR cooperates with teachers, students, parents, and municipal governments in maintaining schools and organized cultural, sporting, and educational activities, and it plays a leading role in disaster preparedness.[12]

The mobilizing ability of the CDR stems from its formal relationship with the Community Party and the government. For example, the CDR maintains close organizational ties with the Committee of Revolutionary Orientation of the Central Committee of the Cuban Communist Party, the Ministry of Interior, the National Police, the CTC, the FMC, other mass organizations, and other ministries and institutes of the government. The organization, because it is organized horizontally and vertically, also links residents across neighborhoods, urban regions, and the nation as a whole. The organizational structure consists of a national directorate, provincial committees, and regions composed of CDR zones, which extend downward to the block level.[13]

In addition to the state-sponsored mass organizations, there are two other types of key organizations. The first is the Junta de Vecinos or neighborhood group, an informal group that deals with neighborhood and housing conditions. These organizations are particularly strong in multistory housing complexes, where residents must work collectively to solve problems, such as broken elevators, water shortages, or building maintenance. That other group includes various religious organizations, especially Santeria, the Yoruba-based African religion. *Cubanos* are a very spiritual people, and religion is an important part of daily life. Santeria appears to be among the most influential of the religious groups, and most *Cubanos* appear either to be practitioners of the religion or have family members who are. Although an Afro-Cuban religion, Santeria is practiced by all Cubans, regardless of race or socioeconomic group.

Participation in civic life strengthened community ties among friends, family, and neighbors; helped define collective goals through the discussion of social issues at neighborhood meetings; and promoted a sense of solidarity in Cuban society. This community ethos has produced a dense network of informal and secondary relationships that have created neighborhoods characterized by trust, solidarity, cooperation, and reciprocity, giving residents significant control over neighborhood life.

## · Creating Safe Neighborhoods

The *rebeldes* believed that strong neighborhoods could evolve only in a safe and secure environment controlled by community residents. They succeeded in their quest to create such places. Cuba has one of the lowest crime rates in Latin America and in the Americas generally, and this translates into neighborhoods where people walk the streets and use public spaces without fear. Most residents attribute Cuba's relatively low crime rate and "livable" streets to the role played by residents, along with the CDRs, in crime control and prevention.[14] The CDR-sponsored Neighborhood Watch Program is one of the main vehicles utilized in the community crime-control strategy. All CDR members are expected to participate in the Neighborhood Watch Program. For example, Omar Cardenas, who lives in Habana Vieja, says the CDR sends out information regularly about participation schedules: who, when, and where to report. When the assigned day arrives, the person reports to the Neighborhood Watch Organizer, signs in, and then goes to his or her designated watch area. Cardenas then laughingly said, "You really don't want anything stolen while you are on watch!"

Residents do not just rely on the Neighborhood Watch Program to make the community safe. They also keep their "eyes on the street, especially older and retired persons, who are at home during the day, and scrutinize the neighborhood for criminal and other inappropriate or suspicious activities." Agustín Cebreco added that when he and some friends, as teens, robbed a warehouse, the police caught them because neighbors saw and reported them. Agustín, however, harbors no ill will. "The neighbors were just trying to protect the community," he said.

According to María Lamparilla, who resides in Alamar, participation in guarding and watching the neighborhood starts in youth. In her community, members of the OPJM guard the neighborhood each year on April 4, Pioneer Day. On Election Day they also "watch" the ballots to make sure no one tampers with them. They perform these tasks because residents believe children are the most trustworthy members in the community. The ideal of community crime prevention also involves the CDR working with schools to determine what kinds of problems children are having and attempting to resolve them with parents. For example, if a child is not attending school regularly, CDR members will check with the family to determine the nature of the truancy problem and work with them to solve it. If teenagers engage in activities that might get them into trouble, CDR members will talk with them and their families in order to keep the situation from becoming serious.

## Helping At-Risk Youth
## and Other Vulnerable Population Groups

One component of crime prevention is identifying and helping at-risk young people. The goal is to reconnect at-risk youth to neighborhood life and culture. The economic crisis spawned unemployment, food shortages, and other hardships. The socioeconomic needs of children and persons with disabilities grew. The number of out-of-school and unemployed, disaffected youth, pregnant teenagers and single mothers, prisoners and ex-prisoners, and senior citizens increased. These socioeconomic factors caused problems such as drug abuse, alcoholism, prostitution, and street crime, long absent from Cuban society, to reappear. Youth were felt to be particularly at risk. Some young people turned to crime and underground market activities and lost faith in the idea of a popular-centered society.

During the 1990s, in response to the increase in socioeconomic problems, the government developed a community-orientated approach to social work based on the establishment of a close working relationship between the social worker and neighborhood residents, representatives of community organizations, and officials from regional government offices. These reforms not only resulted in the creation of Cuba's first university social-work degree program, but also in the start of four paraprofessional social work schools for youth.

In 2000 the *rebeldes* created the first paraprofessional social-work school for youth at Cojímar, in Habana Este (East Havana). The students selected to attend this school were primarily out-of-school and unemployed youth who resided in Cuba's poorest neighborhoods. Members of the Union of Young Communists (UJC) recruited the students. The UJC went door to door searching for young people willing to pursue social-work careers, and the government promised the students jobs with good salaries and the possibility of career advancement. After finishing their training, the graduates (*emergentes*) would work with social problems in their own neighborhoods.

According to three young social workers interviewed at the paraprofessional school in Cojímar, social workers returned to their own neighborhoods because they knew the residents and understood the socioeconomic problems found there, especially those facing young people. Their approach to work, the social workers said, focused on three interactive principles: (1) social work must be people centered.

(2) Go to the people; do not wait for them to come to you. (3) Work in the homes of people. Their home is your office. The goal was to identify problems and develop strategies to solve them in partnership with residents. According to the social workers, they had great latitude in determining how best to approach their work and find solutions to complex problems. "We don't have resources. We have only our ideas and the ideas of those with whom we work. We have to bring these two together to find solutions to problems."

Alejandro Vela, an Afro-Cuban social worker, summarized the role of *emergentes*:

"Cuba is not a paradise. We have many problems in this country and very few resources. Some families and households are very dysfunctional and their children get into trouble. They develop a culture that is antithetical to socialist development. Thus, we must fight the ideas this underworld culture produces. In this respect, we are in a form of cultural warfare—ideas against ideas. Even though opportunities abound in Cuba, for cultural reasons, people do not take advantage of the possibilities. Our goal is to intervene, and move them in a new direction by getting them to embrace a new set of ideas, beliefs and culture."

Alejandro's comments on culture refer to the government's Battle of Ideas campaign, which was designed to strengthen Cuba economically and socially by aggressively challenging an emergent "outlaw culture" through educational and social programs. The *rebeldes* attacked outlaw culture in two ways. First, by incorporating young people into the paraprofessional social-work program, the government immediately reduced unemployment among this group and gave them hope of a better life by providing consistent wages and opportunities to advance up the social-work job ladder. For example, Yuya Lamparilla said all social workers have an opportunity to go on to college and/or to become teachers, professional social workers, or administrators.

Second, by turning thousands of young people into *emergentes*, the *rebeldes* made them frontline workers against the growth of outlaw culture among the youth. Alejandro and his colleagues, for example, said their two most important target populations were young people, between the ages of 16 and 25, who were not working or studying, and young people in prison. He says this is a critical age group because data showed that 58 percent of youth in Cuban prisons were unemployed and not studying at the time of their arrest. Within this context the social workers said they had a twofold strategy. The first point was to get at-risk youth involved in work/study programs, while the second was to prepare young prisoners for reintegration into society.

Thus, the *rebeldes* continually sought to find creative ways to solve neighborhood problems through a participatory process that sought to improve the social functioning of neighborhoods. By recruiting young people from vulnerable neighborhoods, training them as social workers, and then sending them back to work in those same neighborhoods, the *rebeldes* have helped to strengthen the ability of these locales to solve their own problems.

## Socialist Democracy and Neighborhood Development

Participatory democracy is a critical component of everyday life and culture. The electoral system stresses accountability and is designed to maximize community representation in the governance system. In 1976 the government made it possible for eligible voters (those over sixteen who live in the electoral district, excluding prisoners and those declared mentally incompetent) to freely nominate and elect their municipal delegates by secret ballot in competitive elections. There must be at least two and no more than eight candidates and the delegate must win by a majority. If this is not the case, then a second round of elections is held.[15]

Election districts, or *conscripciones*, are small and consist of only one thousand to fifteen hundred voters. In Cuba, candidates do not run campaigns based on promises or platforms. Biographies of candidates are posted in the neighborhoods because "the people want to know what the candidates have already done in the community, rather than what they promise to do in the future," a Universidad de la Habana professor explained. It is past accomplishments rather than promises about future action that drives the election process.

The small size of the electoral district combined with the method of electing delegates to the assembly ensures that representatives are accountable to their constituents. However, of the three levels of government—the National, Provincial, and Municipal assemblies—only the National Assembly has legislative powers, with the budgets for both the Provincial and Municipal assemblies coming from the National Assembly. While the Municipal Assembly's lack of power and resources is a source of frustration for *Cubanos*, this body not only serves as the primary governmental access point for residents, but also plays a significant role in local development. The delegates work with residents to solve local problems and to oversee social, economic, judicial, and political affairs within the municipality, including the selection of managers for local institutions such as public health clinics and schools. Most important, delegates make sure that the Provincial and National assemblies are aware of local concerns and initiatives.

Although these efforts to bolster community participation in local decision making represented an important step forward in the decentralization of power, the *rebeldes* were not satisfied. They felt the gap between the municipal assemblies and neighborhoods was still too great and thus established an intermediate body in 1989, the *consejos populares* (people's councils) in Havana. By 1993, the *consejos populares*, consisting of approximately fifteen contiguous electoral districts within a municipality, had spread throughout the entire country. Although the *consejos populares*, like its counterpart at the municipal level, did not have legislative powers or fiscal resources, it was nevertheless a vital entity that worked with residents to resolve problems, develop the neighborhood, coordinate socioeconomic activities at the neighborhood level, and provide residents with access to the government.

During *El Período Especial* people could no longer depend on the government or the experts to solve their problems. In this moment, when resources were scarce or nonexistent, residents had to set their own priorities, design their own strategies, and then use their own inventiveness and creativity to find solutions. To support this movement toward self-reliance, the government established the *talleres* to encourage the integration of social and physical planning and to promote broad participation in decision making. Toward this end, the government expanded the staff of *talleres* to include sociologists and community organizers in addition to architects and engineers.[16]

### The Pillar of *El Barrio:* Primary Education, the Family Doctor and Nurse Program, and Disaster Preparation

The *rebeldes* used primary education, the family doctor and nurse program, and disaster preparation to anchor neighborhood life and culture. By linking primary education and health prevention and delivery to the neighborhood setting, the *rebeldes* made two of the most important components of social development part of the landscape of *el barrio*. Then, to ensure that the protection of human life during an extreme event was the top priority, they forged a community-based system of disaster preparation. Although much has been written about these celebrated Cuban programs, most of what we know about them is based on top-down viewpoints that reflect the official positions of the government or state-approved studies.

To gain a bottom-up perspective on how these programs have been significant components of neighborhood development in Havana, 249 interviews were conducted with community residents. These interviews bring to the forefront the views of *habaneros* who live in some of Havana's most vulnerable neighborhoods. Most of the interviews were held in communities located in Habana Este, Habana Vieja, and Centro Habana.

## Primary Education

Free education was a top priority in Castro's Cuba because the *rebeldes* believed they could build a revolutionary society only if all its citizens were literate and had the knowledge and skills necessary to participate fully in the life of the nation.[17] Toward this end they sought to build neighborhoods that valued education and supported academic achievement. The Cuban Constitution states that education is a task in which all society participates and made provisions for the involvement of all citizens, not just parents, in the schooling process "through the country's social and mass organizations in the development of its educational and cultural policy."[18]

School attendance is compulsory for students between the ages of six and fourteen. This guarantees that most *Cubanos* will complete their primary and basic secondary education. Primary schools include grades one through six (ages six to eleven years) and a basic secondary school provides for students in grades seven through nine (ages twelve to fourteen years). An additional secondary program, which extends from grades ten though twelve (ages fifteen to seventeen years) consists of pre-university, vocational, and technical school tracks and is free but not compulsory. The students going on to the secondary program are about evenly divided among the three tracks. Following the completion of their secondary program, students either enter the work force or go into Cuba's free university system.

All primary schools are neighborhood based so that students can attend schools close to their homes. The Cuban primary schools have long enjoyed a reputation for high quality, but it was a 1998 report by UNESCO that catapulted the nation's educational achievements into the international spotlight. The UNESCO report showed that Cuban students in the third and fourth grades scored significantly higher than their counterparts in eleven other Latin American countries: Argentina, Bolivia, Brazil, Costa Rica, Chile, Dominican Republic, Honduras, Mexico, Paraguay, Peru, and Venezuela. Even the lowest fourth of Cuban students outperformed their primary-school peers, including those attending elite private schools. So dramatic was the academic performance of Cuban students that the U.N. agency administering the test returned to Cuba to retest the students. The retest confirmed the earlier conclusion: Cuba leads the Latin American region in primary education.

## Why Are Cuban Primary Schools Successful?

How did Cuba, one of the poorest countries in Latin America, outperform its peers, including students from wealthier nations such as Mexico, Argentina, Venezuela, and Brazil? Martin Carnoy and Jeffrey Marshall suggest that the creation of a social environment in which education and academic achievement is valued helps to explain the success of Cuba's primary students.[19] They based their thesis on the role played by "collective" social capital in the educative process, which is a theory originally espoused by James Coleman.

Coleman argues that academic success among students is a layered process in which success is based on the level of support received at the family, neighborhood, and school levels. For example, children with supportive families will likely experience greater academic success than children without such support, and so forth. Thus, children moving through a supportive environment consisting of family, neighbors, and strong schools are likely to achieve greater academic success than students whose support system does not transcend more than one or two levels in the hierarchy.[20]

Carnoy and Marshall agree that the academic success of Cuban primary students might be due to the existence of strong academic support at all three levels in the community support hierarchy. Thus, an examination of these layers not only will provide insight into the academic success of Cuban primary students, but also will deepen our understanding of the intricacies of the social function model of neighborhood development.

## Resident Perception

To interrogate the role of primary education in neighborhood life and culture, ninety-eight household containing primary schools students were interviewed.[21] This sample consisted of racially mixed households, closely divided among whites (37 percent), blacks (32 percent), and mulattos (26 percent), along with a very small number of Asian households. This racial mix is typical of Havana neighborhoods and is reflective of the racial and occupational integration characteristic of neighborhoods.

## Household Structure

In their study of Havana slums Coyula and Hamberg described four types of households: extended (with relatives other than family members), composites (including at least one person unrelated to the household head), nuclear, and single person. The survey information in the Cuba Project study suggests that the household structure is a bit more complicated than this, as a different, but complementary system of classifying Havana neighborhoods was employed.

Most primary students lived in either a multi-generational (57 percent) or traditional family household (18 percent) settings. About 75 percent of the sample households fell into these two categories. For the purposes of the study, *multi-generational households* are defined as units that contain relatives from two or more generations. *Traditional family* refers to a nuclear family in which children live with their mother and father, including stepparent(s), who may or may not be married. The term *partner* is used to describe couples living together. In Cuba, like the rest of the Caribbean and Central America, many couples live in consensual unions rather than marriage.[22] In addition to multi-generational and traditional family households, a few children lived in family-communal households (10 percent). These are households shared by family members within the same generation, including some combination of relatives, such as cousins, brothers, and/or sisters.

The great majority of Cuban primary students, therefore, lived in household settings that included other relatives as well as their parent(s). Overall, primary students lived in households with an average of four persons. Unlike distressed communities in the United States, the number of single-parent households in Cuba is very small. In the population sampled, only 10 percent of children lived in households with one parent, as single mothers usually live with their parent(s), along with other relatives, or in a consensual relationship. For example, of the households surveyed, 52 percent had fathers present, 45 percent grandmothers, 32 percent grandfathers, 28 percent aunts, and 26 percent uncles. In these extended family household settings, single mothers have support with child rearing, which eases the burden of parenting responsibilities.

The primary students in this sample lived in households where members valued work. On average, each household contained at least two workers, along with a few households (6 percent) that contained retired workers. In Havana, it is rare to find households where no one is working. Not only do people work, but many household members also moonlight in either the formal or informal economy. Thus, a culture of work existed in households where primary children lived. The children perceive their families to have a positive view of work and can recognize how this view contributes to the well-being of the household as a whole.

## Community Involvement

Another important component of household social capital is the extent to which household members have relationships with other neighborhood residents. These relationships provide insight into the extent to which families and households are embedded in social structures that provide support, reduce stress, and set normative standards of behavior. To explore this issue further, membership in various organizations was used as a surrogate for household connections with other residents. About 90 percent of the respondents acknowledged membership in the CDR. Many appear to be active participants, with close to 55 percent attending meetings three to four times a year and 23 percent stating that they attend monthly meetings.

Approximately 77 percent of the respondents said they also belonged to the FMC, and 42 percent of this group noted that they attended meetings three to four times a year with an additional 14 percent attending monthly. About 51 percent of the residents said they belonged to the Junta de Vecinos, an important, informal, neighborhood-based organization that grapples with housing and other issues related to the immediate living environment of residents, and the participation rate was quite high for those involved. Residents who live in multistory buildings are most likely to belong to this group. In this sample, 52 percent of the respondents said they met with the Junta once a month, while 34 percent said they met three or four times per year, and 16 percent said they met with the Junta at least once a year. Thus, the data suggest that primary school students live in households with strong collective social capital.

## The Neighborhood Social Environment

Cuban neighborhoods are very stable places where people tend to age in place. On average, households containing primary school students in this sample had lived in their current residence eighteen years. Neighborhoods are safe and relatively free of violence. This is the result of a community-based system of crime control led by the CDR. In addition, in Havana neighborhoods, especially the most vulnerable ones, the Policia Nacional Revolucionario (National Revolutionary

Police Force—PNR) is omnipresent and this, along with the activities of the CDR, serves to discourage criminal activity and keep streets safe. The police presence is not as visible in the outlying neighborhoods as it is in communities such as Habana Vieja, Centro Habana, and Vedado, where the probability of criminal activity is not the greatest.

Not surprisingly, most residents feel their neighborhoods are safe. For example, 70 percent of the respondents said they were not afraid to go out of their houses, and the majority (64 percent) said they did not know anyone who had been assaulted. The number of children who use the street as their playground is probably the best illustration of the perceived safety of Cuban neighborhoods. The normative structure of the community ensures that the many adults who also "inhabit" the street will oversee unattended children, and neighbors will make sure they are kept safe.

## The Hierarchy of Academic Success

Most Cuban households surveyed expressed their belief in the value of education and their support of academic achievement. This is demonstrated, in part, by the large number of respondents who completed primary and secondary school themselves. All the residents in our sample had completed primary school, and 69 percent had gone on to complete secondary school, pre-university, and technical and vocational school. Significantly, 12 percent of the sample indicated that they had obtained college degrees, and an additional 6 percent had completed graduate training. Also, another 8 percent of the sample indicated they had some college training but had not completed their degree. Thus, even in the most vulnerable neighborhoods, with 26 percent of the population having at least some college experience, one finds a well-educated population.

On this point, Juan Casassus, a member of the team that conducted the UNESCO study, noted: "Education has been a top priority in Cuba for forty years. It's a true learning society."[23] The data from our sample supports the idea that primary students lived in "learning environments" where household members believe that education is important. Specifically, 92 percent of the respondents affirmed that their children's education was important to them, and 80 percent of these stated it was very important. Even the remaining 8 percent believed education for their children was somewhat important. The majority, 78 percent, said that doing well in school would offer their children greater opportunities. Only 5 percent said they do not believe education will bolster their children's life chances.

Parents continued to indicate their support for their children's academic success through their awareness and involvement in the daily concerns of schooling. For instance, 98 percent of parents know about homework, how much their children bring home, and how much effort they must provide to assist with its completion. About 47 percent of the respondents said their children had to contend with a great deal of homework, and 57 percent stated that they consistently helped their children with this chore. Another 31 percent said that they did help at times, when the need arose.

Critical to academic support is the connection between parent and teacher. Virtually all parents (99 percent) visit their child's school, with 24 percent saying they visit a great deal and 28 percent saying that they visit often. Also, most parents said they regularly attended conferences with teachers. A small number (5 percent) said they had "very frequent" conferences with teachers, 29 percent said they met "frequently" with teachers, while 49 percent said they "sometimes" had conferences with teachers. Thus 83 percent of those surveyed met with their child's teacher with some regularity. Of those remaining, 15 percent said they met with teachers "only when there are problems." Only 2 percent of the respondents said that they had never met with the teachers of their children.

## Neighborhood Support for Academic Achievement

The neighborhoods in which primary students live are also supportive of academic achievement. Here, all respondents (100 percent) said that they believed their friends and neighbors believed that going to school was very important, with only 7 percent of this total deeming it somewhat important. Moreover, 81 percent of those completing surveys felt that children and youth in their neighborhoods also believed that getting good grades was important. Thus, based on this data, Cuban primary students are living in safe, stable neighborhood environments, where homes are academically supportive and where streets are animated, communal places where people socially interact, and most important, where children are safe to learn and play under the watchful eyes of their neighbors.

## The Primary School

The primary school is the third layer in the community-support hierarchy. According to Carnoy and Marshall, the quality of teachers, physical classroom conditions, and school materials might explain the success of Cuban primary students. While these elements are important, the relational components that foster trust between student and school, parent and school, and the community and the school are critical attributes that turn Cuban schools into supportive environments for students.

Trust is the most important element in the schooling process and represents the connective tissue that ties the school (principal and teachers) to the students, parents, and community.[24] The data indicate that families with primary students trust their children's principals and teachers. When asked if they respected and trusted the principal at their child's school, 91 percent of the residents responded affirmatively, with 28 percent stating that they trusted the principal a great deal. When asked if they trusted the teachers at their child's school, 92 percent of the respondents answered affirmatively. Many teachers live in the neighborhoods where they work, and this helps to explain why many families believe that teachers understand the problems faced by their children and other members of the community. As previously mentioned, many parents regularly visit their child's school and hold conferences with the teachers. One reason this happens is because they feel welcomed and appreciated in that environment. About 94 percent of the respondents said the school makes them feel this way. Only 5 percent of the respondents said that they did not feel comfortable interacting with school personnel.

Trust also has a dynamic quality and is continually shaped and reshaped by the ongoing interactions among principals, teachers, parents, and students. For example, most parents said they felt comfortable talking with their child's teacher (86 percent) and with the principal (82 percent) at their child's school. Parents believed that teachers were excited about their work, 42 percent saying this is often the case, while 51 percent find that they are sometimes quite enthused. Significantly, 61 percent of the parents felt that they did and could influence the curriculum taught at their child's school. Clearly, this data is showing education in Cuba to be a collaborative effort.

Another factor reinforcing the trust between households and teachers is the home visits made by teachers. This factor, perhaps more than any other, illustrates teachers' concern for the academic success of their students. About 54 percent of the respondents said their child's teacher makes home visits. Of this group, 25 percent said the teacher often visits their home, and 58 percent said the teacher will sometimes stop by. Additionally, 17 percent noted that the teacher visits only when their child is having a problem. Given the high levels of trust, it is not surprising that 96 percent of the respondents believe their child's school is a good place to study and learn.

Another component of the school-community relationship deals with the attitude of primary students toward the school and the nature and character of their activities within the school. Most parents felt their child enjoyed going to school, with about 38 percent saying their child enjoyed school a great deal and 36 percent feeling that their child somewhat enjoyed going to school. In Cuba, unlike many schools in the Americas, including the United States, primary students participate in the upkeep of the school. Approximately 92 percent of those surveyed stated that their children participated to some degree, large or small, in the upkeep and maintenance of the school. Only about 6 percent said their child did not participate at all, to their knowledge.

Another critical aspect of creating links between the school and the community is the extent to which there are extracurricular activities that involve the students in community engagement. Again, approximately 90 percent of the respondents said that students in their children's school were involved to some extent in community initiatives. It was also noted that the school was sometimes available for after-school activities. Many households have working members, including parents, and the availability of after-school activities for their children is of some interest. About half of the parents stated that the school was sometimes available for such activities.

In summary, the results of this survey suggest that primary students in Cuba are embedded in a nurturing social environment that is supportive of academic achievement at the household, neighborhood, and school levels. The collective social capital found in Cuban neighborhoods creates a contextual setting that increases the likelihood that primary students will do well in school. Thus, at all levels of the community academic achievement hierarchy, primary students in Cuba encounter a supportive environment and this, in turn, may account for their success when tested against students from other countries, who may not receive these benefits.

## The Medicine in the Community Program

The revolutionary struggle against the Batista regime planted the seeds that ultimately produced the Cuban government's health ideology. In *History Will Absolve Me* Fidel Castro first outlined the *rebeldes'* viewpoint on health care when he stated that no child should die for the lack of medical attention and then further elaborated on the deplorable state of health care in Cuba. The abject poverty and enormous health problems of the rural population greatly disturbed the *rebeldes*, many of whom were physicians, Che Guevara among them. Consequently, when they seized power in 1959, health care became one of the revolution's cornerstones. Good health was indispensable not only in and of itself but also because people needed to be healthy enough "to achieve a high level of education and culture, intellectual and physical development and optimal work capacity." The *rebeldes* thus adopted the World Health Organization's definition of good health, which meant not simply the absence of disease, but also the existence of a state of complete physical, mental, and social well-being.[25]

Informed by this definition, the Cuban government built a health-care system that has received international acclaim. It has achieved developed-country health outcomes despite its developing-country economic status. For example, Cuba spends just 7 percent of its gross national product (GNP) on health care, compared with 14 percent spent in the United States. Health expenditures per person are $193 in Cuba compared to $4,540 spent in the United States. Yet, health outcomes in Cuba are essentially the same as those in the United States in terms of infant mortality and life expectancy.

The *rebeldes* built their health system around three interactive principles: equal access to services, an integrated approach to health care, and popular participation in health initiatives. Equal access meant providing health care, regardless of the level of sophistication, without cost, to all residents. In addition, it meant that the government was responsible for delivering quality health to all parts of the country, including the most vulnerable urban neighborhoods and isolated rural communities. This integrated approach combined prevention, wellness, along with early diagnosis and treatment of disease, into a singular concept of health. Moreover, both mental and physical well-being were considered to be prerequisites for a healthy person. Last, popular participation meant that the *clases populares* would be able to participate in health planning, administration, and implementation through the input provided by their representatives from the mass organizations through regular meetings with policlinic administrators and the municipal health director.

Although Cuba is a developing country with limited resources, its health system is nonetheless physician based; even at the neighborhood level, physicians anchor the system. This is not the case in other socialist or developing countries. For example, in the former Soviet Union, paramedics, known as fedshers, played a prominent role in the health-care system, while in China, a cross between a paramedic and traditional healer, called barefoot doctors, drove primary care. In other developing countries, governments typically use paramedics, especially in the rural areas, to delivery health services. Cuba, despite limited resources, moved in a different direction. The *rebeldes* placed emphasis on the production of doctors. In their medical education program they stressed family medicine with the goal of having specialists-generalists at the point of entry into the health system. In both rural areas and in urban centers, physicians lead the health-care teams.

The success of the health system prompted the *rebeldes* to make medical diplomacy an integral part of foreign policy. Living in a hostile hemispheric environment caused the *rebeldes* to search for allies. This search led to the development of medical diplomacy as a strategy that Cuba could utilize to strengthen its relationship with other developing counties and to ward off ongoing criticism from the United States. Through the provision of medical aid and assistance, Cuba has positively affected the lives of millions of people in developing countries. By the end of 2005, Cuban medical personnel were collaborating in sixty-eight countries across the globe. To sustain these efforts over the years, thousands of developing-country medical personnel have received free education and training in Cuba or by Cuban specialists engaged in on-the-job training courses.

In 1999, as part of its strategy of sustaining high quality health care in developing countries, Cuba established the international Escuela Latinoamericana de Medicina (Latin American School of Medical Sciences—ELAM) as an integral part of the medical diplomacy program. ELAM, with an enrollment of ten thousand to twelve thousand students, primarily from Latin America, the Caribbean, and Africa, might be the largest medical school in the world. Beginning in 2000, ELAM developed a program to accept low-income students from the United States.

In June 2000 a group from the Congressional Black Caucus visited Cuban president Fidel Castro. Representative Bennie Thompson (D-Miss.) described huge areas in his district where there were no doctors, and Castro responded with an offer of full scholarships for U.S. citizens to study at ELAM. Later that year, at the Riverside Church in New York, Castro reiterated the offer of committing five hundred slots to U.S. students who would pledge to practice in poor U.S. communities. By 2004, there were eighty-eight U.S. students at ELAM, 85 percent of them from minority groups and 73 percent of them women. Applicants are required to have a high school diploma and at least two years of premedical courses, to be from poor communities, and to make a commitment to return to those communities.

## The Medicine-in-the-Community Ideal

The medicine-in-the-community ideal, anchored by a neighborhood-based primary-care program, undergirded the Cuban health-care system. This approach recognized the importance of viewing patients as people who are bio-psycho-social beings embedded in a neighborhood setting and thus sought to transform *el barrio* into the prime venue for service delivery and a supportive environment for a healthy lifestyle. In 1984, to strengthen the program, Fidel Castro established a pilot project designed to put doctor and nurse teams on literally every city block and in the remotest rural communities. Each team was to care for 120 to 150 families, or about 600 to 700 people, in clinics consisting of a waiting room, a doctor's office, and an examination and treatment room. These doctor and nurse teams formed the entry point into the Cuban medical system and the link between neighborhood residents and the health-care system. To make these medical teams an integral part of the community in which their patients lived, most family doctors and nurses lived in apartments above their offices.

By the middle of the 1980s the *rebeldes* had established a three-tiered health-care program. Neighborhood-based primary care, delivered in *consultorios* (clinics), represented the first tier of care. A family doctor and nurse team staffed the *consultorio,* which served families in a defined geographic area surrounding the *consultario.* *Policlínicos* (specialty clinics) operated at the community level and provided secondary-level care for a predefined population of twenty-five thousand to thirty thousand people. These clinics consisted of interdisciplinary teams and offered specialty care in a variety of areas, including pediatrics, internal medicine, nursing, social work, dentistry, and physical therapy, and sometimes included cardiology, pulmonology, ophthalmology, neurology, endocrinology, dermatology, and psychiatry. Tertiary care in *hospitales* and *institutos* (hospitals and medical institutes) provided the third tier of care.

The *consultorios,* the entry point in the Cuban health-care system, addresses approximately 80 percent of the health problems of residents and emphasizes health promotion and disease prevention. Typically, in the mornings, family physicians attend patients in their *consultorio;* afternoons are reserved for home visits to patients with acute care needs, rehabilitation of chronic conditions, and primary prevention. The family doctor refers patients who require care beyond the scope of the *consultorio* to a speciality clinic or hospital.

## Resident View of the Family Doctor and Nurse Program

During *El Período Especial* some began to sense that Cuba's highly vaunted health program was suffering and the quality of treatment was beginning to decline. To gain insight into this issue, from the perspective of neighborhood residents, 148 households in Havana were interviewed regarding their experiences with the health-care system.[26] Before asking questions about the family doctor and nurse program, they were first asked to describe their current health status to provide some baseline data. Close to 63 percent said they felt they were in good to excellent health, with 25 percent stating their health was fair and 11 percent in poor health.

## Entering the Health-care System

To obtain a sense of how entry into the health-care system actually worked, the respondents were asked if they had a family doctor and how often they visited the *consultario*, the *policlínico*, and the hospital. About 78 percent of the respondents said they had a family doctor, while 21 percent said they did not. Within a Cuban context, the percentage of resident who stated they did not have a family doctor was surprisingly high. The family doctor and nurse program is meant to cover all neighborhood residents, and thus it was expected that all residents would have a family doctor. There could be a number of explanations for this response. First, some residents may not access health-care services through the intended entry point of the family doctor. They could simply be bypassing the *consultorio* and going directly to the *policlínico* for services. The Cuban health system is hierarchical but not bureaucratic. Those who go directly to the policlinic without a referral from their physician will not be turned away.

It is also possible that the family doctor may be temporarily unavailable due to the recent upsurge in the deployment of doctors to other countries. Anecdotal data obtained from informal interviews suggest that there may have been a reduction in the number of family doctors available in some neighborhoods. One respondent said the doctors in her community "went abroad." To entice doctors to participate in the medical diplomacy program, *medicos* serving abroad receive much higher pay than those in Cuba, along with benefits from the state, such as the right to obtain a car and a "good" house when they return. As a result, some of the best physicians have taken posts abroad. These issues notwithstanding, most residents had visited their family doctor during the past year: 11 percent said they visited the doctor more than seven times during the year, 9 percent said they visited the doctor four to six times, while 55 percent said they visited the family doctor one to three times during the year. Twenty-six percent had not made any doctor visits over the past year.

## Secondary and Tertiary Levels of Care

Under the Cuban health system, the *policlínicos* represent the second tier in health care. Theoretically, patients go to the family doctor, who then refers them to the policlinics if they need a more advanced level of care. The surveys indicated that 86 percent of the respondents visited the *policlínico* at least once during the previous year. Of this group, about 13 percent of the respondents said they visited the policlinic more than seven times, 24 percent visited it four to six times, and 32 percent had visited two to three times. About 18 percent of the respondents said they visited the policlinic once. Only 14 percent of the respondents said they did not visit the policlinic during the year.

These findings are somewhat surprising. Because the *consultorio* is the entry point into the health-care system, one would anticipate that the family doctor would have the highest percentage of visits. However, a higher percentage of respondents visited *policlínicos* than *consultorios* (86 percent vs. 75 percent). This suggests that, as suspected, some respondents may be bypassing the family doctor and going directly to the *policlínico* to see a physician. Though 26 percent of the respondents said they had not visited the family doctor, only 14 percent stated they had not visited the policlinic. Both the *consultorios* and *policlínicos* are within walking distance in most neighborhoods. Therefore, given the flexibility within the health system, it is reasonable to assume that, for whatever the reason, some *habaneros* go directly to the policlinics rather than visit their family doctor.

The hospitals provide the third tier of health care in the Cuban system. About 61 percent of the respondents said they visited the hospital at least once during the year. Of this group, about 22 percent said they visited the hospital at least once, while 19 percent said they visited it two to three times. About 20 percent of the respondents said they visited the hospital more than four times during the year. Thirty-nine percent had not visited the hospital at all during the past year.

## Trust and the Family Doctor

Health professionals recognize trust as being central to the establishment of a good patient-doctor relationship. In the world of health care, the absence or presence of trust in patient-doctor relations can have life-altering consequences. People are more likely to seek care, comply with treatment recommendations, and return for follow-up services if they trust their provider or health service. The respondents were asked a series of questions to gain insight into the key issues that influence the establishment of a trusting relationship between the family doctor and his or her patients. In terms of physician competency, it was discovered that the majority of people (58 percent) were basically satisfied with the quality of care received from their family doctor. Eleven percent stated they were very satisfied, 23 percent were satisfied, and 24 percent were somewhat satisfied

However, 30 percent of the residents noted that they were dissatisfied with their family doctor. About 12 percent of the sample had no opinion on the question. The anecdotal data obtained from the interviews shed some light on concerns that exist about the family doctor program. One respondent, for example, complained that the family doctors "are young doctors without experience." In a similar vein, another respondent said, "Because some of them are so young, they don't pay attention to their work." Yet another respondent worried, "Sometimes, because the doctors are incompetent, lack motivation, or don't want to work, they make fatal mistakes." Further concern is evidenced by this sad tale: "My father was sick and we took him to the family doctor. They sent us to the policlinic. The doctors at the policlinic found nothing and sent him home. Three days later, a neighbor and I took my father to the hospital. The hospital doctors said he had had a heart attack three days earlier. After several days in intensive care, my father died."

Concurrently, a number of respondents spoke positively about their experiences with the family doctor. "The family doctor visits my home regularly because my father has colon disease and arteriosclerosis," a respondent said. Another respondent said," My husband was disabled for five years before he died, but I cannot complain because the family doctor attended him very well." Still another respondent said, "Everyday I have pains, but the nurse comes every two days." Thus, there appears to be an uneven quality in the delivery of health services at this initial level as noted by those surveyed, with many expressing concern, while others were very pleased.

Next, respondents were asked to evaluate the effectiveness of the family doctor program in terms of (1) providing education and counseling on maintaining personal health; (2) protecting the community against communicable diseases; and (3) providing health-care services for neighborhood residents. About 91 percent of the respondents said the family doctor and nurse program provided effective health education and counseling for the community. About 5 percent said the family doctor and nurse program was not effective in this area, while about 5 percent of the respondents said they did not know. This aspect of the health-care delivery system appears to be an effective one.

The respondents were also predominately positive about the role of the family doctor and nurse program in providing effective protection against infectious diseases in the neighborhood, with 70 percent believing the program was effective to very effective. Another 38 percent of the respondents thought this component of the program was somewhat effective in protecting the community against infectious diseases, and 5 percent of the respondents said they did not know. When asked about the effectiveness of the family doctor and nurse program in improving medical service for the neighborhood, about 86 percent felt the program produced favorable health outcomes for the neighborhood. About 9 percent of the respondents said the services were not effective, while 5 percent said they did not know.

Next, to gain additional insight into the trust question, we wanted to probe the interpersonal communication between the respondents and the family doctor, which refers to the doctor's concern for the well-being of his or her patients, the ability to get them to communicate concerns, and the overall comfort level that exists between doctor and patient. Residents were asked if they believed the family doctor placed their health and welfare above other considerations, such as making more money or working in a better position. Of this group, 12 percent said the family doctor always placed their health and welfare above other concerns, while 26 percent said they placed them first most of the time. Another 26 percent said the family doctor occasionally placed their health and welfare above other concerns. About 19 percent of the respondents said the family doctor never placed their health and welfare above other concerns, and 16 percent of the respondents said they did not know.

An essential part of the communication between doctor and patient is openness. Toward this end, we wanted to know how relaxed, or at ease, the respondents were with their family doctors. About 51 percent said they were at ease with the family doctor and nurse, while 32 percent said the family doctor team sometimes made them feel comfortable. On the other hand, 14 percent of the respondent said the doctor-nurse team made them feel uncomfortable, and 3 percent had no opinion on this question. The next question focused on being able to discuss most issues with the family physician. About 52 percent of the respondents felt they could discuss any issue with their family doctor, and an additional 28 percent said they felt comfortable talking with the doctor some of the time. Ten percent of the respondents said they never felt comfortable talking with the family doctor, while another 10 percent said they did not know.

Another critical component of trust is the extent to which the patient believes the doctor knows and understands the conditions of life they face. The *rebeldes* wanted the doctors and nurses to live in the communities they served not only to increase their access to residents, but also to deepen their understanding of the neighborhoods in which their patients lived. Thus, residents were asked how likely they were to see the family doctor in their neighborhood. Eight-four percent of the respondents said it would not be unexpected to see the family doctor in their neighborhood. Only 9 percent of the respondents said there were not likely to see the family doctor in the neighborhood, and 8 percent had no opinion. The respondents were also asked how likely it would be to see the family doctor at a neighborhood meeting. About 73 percent of the respondents stated they had seen the family doctor at meetings, but about 20 percent said they did not think this was likely. Seven percent of the respondents had no opinion.

Next, we wanted to know if the respondents believed that the family doctor understood the issues facing their neighborhoods. Approximately 18 percent of the respondents said the doctors greatly understand the issues facing their community. Thirty-five percent said the doctors understand their community's problems, while 28 percent said the doctors somewhat understand the neighborhood issues. About 18 percent of the respondents said the family doctor did not understand the conditions facing their community.

The overwhelming majority of respondents felt the family doctor was an important factor in making their neighborhood a good place to live. Eighty-six percent of the respondents said the family doctor was an important asset to the neighborhood, with only 7 percent stating that the family doctor was not an important factor. About 5 percent of the sample said they did not know. This data suggests that a significant level of trust exists between family doctors and their patients, although some respondents have concerns about the quality of care. These reservations notwithstanding, the majority of residents believe that the family doctor is an effective service provider, one who makes them feel at ease and one with whom they can discuss most issues. Moreover, the respondents believe the family doctor understands their problems and the conditions faced by the neighborhood. The respondents might feel this way because the family doctor spends time in the schools, in the work place, and also lives in the community where he or she works. Thus, the residents are likely not only to see the doctor on the streets, but also in community meetings. Taking these results as a whole, it is not surprising that the overwhelming majority of residents, despite the reservations of some, believe that the presence of the family doctor makes the neighborhood a better place to live.

## Access to Health Services

Cuba has gone farther than any other developing country in creating access to health-care services for its citizens. Accessibility to health-care services typically involves the interplay of four factors: geographic accessibility, service availability, financial accessibility, and quality of care. The medicine-in-the-community model virtually eliminates the geographic accessibility issue. In *el barrio*, the *consultorios* and the *policlínicos* are within walking distance in most neighborhoods. In addition, most specialty hospitals are centrally located, which makes them also easy to reach. Adding to the accessibility factor are home visits made by the family doctor and/or nurse, especially for patients with acute care issues. For example, 30 percent of the respondents said the family doctor sometimes visits their home, and 8 percent said the doctor visits their home regularly.

Moreover, family doctors also closely follow all pregnant women and newborns, children, those with chronic illnesses, the elderly, and those recently released from hospitals. Family doctors are linked to neighborhood policlinics, the work place, and the schools. Geographic accessibility and the availability of services are not issues in Havana. About 91 percent of the respondents said their families received the health services they needed. Moreover, as mentioned previously, interpersonal communications between the patient and doctor are generally good, and most respondents believed the family doctor-nurse team understood the issues facing their community.

Although health care is free in Cuba, I still wanted to determine the extent to which financial issues influenced both access and quality of care. Informal conversations with numerous *habaneros* indicated that this could sometimes be problematic. Therefore, respondents were asked if they would receive better care or faster service if they offered the family doctor money. Thirty-four percent of the respondents said no, but 31 percent said this would happen, and 16 percent said this would occur at times. Eighteen percent said they did not know. Thus, although *Cubanos* do not have to pay to receive medical services, about 47 percent of the respondents said they believed they would receive better or faster service if they paid the family doctor. While medical care is free, patients do have to pay for their prescriptions, even if the cost is nominal. About 46 percent of the respondents said getting their prescriptions was not a problem, while 43 percent said sometimes it was an issue. About 11 percent of the respondents said they consistently had difficulty getting prescriptions filled.

*El Período Especial*, however, generated considerable challenges to the family doctor and nurse program, creating a tension between the ability of the *rebeldes* to foster a medical diplomacy strategy that sends thousands of doctors abroad and concurrently to maintain a high quality of service at home. Within this context residents were questioned about their views on the quality of medical service over the past five years. About 48 percent of the respondents felt that medical service had either improved or remained the same over this period of time. However, 41 percent felt that services had declined, and, among this latter group, 22 percent said the service declined a little, while 18 percent felt that medical services had declined greatly.

It is not surprising that many *habaneros* are pleased with the family doctor and nurse system. Infant mortality and life expectancy are internationally recognized indicators of human well-being because they tap into both the quality of health care and access to food and other variables that promote social well-being. Despite the great challenges encountered during *El Período Especial*, the infant mortality and life expectancy rates in Cuba continue to be the same as those in the United States. Nonetheless, the numerous concerns expressed by the respondents and others informally interviewed suggest that there are cracks in the vaunted family doctor and nurse program.

The problem might be a result of the *rebeldes'* desire to deploy doctors abroad and also meet the needs of neighborhoods at home. For example, because of the many doctors sent abroad, those left behind are sometimes stretched thin and overworked, resulting in a decline in the quality of care. On this point, Agustín Cebreco, reflecting on the viewpoints of neighbors, said:

> "Before [*El Período Especial*] there were more doctors for less people. Right now, there are a lot of doctors in Venezuela, Pakistan, Honduras, and Bolivia. In these countries, they are helping the people. Now, these doctors [the ones left behind in Cuba] have more people. Therefore, they pay more attention to people with more serious problems, such as old people. When you go to see the family doctor, they are not there. They have gone to someone's house to help them. Now, some people, instead of going to the family doctor, will go to the policlinic. If there is a big problem, they will go to the hospital."

A forty-five-year-old nurse in Camagüey province said she has worked without a doctor in her *consultorio* for more than two years, ever since the physician was transferred to another clinic to replace a doctor sent to Venezuela. "My patients complain every day. They want me to act as a doctor, but I can't," she said. "The level of attention isn't the same as before. It's not fair . . . to take from us to give our neighbors. People are now saying, 'I've got to get a ticket to Venezuela to get healthcare.'"

Cuban doctors and nurses have worked overseas in humanitarian missions for many years, but over the past few years, as Castro's and Chavez's cooperation has blossomed, and the petroleum-rich Venezuela has become an invaluable trading partner, Cuba has significantly increased the number of doctors sent to that country. This has led to the growing complaint that quality and access are suffering as tens of thousands of medical workers are lost to Venezuela in exchange for cheap oil, which the country desperately needs. At the same time, Venezuela is one of Cuba's most important allies and plays a central role in keeping the island stable. Venezuela has provided Cuba with 100,000 barrels of oil a day at a reduced rate and has provided the country with more than $2 billion in financing. Concurrently, exports from the island to Venezuela rose from just $25 million in 2002 to $300 million by 2004.[27] Cuban physicians have also played an important role in bringing primary health care to Venezuela's poorest inhabitants. More than twenty thousand Cuban medical personnel—doctors, nurse, dentists, and others—have been the backbone of the program. Thus, despite the contradictions, it is not likely that Cuba will abandon its medical diplomacy program in Venezuela and elsewhere.

## Risk Reduction and Disaster Preparation

Cuba's geographic location leaves it at high risk to hurricanes, so it is not surprising that the *rebeldes* prioritized risk reduction and disaster preparation. The result has received international acclaim. The United Nations Development Program (UNDP) and the International Federation of the Red Cross and Red Crescent Societies (IFRC) have repeatedly pointed to Cuba as an example for other countries to emulate in the area of risk reduction.[28] In the wake of Hurricane Katrina, even scholars and reporters in the United States are now suggesting that the country might learn from examining the Cuban experience.[29] Interest in the Cuban approach to disaster management is a result of the growing number of deaths worldwide from weather-related disasters. In the fourteen years between 1985 and 1999, natural disasters have killed over half a million people. Against this backdrop, a growing number of people, especially in developing nations, began examining the Cuban approach to risk reduction and disaster management because of its success in saving lives.

## Residents' Perception of Cuba's Risk Reduction and Disaster Preparation System

Understanding the dynamics of neighborhood life and culture is crucial to unraveling the secret to Cuba's highly efficient system of risk reduction and disaster preparation. Without stable and highly organized neighborhoods, the Cuban system of risk reduction and disaster preparation probably could not exist. The reason is that a combination of community-level disaster preparation, along with the ability to communicate with and quickly mobilize thousands of residents, lies at the core of the country's disaster management system. Thus, disaster preparedness, because of its community focus, is but another component of the *rebeldes'* social function model of neighborhood development. For example, neighborhood stability and communal values have produced the trust and solidarity that enable residents to work together and follow directives in an emergency, while the linkages and interactions among people, organizations, institutions, and the government make it possible for all groups to operate as a unit during extreme events.

## The National Organizational Framework

The interplay between government intervention and popular participation is the crucial element in the Cuban system of risk reduction. Although headed by the Ministry of Armed Forces, the *rebeldes* nevertheless structured the National Civil Defense system so that it blended centralized decision making with decentralized implementation and mass participation. In this context, rather than create a "separate" civil defense bureaucracy, the *rebeldes* made civil defense another responsibility of leaders and organizations at the local level.

At the provincial and municipal levels, local leaders run civil defense and use the same organizational and institutional structures for civil defense that they employ in everyday life. For example, by law all heads of provinces and municipalities are also the local civil defense directors who are in charge of organizing, coordinating, and monitoring all work related to prevention, mitigation, emergency response, and reconstruction in their communities. In the event of an emergency, all heads of work places, hospitals, schools, and businesses assume their responsibilities to direct their staff in carrying out civil defense measures. At the neighborhood and block levels, the CDRs and FMC take the lead in organizing civil defense committees or coordinating emergency activities.

These organizations, especially the CDR, have considerable freedom in determining how to respond to situations on the ground. In order to make this local leadership effective in risk reduction, the government invests in the development of skills in disaster preparedness among the residents and neighborhood leaders. This reliance on local leadership optimizes knowledge, strengthens social cohesion, and enhances participation at the community level. To gain deeper insight into the operation of the Cuban risk-reduction and disaster-management program at the neighborhood level, 148 households were queried about their views on disaster preparation.[30]

## Residents' Perception of Reduction and Disaster Preparation

The *rebeldes'* deep commitment to the preservation of human life provides a basis for creating a high level of trust between the government and the people during a time of emergency. Concurrently, the population must have confidence that the emergency system is effective and that they will have access to the necessary support and assistance. When it comes to risk reduction and disaster management, *Cubanos*, regardless of their views of the government, believe the government knows what it is doing and is committed to saving lives. Ninety-eight percent of the householders said the Cuban system of risk reduction and disaster management was effective, with 57 percent of these respondents believing that the government's approach is very effective. Moreover, 98 percent of the respondents also said the government was committed to saving lives during a disaster, with 70 percent saying the regime was very committed to this goal. Castro stressed this point as the island nation faced Hurricane Michelle in 2001. "We will overcome this problem no matter how big the damage. For us, victory means having a minimum loss of human life."

Neighborhood residents also believe that active participation in disaster preparedness is part of their responsibility as citizens. When asked about the importance of their role in an emergency, 63 percent of the respondents said their participation in disaster preparedness and response during an emergency was important. Some respondents said citizen participation was significant because it helped to "make the hospitals, schools, stores, and whole country safe." Others said their role was important because "it helps to save lives and avoid accidents." A number of residents also felt it was vital to help clear the streets and assist with the cleanup after a storm.

Not everyone, however, thought his or her role in an emergency was important. Thirty-five percent of the households said either their role in disaster preparedness was unimportant (23 percent), they did not know (10 percent), or they refused to answer the question (3 percent). Nonetheless, the large number of people who believe the disaster-management system is effective, that the government is committed to saving lives, and that their role in helping prepare for disasters and cleaning up after storms helps to explain the high levels of popular participation in risk reduction and disaster preparedness.

In their report on disaster preparedness in Cuba, Oxfam America reported: "Regardless of their role, everyone was clearly aware of what measures and procedures they needed to follow in case of a hurricane. They knew the stages of emergency warning, where to get information, how to secure their house, and where to go for shelter if they needed to evacuate."[31] The data here confirms this viewpoint. When asked if they knew what to do in case of a hurricane or some other natural disaster, all householders answered affirmatively, with 89 percent of the respondents saying they were knowledgeable to very knowledgeable about what to do. Ninety-seven percent of the respondents knew the stages of emergency warning, 90 percent of the householders knew how to secure or make their homes safe for a hurricane, and 66 percent said they knew where to go for shelter if they had to evacuate their home.

During an emergency most respondents ranked television and radio as their most important sources of information, followed by the CDR, family, friends, and relatives. The high level of electrification in Cuba makes it possible for the *rebeldes* to use the media for mass communication during an emergency. About 95 percent of Cuban household have electricity, and most Cubans own a television and/or radio. Outside the media, most respondents said the CDR, civil defense officers, the FMC, along with friends and family members, were the most likely sources of information during an emergency.

For a population to reduce its vulnerability to risk, it is critical that the people know how the disaster-management system works, how to access it, and who is responsible for managing the various activities. In this regard 78 percent of the householders knew who in their block, apartment, or neighborhood was responsible for identifying vulnerable populations and getting them help. Most respondents identified the CDR as the main group responsible for knowing who in the neighborhood needs help during a disaster. This is understandable, since part of the CDR mandate is to know the composition of every household in its jurisdiction, including which houses are most vulnerable to hurricane damage and which can act as shelters.

The FMC representative keeps track of the women in the neighborhood, including those who are vulnerable or need special assistance; the family doctor keeps track of people who are ill or have special physical or psychological needs. The CDR is responsible for collating this information from the relevant actors and putting it into the emergency plan. Thus, when a hurricane or disaster is imminent, the CDR assumes responsibility for making sure vulnerable population groups, as well as all residents, are safe. While some *habaneros* might regard the CDR as government busybodies during normal times, most residents appreciate the organization during a crisis. Only

22 percent of the householders said they did not know who in the neighborhood was responsible for knowing the whereabouts of people who might need help during a natural disaster.

Most people know what to do during an emergency because they participate in the formulation of neighborhood emergency plans. Sixty percent of the respondents said an emergency plan existed for their community, and 41 percent of these respondents said they had participated in its formulation. According to Holly Sims and Kevin Vogelmann, *Cubanos* not only participate in the development of local emergency plans, but they serve on civil defense committees at the community, neighborhood, and block levels. They visit each shelter to ensure it contains adequate food, water, blankets, and other provisions.[32]

The development of a culture of safety in Cuban neighborhoods stems from the *rebeldes'* commitment to raising people's awareness and knowledge about risk reduction and disaster preparation. About 36 percent of the householders said they had received formal training in civil defense, while 36 percent said they learned about disaster preparedness from friends and family, 29 percent from work, and 21 percent from school. In addition, disaster preparedness, prevention, and responses are part of the curricula in all schools and is included in the curricula of many disciplines at the university. Since all Cuban children attend school through ninth grade by law, young people are made aware of risk reduction.

The foundation of Cuba's successful risk-reduction and disaster-preparedness system is its social function model of neighborhood development. Stable and highly organized neighborhoods with a rich storehouse of social capital produce "multiplier effects" for national efforts in disaster mitigation, preparation, and response. The ability of the civil defense system to depend on community mobilization at the grassroots level under the leadership of local authorities along with the widespread participation of the population in disaster preparedness and response is the result of accumulated social capital.

# 4

# USING CAPITALISM
# TO SAVE SOCIALISM

## Making Ends Meet during the Special Period

The abrupt collapse of the Soviet Union fundamentally changed the context that shaped everyday life and culture in Cuba and altered the environment in which *habaneros* struggled to make ends meet. A central feature of the Cuban revolution was the individual's entitlement to a basic standard of goods and services. Access to these goods and services was not determined by low salaries or wages earned; rather, it was based on a principle of socioeconomic inclusion that viewed food, housing, health care, and education as basic human rights.[1] The *rebeldes* enshrined this principle in the actions of the state operating in partnership with its people and anchored it with highly functional, stable, and well-organized neighborhoods that were rich in social capital. Their ultimate goal was to build a society where moral rather than material imperatives motivated citizens, who willingly subordinated their personal interests to the broader interest of the collective.

Between 1959 and 1989, because of favorable trade agreements with the Soviet Union, the *rebeldes* had the resources to develop their model of a people-centered society, and Cuba flourished. During this thirty-year period an interactive link existed between individual and collective benefits, and people saw congruence among the maintenance of the state, the economy, and their own family's livelihood. Within this framework a quasi-paternalistic approach to governance emerged, and people came to depend on the state to provide them with necessary goods and services.

The Special Period ended Cuba's Golden Age. Quasi-paternalism broke down, and people began to recognize that the government could not always provide for their basic needs. Now they had to take greater responsibility for their survival. The catastrophic economic crisis, however, did not terminate the interactive relationship between neighborhoods and the state; it was refashioned. The readjustment process altered not only this relationship, but also the relationships between the residents and their community institutions. In this new environment a genuine partnership emerged between the state and the people as they worked together to overcome the crisis. The driving forces behind these changes were the rise of *turismo* and the dollarization of the economy. (*Dollarization* here refers to the establishment of market-based reforms and the movement toward the establishment of a socialist market model in Cuba.) Although legalization of the U.S. dollar spawned the use of the term, the concept has a much broader meaning than simply using the dollar in transactions. In 2004 the Cubans eliminated the use of U.S. dollars in transactions in Cuba. Dollars must be changed into Cuban *convertibles*. The government charges a 20 percent tax on the exchange of U.S. currency.[2]

## The Context: Using Capitalism to Save Socialism

The fall of the Soviet Union and the Eastern European Communist Bloc in 1989 was the cause of the economic crisis in Cuba. Almost overnight, the country lost close to 75 percent of its international trade. Living conditions declined, and *vida no es fácil* (life is not easy) became a common refrain. In this deteriorating environment Fidel Castro turned to international tourism to save the island. As he explained: "We have to develop tourism. It is an important source of foreign currency. We do not like tourism. It has become an economic necessity."[3] The goal was to secure hard currency and the resources needed to stabilize and maintain the existing social and political structure. By adopting international tourism, Castro was attempting to use capitalist strategies to save socialism.

It is both ironic and paradoxical that Castro bet on international tourism to rescue Cuba from an economic and political catastrophe. The *rebeldes* viewed *turismo* as the quintessential example of the evil of capitalism. Prior to the Revolution, the U.S. mafia controlled the international tourist industry in Cuba and anchored it in gambling, prostitution, and drugs, along with the attractions of sun, sea, and sand. Tourism was purely about pleasure, and thousands of visitors from the United States and around the world came to Cuba in search of it. Between 1948 and 1957 tourist arrivals in Cuba grew by 94 percent. On the eve of the Revolution, arrivals from the United States alone accounted for approximately 86 percent of the visitors to Cuba. However, the realities of tourism and the sugar industry painted Havana's social landscape with misery and pain. There were more than five thousand beggars walking the streets of the city in 1958, many of whom were homeless women with children. Crime was on the rise, and so was juvenile delinquency.

Arthur Schlesinger, Jr., recalled a visit to Havana during the Batista epoch:

> I was enchanted by Havana—and appalled by the way that lovely city was being debased into a great casino and brothel for American businessmen over for a big weekend from Miami. My fellow countrymen reeled through the streets, picking up fourteen year-old Cuban girls and tossing coins to make men scramble in the gutter. One wondered how any Cuban—on the basis of this evidence—could regard the United States with anything but hatred.[4]

Thus, when the *rebeldes* seized power, they understandably shunned international tourism, and it all but disappeared from the island. Concomitantly, they believed that leisure time was a basic human right and made domestic tourism one of the cornerstones of national development. In November 1959 the government established the Instituto Nacíonal de la Industria Turístic (National Institute of the Tourism Industry—INTUR) to expand and develop domestic tourism in order to help *Cubanos* acquire knowledge of their country, to provide them with opportunities to enjoy it, and to emphasize the revolutionary reality that Cuba belonged to them—the *clases populares*.

## Resurrecting International Tourism

The economic crisis hit Cuba with the force of a sledgehammer. Teetering on the brink of economic and political disaster, and without other viable options, Castro and the *rebeldes* felt they had to embrace international tourism, however reluctantly. Blending pragmatism with their idealism, they adopted the necessary policy reforms to integrate tourism and foreign investment into the economy. Boldly, the *rebeldes* embarked on this new and infinitely more complex phase of building a people-centered society. Thus, at the very moment when *Cubanos* faced economic disaster and extraordinary hardship internally, the *rebeldes* invited thousands of visitors, with money to spend on pleasure, to the island.

This new direction was dramatic. International tourist arrivals in Cuba fell from a peak of 272,000 in 1958 to less than 4,000 annually between 1959 and 1973. By 1975 Cuba had begun to promote tourism, attracting over 300,000 visitors annually by 1990. As *El Período Especial* began, the industry exploded, and by the year 2000 the number of tourist arrivals to Cuba had doubled. By 2004 the number of visitors to Cuba surpassed the 2,000,000 mark for the first time (see Table 4–1).[5]

**Table 4–1.    Tourist Arrivals 1945–2005**

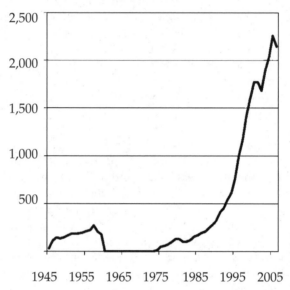

The new tourists to Cuba came mostly from the capitalist countries of Canada, Spain, Italy, Germany, France, the U.K., and the Netherlands. Prior to the Revolution the majority of visitors came from North America (principally the United States). After 1975 the number of North Americans averaged about 25 percent of all visitors. Many U.S. citizens also traveled to Cuba during this period—including Cuban Americans and those traveling both with and without permission from the U.S. government. During the 1980s the number of visitors was shared equally among North America, Western Europe, Eastern Europe, and Latin America. By 2000 approximately one-half of all visitors came from Western Europe. With the arrival of thousands of tourists, the gross revenues from tourism increased from US$1.1 billion in 1995 to US$1.9 billion in 1999 to US$2.25 billion in 2004.[6] By 2003 revenues reached US$2.1 billion, almost half of Cuba's total hard currency. During this period, tourism surpassed the sugar industry as the prime source of hard currency and became the engine driving the economy.

## Reinventing Cuba:
## A New Framework for Socioeconomic Development

The *rebeldes* hoped to develop a wholesome brand of tourism and encapsulate it, along with other foreign investments, so that *turismo* would not undermine Cuban society. The goal was to separate tourism and the leisure and hospitality industry from the daily lives of ordinary *Cubanos,* thus shielding them from the negative impact of tourism. From 1992 to 1995 the *rebeldes* introduced a package of reforms to facilitate international investment, accommodate *turismo,* and generate hard currency. The key measures were (1) to open the economy to foreign capital by making mixed ownership possible, and (2) to legalize the U.S. dollar, family remittances, and limited forms of self-employment.[7]

However, these reforms unlocked a Pandora's Box that sent socioeconomic ripples throughout Cuban society, with racially differentiated effects. The legalization of the dollar meant that *Cubanos* could freely engage in transactions with U.S. currency. In addition, it encouraged family members abroad, especially in the United States, to send relatives money to help make ends meet.[8] With most of the Cuban diaspora consisting of white émigrés, it was the white families that generally received most of the dollars.[9] The legalization of the U.S. dollar also affected Cuban society by triggering the growth of government retail stores expressly to "capture" dollars. Thus, lifestyle differences resulting from the allowance of remittances, higher wages and salaries, and the establishment of dollar retail stores furthered the racial divide that was growing during the *El Período Especial*. By expanding the scope of international tourism and providing a labor market and opportunity structure to support this industry, Cuba reluctantly fostered a dependence on the dollar (hard currency) and created a dual economy in which new social groups were being formed.

From the outset the idea of isolating foreign investments and international tourism from the social fabric of Cuban society was naive and ultimately unworkable. The government could not introduce international tourism into the economy without simultaneously making a series of economic reforms to accommodate the industry, and these policies affected all aspects of everyday life and culture. Reconstructing the policy framework to incorporate tourism refocused the socioeconomic and physical development of Cuba in significant ways.

## Tourism Occupations and Segmented Employment

The emergence of the tourist industry combined with self-employ-ment to produce new occupational groups; by 1997 approximately 130,000 Cubanos were employed, directly and indirectly, in this in-dustry.[10] Jobs materialized in hotels, restaurants, museums, tourist shops, entertainment centers, nightclubs, travel agencies, and airports. In addition, positions opened up in corporations organized to pro-vide services to the tourism, leisure, and hospitality sector. Interac-tion with tourists and access to the dollar made work in the tourist industry extremely desirable.[11] Although typically paid in *pesos*, these workers nevertheless obtained dollars for tips or as "gifts" from the tourists. Moreover, workers in the tourist industry, because of their interactions and friendships, were exposed to the experiences, cul-ture, and world view of tourists. To stem the growing popularity of *turismo* jobs, in February 2005 the Ministry of Tourism established regulations that forbid Cubans to receive tips, gifts, or accept dinner invitations from foreigners.[12] However, it is doubtful that all tourist workers consistently abide by these new regulations.

Although strategically located in hotels, restaurants, and similar service areas during the 1980s, Afro-Cubans did not become integrated into the international tourist industry during the Special Period. In a 1994 survey conducted in Havana and Santiago de Cuba, 40 percent of the respondents said that blacks did not have the same opportuni-ties as whites in the tourist sector.[13] Thus, in reinvented Cuba, Afro-Cubans found themselves at the margins of *turismo,* with limited access to the dollar. At the same time, some of the most important tourist venues were located in the communities where they resided. Given this context, it is not surprising that Afro-Cubans became over-represented in the informal sector of *turismo.*

Allowing opportunities for self-employment led to the develop-ment of microbusinesses, such as restaurants, automotive repair shops, beauty shops, taxi and bicitaxi driving, shoemaking, video produc-ing, and the opening of *casas particulares*, the Cuban version of the U.S. bed and breakfast. By 1995, 138,000 Cuban workers were self-employed. The government had two interrelated reasons for foster-ing self-employment. First, it represented yet another way to "capture" dollars coming into the country (by taxing self-employed workers). Second, self-employment enabled *Cubanos* to provide a range of ser-vices for residents that the government could not afford to supply. Tourism also stimulated the development of new economic activities within the informal economy, especially for unlicensed taxi drivers, informal tourist guides, and other "street" workers, who offered a range of services to tourists.[14]

The segmented labor market generated significant wage differentials among *Cubanos*. For example, private-sector employment consisted of jobs in the tourist industry, self-employment (including the private farmer), and work in the informal sector. Private-sector wages were much higher than those paid in the public sector, regardless of education and/or skills required for the occupation.[15] Economist Carmelo Mesa-Lago, for example, says that the poorest farmers tended to have incomes that were four to five times those of engineers or university professors employed by the state, while owners of *paladares* (family-owned restaurants) could make even more. Even private taxi drivers, waiters, and hotel janitors in *turismo* made more than many public sector workers. Certain workers in the informal sector, particularly prostitutes and hustlers, earned very high wages by providing services to *turistas*.[16]

These realities led to the emergence of a tri-level economy characterized by a peso-based state sector, a dollar-based private sector, and an informal sector linked to the tourist industry, with each sector having distinct pay scales and working conditions. Under these changed circumstances, a connection developed between one's life chances and the economic sector in which one worked. Racially speaking, because whites and mulattos were more likely than Afro-Cubans to have jobs in the private sector, as well as to obtain remittances, the new economy gave rise to differentials in lifestyle and living conditions based on race and skin color.

The segmented labor market differentials created a type of skills mismatch. Many of the professional jobs and occupations that might be attractive to *Cubanos* do not pay as much as occupations in *turismo* or self-employment. These higher paying jobs often do not require as much education and training as those in the professions. Consequently, many public-sector professionals abandoned their chosen professions for the higher paying but lower skilled jobs that paid more.

## The Dollar Stores: Segmented Consumption

The influx of dollars into the economy, both from exile remittances and tourism, meant that the government had to develop a mechanism to capture them. The purpose of legalizing the dollar was to generate the hard currency needed to pay for imports, subsidize social services, and to increase the supply of goods and services into the country, all in hopes of providing increased economic stability. Cubans were anxious to spend the dollars they were receiving from abroad on products and services inside Cuba. If the government did not establish retail outlets to capture dollars, the black market would. Recognizing this, the government opened retail stores in every neighborhood throughout the country.

These retail outlets sold an exclusive variety of foodstuffs, alcohol, cigarettes, televisions, cameras, electronics, toys, jewelry, and other imported items at high prices. Concurrently, in an attempt to shield *Cubanos* from inflation and high-priced merchandise, the government maintained the peso stores. This established a de facto segmented commercial and labor market resulting in, regardless of government policy, people with access to dollars being able to participate in a lifestyle and living standard that was not available to those who did not. This unequal access to remittances, higher wages, and tourist dollars created conditions that weakened the carefully crafted egalitarian distribution of income. International tourism continued to grow within the context of these domestic socioeconomic reforms.

## A Society in the Balance

### The Failure of Tourist Apartheid

The *rebeldes* recognized the dangers emanating from the tourist industry and hoped their continued emphasis on revolutionary ideals would protect society from the "tourist virus." Fidel Castro said:

> The technocrats and bureaucrats suffered from and transmitted a sort of ideological AIDS, something like AIDS that was destroying our revolutionary defenses. Now that we are strengthening our defenses, can we succeed or not? Or are we going to let them buy us for four dollars? Or is it that anyone can come and buy us for four dollars and corrupt us? With our defenses strengthened, as we are strengthening them now, and with the capacity of our people, their integrity, their virtues, I am sure that we will be able to be good hosts to as many tourists as are necessary.[17]

To the *rebeldes*, strengthening defenses also meant forging strategies to isolate the population from *turistas* for two interrelated reasons. First, they did not trust fully that revolutionary ideology would keep *turismo* from contaminating the people. Thus, they sought to separate *Cubanos* from *turistas* in order to shield them from the harmful effects of *turismo* (prostitution and consumerism). Second, the government wanted to protect *turistas* from possible criminal activity. If the media projected Cuba as a dangerous place, many tourists would choose another travel destination. Thus, the government adopted a strategy, popularly called tourist apartheid, as a way of immunizing Cuban society from the "virus" of international tourism, while simultaneously protecting *turistas* from crime. The most conspicuous dimension of this policy was the harassment of Cubans, especially young black men, publicly seen with tourists. Police would often stop these young men, question them, ask for identification, and sometimes even arrest them.

The government policy of separating *Cubanos* from tourists was unsuccessful. The distribution of tourist facilities throughout the city meant that numerous opportunities existed for *habaneros* to encounter *turistas*. For example, in *paladares*, bars, nightclubs, taxis, and on the streets, many opportunities existed for *Cubanos* and *turistas* to encounter one other. One of the most important personal forms of contact occurs when *turistas* hire a *habanero* as an informal tourist guide. These *guías* are usually young black men with an intimate knowledge of the city; they serve as translators and provide the tourist with a variety of services. The government is aware of these "illegal" activities and often takes a lenient attitude toward them. It realizes that many people are simply trying to make ends meet. Thus, as long as these activities stay below the threshold of social disruption, the authorities adopt the "Whitney Houston rule," that is, "it's not right, but it's okay."[18] Thus, despite efforts to keep them separate, *Cubanos* and *turistas* find endless ways to meet and get to know one another.

### The Transition to Consumer Culture

*Turismo* is a unique industry because it turns a country's natural resources and urban assets into pleasurable experiences that are sold to consumers with discretionary income. Thus, the island beckons to the *turistas*, and they are offered "un mundo de experiencias ... la buena mesa, la exclusividad, lo natural, la aventura, o una noche inolvidable [a world of experiences ... good food, exclusivity, nature, adventure, or an unforgettable night]."[19] To create this world of unforgettable experiences, *turismo* transformed Havana's infrastructure into a tourist icon. This was bound to happen. To entertain and accommodate the mostly European and North American visitors, the *rebeldes* restored historical sites; built fancy hotels, elegant restaurants, exciting entertainment venues, and exotic public spaces; and set up retail shops with enticing window display; these merged to form a symbolic environment that celebrated consumerism and epitomized the "good life."

In this world the *turista* became the new elite in Cuban society. Moreover, the symbolism associated with international tourism made its way into everyday life and culture by transforming the lifestyle of tourists and the facilities developed for them into icons that symbolized and reinforced consumerism. Several examples illustrate this point. During the 1990s the government built numerous luxury hotels across the island to provide *turistas* with an upscale living environment during their stay. They had rooms with fashionable décor that were constructed with high-quality materials. These facilities had exquisitely designed lounges and public spaces, abundantly decorated with fresh flowers and plants, lavish dining facilities, and elegant bars, patios, swimming pools, and chic nightclubs and/or discos. In addition, some buildings, such as Hotel Nacional de Cuba in Havana, had magnificently landscaped gardens situated in a park-like setting. Some resort hotels even had golf courses and offered scuba diving, snorkeling, and horseback riding.

The restaurants, including those located in hotels, illustrate the ways in which *turismo* influenced everyday life and culture. The phrase *La mejor comida en el mejor ambiente* (the best food in the best environment) captures the message restaurants wanted conveyed to *turistas*. Although meant for *turistas*, *habaneros* intercepted and translated these messages, as well. In the hotels and restaurants *habaneros* saw the *turistas* eating foods such as lobster, veal, steak, even hamburgers, that are not available in *mercados* or farmers' markets and that they could not afford even if they were available. The ceremonial manner in which the wait staff served the food augmented its significance. The cooks laid out the food on beautifully garnished plates that were presented on elegant trays. People sat at candlelit tables, adorned with tablecloths. *Mojitos* were served in tall, stylish glasses, wine was poured into elegant goblets, or rum was splashed over ice. These amenities filled the restaurants creating an exotic, serene, and romantic atmosphere. In the upscale hotel and restaurant setting, these food experiences came to symbolize the good life.

Such symbols were not lost on *Cubanos*, and they influenced everyday life and culture by imbuing it with consumerism and material-based notions of self-realization and identification—equating personal happiness to the purchase of goods and services and the use of material possessions to shape and reinforce identity and define social status.[20] Like the *turistas*, *Cubanos* not only wanted the products but also desired the experiences they represented. For example, Andrea Colantonio and Robert B. Potter tell the story of a seventeen year old who hangs out on the Malecón with his friends so they can meet tourists. The youth says many of his friends attempt to barter cigars and cheap rum with tourists in exchange for designer or trendy clothing that they cannot easily purchase in Cuba. These teenagers do not necessarily need clothes, but they *want* garments that make them feel and look like the *turistas*.[21]

*Turismo* has even turned certain foods into iconic symbols that Cubans now desire for their social rather than nutritional value. For example, after paying my friend Omar for helping with a project, he asked if I would go shopping with him at a large food market in the western suburb of Miramar, where many diplomats and foreign workers live. At the market he purchased a large quantity of steaks. I asked why he was spending so much money on red meat when he could purchase more than a month's supply of food for the same amount. "I want to eat what you eat," he replied. "But it's not healthy," I responded. He was adamant, "I don't care; I want to eat it anyway." To him, steaks were symbols of affluence and the good life. Consuming them made him feel good because then he was eating like a *turista*. These two stories reflect the sentiments of many *Cubanos*.

Through tourism, Cubans are beginning to share a ubiquitous phenomenon present in the contemporary world, where products serve as symbols and are evaluated, purchased, and consumed based on their symbolic content and perceived social meaning. The dollarization of the economy intensified the trend toward consumerism, reinforced the materialistic icons produced by *turismo* and led to the emergence of a new retail sector in Cuba. Before 1993, the retail sector processed transactions only in pesos and sold mostly recycled clothes, inexpensive apparel, and new and used appliances. The store environments were drab and colorless, with no stylish in-store or window displays to encourage buying. The new retail sector, developed during the resurrection of international tourism, mimicked the design of retail shops in market-based consumer societies.

On the surface the *rebeldes* appear to be enthusiastic supporters of this trend toward consumerism. For instance, in the entranceway of Tienda Carlos Tercera, a Central Havana shopping mall, a sign announces, "Sales + economy + efficiency = revolution." In this shopping complex and many other stores throughout Havana, *habaneros* must make purchases in dollars or Cuban *convertibles*.[22] While the *rebeldes* seem to be promoting consumerism, an alternative explanation may be that they are encouraging *habaneros* to buy goods in retail shops rather than on the black market. According to Mona Rosendahl, an urban anthropologist, before 1990 the black market in clothing was widespread in Cuba, especially in places like Havana. She says that a t-shirt that cost $2 or $3 dollars in the United States sold for about $65 to $70 on the streets, while a pair of U.S. jeans could sell for as much as $200. During this earlier period many Cubans had discretionary funds and could afford to purchase this type of apparel. But even today there are underground *casas de ropas* (clothing stores) where *habaneros* can purchase expensive designer clothes that are not available in department stores.

Today, however, while most *Cubanos* do not have the money to buy merchandise in the new retail outlets or even on the black market, there are some *habaneros* who do. In this sense the availability of an assortment of apparel, appliances, and electronics in retail shops may keep dollars out of the black market. Regardless, the *rebeldes* are trapped in a vicious cycle. They need the market-based retail shops to counteract the black market and capture dollars. Conversely, the establishment of this sector reinforces a culture of consumerism, which spreads values that are contrary to revolutionary ideology. Thus, regardless of original intent, *turismo* caused consumerism and materialism to become significant cultural forces in the development of Cuban society during the 1990s.

### *Making Ends Meet in* El Período Especial

The dollarization of the economy and the rise of consumerism merged to restructure the framework in which *habaneros* struggled to make ends meet. Getting by during the Special Period differed significantly from getting by prior to 1989. Before *El Período Especial* wages and salaries alone did not determine access to goods and services, nor did they determine one's lifestyle or living standard. That changed in the post-Soviet era. Yet, because of the complexity of Cuban society, determining how people make ends meet is a complicated process. During *El Período Especial* getting by not only depends on wages from pesos and access to other revenue sources such as remittances, self-employment, and economic activities in the informal economy but on social relations. Social contact with tourists can be lucrative but for those outside of this network, it is also important to recognize the intrinsic value of community. Cuban neighborhoods are close-knit places undergirded by cooperation, reciprocity, and support from family, friends, and neighbors. Communities that operate in this way provide the social capital that helps to maintain a level of emotional and economic stability in times of crisis. Thus, one must consider a variety of interactive factors before fully understanding how *habaneros* make ends meet in a people-centered society infused with both dollarism and consumerism.

Cuba is a highly subsidized society in which many goods and services are free or available for only a nominal cost. The two-currency economy, bred by tourism, has resulted in a variety of establishments, some accepting only dollars, some only pesos, and others accepting both. However, most establishments accept only pesos for the most essential goods and services, such as rationed items, transportation, rent, or housing loan credits. This means that *Cubanos* live in two interactive worlds; this typically requires the use of both pesos and dollars (hard currency). Thus, in Cuba's dollarized economy, most household budgets include both pesos and dollars. Increasingly, the ability to make ends meet and to live the good life requires access to both types of currency.

The problem is that most state and private employment generates wages only in pesos. The only way that most people can legally gain access to dollars is through remittances or access to *turismo*, by either working in the industry or by forging friendships with *turistas*. However, *Cubanos* can acquire dollars though engagement in economic activities in the informal economy. Against this backdrop, in assessing crisis-time coping strategies, it is critical to note that the cohesive nature of Cuban neighborhoods, where communal values and reciprocity are the norm, allows for a significant amount of latitude and flexibility in formulating options for survival.

For these reasons, using the dollar equivalents of peso prices will not always accurately reflect real buying power, cost equivalents, or the actual income of *Cubanos*. Such equivalents tend to hide more than they reveal, thus the following analysis, investigating how *Cubanos* make ends meet, presents income and expenditure data in terms of both pesos and dollar equivalents. Whenever such references are made, the CADECA (Casa de Cambio SA) exchange rate of 26 pesos to the dollar is used. The following examination includes the 398 households surveyed to examine more closely the process of getting by through the eyes of *habaneros* in some of Havana's most vulnerable neighborhoods.[23] At the same time it is important to note that many households do acquire dollars, by various means, and use them in numerous transactions. *El Período Especial* has etched this duality into the landscape of everyday life and culture in *el barrio*.

### The Household as an Economic Unit

Knowing how *habaneros* make ends meet in the complexity of *El Período Especial* requires an understanding of the organization and structure of households, and it requires viewing them as economic as well as social units. Though the government does not maintain data on wages and salaries, including household income, some researchers have been able to shed light on the wage level of individual workers and the issue of income inequality.[24] However informative and insightful, this data nonetheless leaves lacunas in our knowledge on how *habaneros* get by in Cuba's dollarized socioeconomic environment. Most *Cubanos* live in households with other people, and since the household unit is the locus of daily and long-term social repro-duction, looking at the household rather than the individual in terms of income and expenses is most useful and informative.

During the Special Period individuals and families worked together to create households capable of meeting their daily needs. Increas-ingly, instead of the state, households came to rely on family and so-cial networks to secure necessary goods and services and to enhance their standard of living and quality of life. For example, in this sur-vey single-person households made up only 3.5 percent of the total households. Instead of living alone, most *habaneros* (73.6 percent) re-sided in multi-generational, communal, and traditional family house-holds with an average of four members. These households, with 91 percent of these homes being owned by the residents, exist in es-tablished and well-organized neighborhoods, rich in social capital. Thus, household members, through their participation in mass orga-nizations and their relations with friends and neighbors, create an everyday life built on dense social networks and strong links to the community. This leads to numerous valuable though non-monetized activities within the home and among household members and their friends and neighbors.

### The Occupational Structure of Households

Class analysis is not a very useful endeavor in the Cuban context. A class system, similar to those found in capitalist countries, simply does not exist in Cuba. An occupational hierarchy, however, does, and knowing the types of work that occupy household members pro-vides insight into income levels and the ability of household units to make ends meet. After 1993 a mixed economy emerged that distrib-uted the work force across the public, private, and informal sectors. A unique feature of the economy was the "inverted" skills match, men-tioned earlier. Some of the higher paying jobs, located within the tourist industry, did not require much in the way of skills or education. Other positions, which did require greater skill and educational levels, paid little compared to occupations in *turismo*.

*Cubanos* prized jobs in *turismo* because they afforded access to dol-lars and the opportunity to obtain gifts from tourists. Other occupa-tions, such as mechanic, refrigerator repairperson, carpenter, and tobacco-factory work, while not linked to tourism, were desirable be-cause they lent themselves to moonlighting in either the formal or informal economy. For example, according to Ana Julia Jatar-Hausmann, those workers with a degree from a technical high school had the highest level of earnings among the self-employed. Moreover, because of their composition, some households had a greater capability to generate home-based economic activities or provide goods and services on an informal basis for either internal household consumption or to barter with friends and neighbors. For example, a household member might develop television antennas or other such small household technologies to improve their own or a neighbor's house, baby sit for a neighbor, or trade a pair of shoes for soap or detergent.

## A Tradition of Work

A tradition of work exists in Havana, even in the most vulnerable neighborhoods. In the typical household three out of four members are working and receiving wages. Comparatively speaking, Cuba has a well-educated work force and the level of schooling completed among respondents confirms this viewpoint. Among the 246 households that were questioned regarding educational attainment, most respondents (86 percent) had finished high school, including technical school, and about 25 percent either had some college, had completed their university training, or had obtained an advanced degree. Thus, in Havana, the average household consists of well-educated workers who base their survival strategies on multiple, rather than single, incomes.

This survey did not differentiate public-sector from private-sector jobs, nor did it seek to identify occupations in the tourist industry. However, an examination of the different types of jobs listed by respondents indicates that a wide assortment of occupations was distributed across households. Most household members seem to be working in the public sector, although households with private-sector workers were not rare. Some of the occupational categories found were professional: chemical engineers, lawyers, doctors, dentists, nurses, medical technicians, elementary school teachers, university professors. Others were service and factory oriented, such as cafeteria workers, electricians, tobacco-factory workers, and tourist-related occupations such as owners of *casas particulares*, domestic workers, taxi drivers, bus drivers, bartenders, entertainers, and even prostitutes and hustlers.

Occupational diversity gives households great flexibility and latitude in forging survival strategies. For example, one twelve-member household included a nurse, baker, construction worker, shoe-factory worker, and a prostitute. A four-member household contained a housekeeper, security guard, university professor, and dancer. Another four-member household contained a self-employed worker, a security guard, a social worker, and a maintenance worker. A three-member household contained a bus driver, oil-refinery worker, and student teacher.

### Household Income: The Wage Hierarchy

Determining household income among *Cubanos* is a complex task. Typically, the most basic component of household income is wages. However, not only do wages vary greatly between the private and public sectors, but there is also variation within occupational categories. For example, wages in the tourist sector, regardless of occupation and skill, tend to generate more income than jobs in the public sector. Mesa-Lago reports that a domestic servant in the tourist industry has a salary that ranges from 520 to 1,040 pesos a month, while an engineer or physician in the public sector makes between 300 and 600 pesos monthly. Thus, the peak earning potential of a domestic servant in the tourist industry is almost double that of the peak earning potential of a physician or engineer.[25]

Because most *Cubanos* live in households with other people, the wages of individual workers are only part of the story in the quest to make ends meet. Among the survey population, 344 workers stated that their monthly household income from wages ranged from 62 to 10,100 pesos, the median figure being 499, and the average income being 598 pesos. This equates to a per capita monthly income of approximately 150 pesos for a household consisting of four members. These figures are comparable to a survey of the economic conditions of households in Havana reported in March 1999 by the Cuban economist Viviana Togores González.[26]

While noting the per capita breakdown is helpful when looking comparatively at earlier studies, this perspective can be misleading. Understandably, the more money coming into a household, the greater the flexibility household members have in obtaining needed commodities. However, the communal nature of households, where members share expenses as well as skills and resources, is extremely advantageous in solving the common daily challenges of making ends meet. Most individuals live in households that not only have multiple workers but are also embedded in neighborhoods that operate on the basis of solidarity and reciprocity. For this reason this analysis locates the individual within a household and neighborhood setting.

Within this framework, a wage hierarchy does exist among households in Cuba's most vulnerable neighborhoods. For example in this sample, about 50 percent of the households had monthly incomes below 499 pesos; 23 percent had monthly incomes between 502 and 699 pesos; 13 percent had monthly incomes from 702 to 899 pesos; and about 13 percent had monthly incomes from 900 to 10,085 pesos.

A closer look at household size in relation to income does not result in any clear associations between the two, interestingly enough. The mean household size of four was spread quite evenly across all income levels, though household incomes over 1,000 pesos per month were half again more likely to have five or more people in residence. In keeping with the revolutionary belief regarding the basic rights of citizens, all households receive essentially the same package of subsidies. Higher-wage earners also receive government support, and this adds to the greater availability of disposable income, both collectively and individually, for these households to spend on items such as home repair, appliances, or entertainment.

### Beyond Wages: The Informal Economy and Remittances

Wages, however, tell only part of the household income story. Having a sense of the revenue obtained from participation in the informal economy and through remittances from family and friends who live abroad is crucial to understanding how *habaneros* make ends meet. This is particularly important since most *Cubanos* obtain access to dollars outside of work. Thus, it is important to account for these two revenue streams to get a clearer picture of actual household income.

In this study the term *informal economy* captures a wide range of economic activities that take place outside the formal work place. This study does not attempt to classify or categorize these activities beyond noting that they do exist. In addition, the nonmonetary activities that occur within the home or among neighbors, such as bartering or sharing goods and services, are construed here as social capital and as such reflect the values of cooperation and reciprocity. Although these types of activities are incorporated into the meaning of *household economy* and are critical to understanding how *habaneros* survive day to day, it is best to conceptualize these actions as social rather than economic because they best illustrate the contributions of social capital.

In addition, no effort was made to separate moonlighting in the formal sector from economic activities in the informal economy. The primary goal here was to determine the level of income generated outside of regular wages rather than study the informal economy per se. Many *Cubanos* insist that virtually everyone works in the informal economy or moonlights at some level. They argue that no one in Cuba can survive with just one job. The analysis here is an attempt to investigate the veracity of this street credo.

Detailed information on income and expenses was obtained from 118 out of the total 398 households.[27] Respondents were asked if they received revenue from sources other than their regular jobs and, if so, how much. Approximately 46 percent of the respondents indicated that their household generated revenue from moonlighting. About one-third of these households described their moonlighting as *negocios* (business) and would not indicate how much income they generated. Thirty-seven of the householders engaged in moonlighting were willing to disclose the income they received from their activities. Their revenue ranged widely, from 15 to 2,110 pesos monthly, with half of this group stating that they brought in 400 pesos or less. A handful of households were willing to disclose their moonlighting income in dollars. The dollar income from moonlighting ranged from $10 to $500 monthly, with a median of $100 and a mean of $77 monthly. However, the number of households with members who work outside their formal positions may be higher than that actually reported. For example, fourteen of the households that said they received only wages also said that they expended more than US$30 monthly on various consumer items. Since these households said they received no remittances, moonlighting may be the source of these dollars.

Although the number of respondents willing to share information on revenues generated from moonlighting is too small to draw any strong conclusions, the data suggest that such activities are common and can significantly augment the income of participating households. Hence, those households with revenues generated from both wages and activities outside their regular jobs had an economic advantage over households that generated only wage-based income.

Some families also augment their income with the receipt of remittances. While researchers disagree over the level of remittances coming into Cuba, especially from the United States, they do agree that the amount is significant and ranges anywhere from US$400 million to US$1 billion annually. One big problem in determining, with any accuracy, the level of remittances from abroad is that many households receive these resources through informal channels via friends or relatives instead of through official channels.

These issues notwithstanding, researchers also agree that families receiving remittances have an economic advantage over those families who do not. Within this framework several researchers have tried to determine the income from remittances on an individual household level. In a 1998–99 study of recent émigrés from Cuba, conducted by Churchill Roberts from the University of Florida, about 37 percent of the respondents said they received cash remittances at a weighted average remittance level of US$72.12 monthly, or US$853 per annum. In a 2000 study of 334 households in Havana, Sarah Blue found that 34 percent of the respondents received cash remittances, which ranged from US$20 to US$3,900 per annum per household, with a mean of US$752.[28]

Our findings are consistent with the conclusions of Roberts and the Blue studies. In the present study, about 40 percent of the respondents said they received cash remittances from abroad, which ranged from US$10 to US$690 per household monthly, with an average remittance level of US$99, or US$1,188 per annum. Of those receiving cash remittances, about 46 percent of the households said they also received non-cash items from friends and relatives, mostly clothes and medicines. Since remittances represent a form of unearned income and also provide access to dollars, the households receiving them again have a decided economic advantage over those families that do not have access to this revenue source.

There is a street saying that everyone in Cuba is involved in some type of activity considered illegal by the state, and while this may be an overstatement, the suggestion that Cuba is awash in people engaged in economic activities beyond their regular jobs is probably true. About 69 percent of the households in this sample augment their income by moonlighting and remittances. Some lucky households even had an income "trifecta"—about 14 percent of the households said they received income from all three revenue sources, that is, wages, remittances, and moonlighting. Clearly, the trifecta households had an economic advantage over those households (31 percent in this survey) that must rely solely on wages or pensions. Given the dollarization of the economy, comparatively speaking, these "wages only" households are more economically challenged than are those units with multiple sources of household revenue (see Table 4–2). Although most households received income from moonlighting or remittances, wages from formal employment were still the income base for 92 percent of the households.

**Table 4–2. Sources of Household Income in Havana**

| Income Source | Number | Percentage |
|---|---|---|
| Wages only | 38 | 30.5 |
| Wages and moonlighting | 31 | 27.1 |
| Remittances only | 2 | 2.5 |
| Wages, moonlighting, and remittances | 16 | 13.6 |
| Wages and remittances | 23 | 19.5 |
| Remittances and moonlighting | 4 | 3.38 |
| Self-employment or informal economy | 4 | 3.38 |
| **TOTAL** | **118** | **100** |

Determining the accurate level of household income is a challenge because many householders will not reveal the revenue amount that they receive from economic activities outside of their regular employment. Moreover, some households will not reveal the level of remittances received from abroad, or the level they reported might be understated. This is suggested due to the larger amounts, over the income figures, often quoted as being spent in these same households. This caveat notwithstanding, the available data, especially the information on wage level, indicate that many households are receiving revenues from these other sources. Moreover, the data also suggest that the refrain that everybody in Havana works in the informal economy appears to have some validity. Whether due to necessity, cultural preference, or a combination of both, many *habaneros* operate beyond the structure of formal employment.

### Race and Household Income

The severe crisis of the 1990s reversed some of the previous gains of Afro-Cubans and created new inequalities. Although remittances are important sources of revenue for *Cubanos*, proportionately fewer blacks received them, and those who did received less than one-half the dollar amount received by whites. Afro-Cubans are also under-represented in the tourist industry and among the self-employed. Consequently, the household income disparity between Afro-Cubans and whites has widened during *El Período Especial*, and this income disparity enables whites to experience a lifestyle and living standard that differs significantly from that of Afro-Cubans. Researchers assume that the black and white income differential in Cuba exists in the most vulnerable neighborhoods, as well as in the general society. Thus, even in at-risk neighborhoods, where blacks, whites, and mulattos live together, it is assumed that the black and white income differential is present.

Race was determined in 381 of the households in this survey. Although Afro-Cubans are over-represented, they share residential space in these vulnerable neighborhoods with whites and mulattos. Whites constitute 38 percent of the survey population, blacks 31 percent, and mulattos 27 percent. Significantly, however, Afro-Cubans, with a monthly household income of 590 pesos, exceeded the monthly household income of both whites (492 pesos) and mulattos (482 pesos). Within this context, white households were more likely to receive cash remittances than either Afro-Cubans or mulattos. About 17 percent of white households, 9 percent of mulatto households, and only 5 percent of Afro-Cuban households stated they received cash remittances. While remittance revenue does not help to explain the higher income of black households, these households (29 percent) were more likely than both white (21 percent) and mulatto (13 percent) households to engage in economic activities outside of formal work. Given that actual revenues received from outside work were often not shared, the differential between the household incomes of Afro-Cubans and whites and mulattos could well be even greater. It is important to remember that monthly income figures noted on the surveys report income earned from wages and are not inclusive of these other forms of revenue. Incomes from other sources were identified separately.

The reality that, in this sample population, the income of blacks is higher than that of whites may be surprising but in some respects understandable. Before 1959, Afro-Cubans and working-class whites were over-represented in the city's most vulnerable neighborhoods. For the most part the Revolution "froze" population groups in place. That is, although the *rebeldes'* goal was to improve the quality of housing for all residents, black, white, and mulatto, they did not use a population redistribution strategy to achieve this objective. Later, in neighborhoods like Habana Vieja, Centro Habana, and portions of Vedado, many people did not want to move to a different neighborhood because they valued their proximity to the *turistas* and the jobs and opportunities afforded in these places. Moreover, because of the importance of social networks, many *habaneros* wanted to remain embedded in their existing complex of friends and relations.

After the Revolution, improvement in the socioeconomic conditions of Afro-Cubans did not trigger the migration of the most successful group members to other parts of the city. Most often, as their socioeconomic conditions improved, they remained rooted in the same neighborhoods, as did the mulattos and working-class whites. It is important to recognize that this survey mostly samples Afro-Cubans, whites, and mulattos who lived in the most vulnerable neighborhoods in Havana and not in neighborhoods such as Nuevo Vedado, Vedado, and Miramar, where higher income groups have historically lived. Thus, a combination of wage income and income derived from the informal economy might explain the income differentials among blacks and whites and mulattos.

### Expenditures

Understanding household consumption and expenditure patterns is crucial to gaining insight into how *habaneros* make ends meet. Surprisingly, given the viewpoint of some researchers that *Cubanos* have trouble just getting by, very little is known about consumption and expenditure patterns. There are few reliable published statistics on household finances, but some sense of family budgets comes from a study by Ferriol Muruaga and others based on a 1996 household survey.[29] There is also a consensus in the literature that *El Período Especial* produced a hierarchical employment structure in which the ability to make ends meet differed among various occupational groups. Those who earn dollars, receive bonuses in *convertibles* or dollars, or obtain remittances from abroad, and have substantial bank savings, can easily manage economically.

Mesa-Lago argues that four factors have contributed to the decline in the living standard of *Cubanos* since 1993: (1) a decrease by 44 percent in the average real wage and in its purchasing power; (2) the reduction in rationing quotas (goods subsidized at a price below production cost), which now cover only about 10 days per month, forcing people to purchase essential foodstuffs in other markets for the remaining 20 days; (3) excessively high prices for essential goods, due to a 140 percent sales tax plus huge profit-taking in dollar shops (TRD); and (4) the high prices still charged in agricultural free markets despite the declining trend of such prices in 1995–2001.[30] While this information deepens our understanding of the socioeconomic context in which households operate, it does not provide insight into patterns of household consumption and expenditures, nor does it tell us anything about the strategies households employ to handle these challenges.

Cuban economist Viviana Togores González stated in 1999 that "income is insufficient to meet basic needs of a typical family of four persons, and some groups of the population are very badly affected; this refers to minimum needs for food and hygiene and exclude expenses such as rent, electricity, clothing, transportation, and other essentials."[31] Mesa-Lago accentuates this point. He says that at the beginning of 2002, Chinese televisions, "Pandas," were sold for 4,000 pesos in the state non-rationed market, a price equivalent to 1.5 times the average salary of a state worker; some sets were even sold in the dollar stores for $470 (equivalent to 12,000 pesos).[32] Mesa-Lago is addressing the relationship between wages and expenditures. However, in the Cuban context, studying the relationship between household expenditures and peso wages is not only complicated, but also provides only a part of the whole story. As previously mentioned, many households augment their wage incomes with commercial ventures in the informal economy, through remittances, bartering, and trading, and through a complex web of reciprocal actions.

Determining what Cubanos can afford simply by comparing the level of peso wages to the price of commodities can be misleading. In the daily life of neighborhoods, where people, to coin a popular *Cubano* phrase, "move like a snake," determining how people actually get by requires thoughtful detective work. For example, high prices notwithstanding, field visits to farmers' markets and dollar stores in Centro Habana and Habana Vieja over the past six years (2001–07), reveal that shoppers buying foodstuffs and a variety of other items fill these establishments on a regular basis. Restaurants that cater primarily to *Cubanos* are also typically filled, especially on the weekends, with *habaneros* dining out and paying for their meals with *convertibles*. In one way or another, many *Cubanos* are finding a way to purchase needed items as well as partake of dining-out experiences with their families and friends.

In the earlier statement Mesa-Lago implies that owning an expensive television is beyond the economic reach of most *habaneros*. However, many *Cubanos* do own televisions. One five-person household, composed of a mother, two adult daughters, and two small children, has a low household income by Cuban standards. The mother works part time, one daughter sells flowers, and the other does not work. According to the mother, the family does not receive any remittances and only minimally participates in the informal economy. The mother says that she occasionally will sell cakes to friends. Yet, the family owns a washing machine and recently purchased a television and had it hooked up to the satellite so they could receive cable service. This household is not unique. Surveying the rooftops of the homes in Centro Habana reveals numerous TV antennas and along Havana neighborhood streets at night, the murmur of television voices through open doors and windows is omnipresent.

A closer inspection of household consumption and expenditure patterns deepens insight into the complex reality of how *habaneros* actually get by. Toward this end, data was obtained on household expenditures for 152 of the 398 households surveyed in this study. In the case of 118 households, information was obtained on their expenditures in both dollars and pesos. Determining what items are paid for with dollars and what items are paid for with pesos helps to explain how the dollarization of the economy has affected *Cubanos* at the household level. Because the specific income from remittances and economic activities in the informal economy is missing from a number of surveys, direct comparisons between expenditures and household income are not possible. Instead, the goal here is to gain a deeper understanding of the consumption and expenditure patterns of households and to acquire insights into the ways householders negotiate Cuba's dual economy.

The following areas, outlined in Table 4–3, are addressed in this section. Household heads were asked to estimate the amounts the household typically expended in the areas listed below in both pesos and dollars. Since these are personal estimates, it is expected that some will be a bit high, others low, and still others probably quite accurate. This should be kept in mind when interpreting the outcomes.

**Table 4–3.    Patterns of Household Consumption and Expenditures**

| Basic Needs | Household Needs |
|---|---|
| Housing | Cleaners |
| Electricity | House repairs |
| Water | House improvements |
| Gas/kerosene | Organization dues |
| Transportation | Child care |
| Food | |

| Personal Needs | Wants |
|---|---|
| Health/medicine | Cigarettes/cigars |
| Clothing | Alcohol |
| Toiletries | Telephone |
| Hair treatment | Recreation |
| Bathing needs | |

*Basic Needs Expenditures*

*Housing Consumption*

The most striking aspect of this analysis is the fact that *Cubanos* spend so little on housing. About 93 percent of the respondents said they spent no money on rent or mortgages. About 91 percent indicated that they owned the dwelling units in which they lived. These householders appear to own their homes outright, without any outstanding loan payments. In addition, many "renters" live in lease-free housing units. For those with housing expenses, the mean expenditure is only three pesos per month. The limited amount spent on housing, however, must be qualified by the fact that many of these units are quite dilapidated and in need of many repairs.

According to Coyula, the greatest concentration of poor housing in Havana is found in five municipalities—Habana Vieja, Centro Habana, Arroyo Naranjo, San Miguel del Padrón, and Diez de Octubre—the very locations from which most of these surveys were drawn.[33] However, only twenty-two households (14 percent) expended household revenue on housing repairs; the remaining 86 percent of the households said they had no housing repair expenditures. In addition, the twenty-seven households that did note these types of expenditures spent an average of US$83, monthly. This may indicate that many households may not be able to afford housing repairs or they may choose to expend their resources on other items until or unless confronted with a housing emergency.

From the perspective of necessary costs of living, households do seem to have leeway in deciding when and how much to invest in home repairs. In addition, many *habaneros* live in multiple family units, and the most urgent repairs may relate to the entire building rather than to individual apartments. Because of these circumstances *juntas de vecinos* (neighborhood groups) have been formed so that neighbors can work together to solve these larger housing issues. In still other instances householders barter to get repairs done or do the repairs themselves at little or no cost. Then, there are instances in which *habaneros* turn to friends and family outside the country to help. For example, in an East Havana community, a householder living on the top floor of a five-story apartment building had a serious leak in her roof. She contacted a relative in the United States who provided her with the resources to fix the roof.

Thus, most *habaneros*, regardless of the size, quality, or value of their dwelling unit, pay very little for housing, though many of these units are in serious need of repair. However, ownership does provide them with the leeway to dictate if, when, and how they want to make improvements. Most important, wage levels do not dictate where *habaneros* live. Housing is affordable to all and does not require participation in the dollar economy.

### Housing Utilities Consumption

Moreover, the monthly cost of housing utilities is also very low. For example, the mean monthly expenditures for water are 5 pesos, gas/kerosene about 10 pesos, and electricity averages 27 pesos. About 35 percent of the householders said they paid no money for water and 4 percent said they paid no money for electricity. It is not unusual for residents in some of the worst housing units to tap illegally into the city's power grid. About 25 percent of the households did not list any expenditure for cooking gas or kerosene. This is not surprising. Cooking gas is in short supply, and because kerosene is so costly and unhealthy, the government is working to eliminate its use. For example, in 2005, Castro gave out 100,000 pressure cookers in Havana. Clearly, this data indicates that housing and utility costs are very manageable issues for *habaneros*. Significantly, all critical housing costs (rents, loans, water, gas, kerosene, electric) are paid in pesos.

*Cubanos* do not need dollars for these types of expenses. While there have been increases in the cost of utilities, because of the high subsidy, they are still quite affordable.

### Transportation Consumption

The cost of transportation is also very low, although that cost varies depending on where in the city people live. Householders living in the outlying neighborhoods probably pay more for transportation than families living the central areas of the city. Regardless, transportation is inexpensive in Havana. Bus transportation costs, including the *camellos* (a truck cab and chassis attached to a bus body that carries over two hundred passengers), are only about one-fourth to one-half peso a ride. Many people walk, ride bicycles, or use bici-taxis for short trips, while others hitchhike or take an *almendrone* (privately owned U.S. cars from the 1950s that run along the main routes of the city at a fixed rate of ten pesos a ride). About 41 percent of the respondents said they paid nothing for transportation. This is not surprising, given the options that *habaneros* have for getting around the city and that many of those living in the central neighborhoods (Habana Vieja, Centro Habana, and Vedado) frequently walk to their destinations. Also, hitchhiking is very popular, and drivers of government-owned vehicles are required to pick up hitchhikers if they have room.

### Food Consumption

In many respects food consumption is the single most important expenditure for Cuban households. Food consumption has been viewed as the most important marker to determine if a population has the resources to meet its basic needs. During the early days of *El Período Especial*, a dramatic drop in per capita food consumption occurred as scarcities were pervasive. The government launched a series of programs to attack aggressively the problem of food availability. Concurrently, the government expanded its maternal-care program by providing special food allocations and meals for expectant mothers, along with expanding services for this special population. Within this context the development of a sustainable urban agriculture program dramatically increased the availability of food for the urban population. By 1996 some scholars argued that Cuba had entered a post critical stage in per capita food availability.[34] In essence, *Cubanos* are now able to access the quality and quantity of food necessary to maintain a healthy, nutritional diet.

This survey of household expenditures indicates that food consumption, by a wide margin, is the largest single expenditure for households. The mean monthly food expenditures were 345 pesos, with a median of 260 pesos. Significant portions of these food purchases were made through the *libreta* (food rationing book). For example, 58 percent of those in the sample population said they obtained 50 percent of their food purchases with the ration book. Most observers argue that the food purchased through the *libreta* covers only about two weeks or half-a-month food supply for a typical family.

According to Ferriol Muruaga, the greater part of people's nutrition is still provided by the state. She states that 89 percent of the calories, 93 percent of the protein, and 80 percent of the fat are obtained through the ration system, meals offered at workers' dining rooms, schools, or hospitals. Castro himself said in an interview that his government tried to keep the supply of food from free markets to within 20 percent of total production, so that people could purchase food within their salaries.[35] However, the fact that most households indicated that the *libreta* covered only half of their food costs suggests that at least half of food supplies had to purchased at non-subsidized prices. Yet food consumption represented only about 30 percent of the total reported expenditures for households in this sample. This would indicate that most households could meet their food consumption needs within their peso wage.

Concurrently, about 31 percent of the households in the sample spent more than US$25 a month on food. These households chose to augment their food budgets with purchases in dollars. There is no evidence to suggest that households making food purchases in dollars had diets superior to those households that made food purchases only in pesos. However, it is reasonable to believe that they did have wider food choices and that access to dollars enabled these households to develop a pattern of food consumption that those without access could not afford. In this instance, availability of dollars allowed certain households to attend to their wants rather than just their dietary needs.

### Personal Needs

Personal needs, while not as critical as basic needs, are still important, especially those expenses related to health and medicine. Health care is free in Cuba, but people must pay a nominal fee for medication. The households surveyed stated their mean expenditures for medications are 30 pesos, but 22 percent indicated that they expended no money at all on medicine. Dollar purchases of medications were not a factor. Thus, in the most critical personal need area, expenditures were made in pesos. However, many households did note that they obtained non-cash remittances in the form of medicine, which would give them a favored position over those who do not have these resources available to them.

Households spent little on other personal needs items. The monthly mean expenditure was eight pesos for toiletries, twenty-five pesos for bathing needs, and forty-nine pesos for hair treatments. About 84 percent of the respondents said they did not spend any pesos on toiletries and 72 percent did not expend peso resources on bathing soap or shampoo. Most of these items are obtainable through the *libreta*, and many people can obtain needed items through bartering and the provision of reciprocal services to friends. Some households did expend dollars to purchase these items. For example, eighty-three households expended dollars on toiletries, ninety-two households spent money on bathing needs, and twenty-two households on hair treatments. Less than ten dollars (mean monthly dollars) was spent in all of these areas. In addition, about 93 percent of the households indicated that they do not pay any pesos for child-care services, and no households expended dollars for these services.

Some *habaneros* believe that toiletries purchased in the dollars stores are superior to those purchased through the *libreta*. For example, a Cuban friend finds Cuban toothpaste to be very unpleasant and purchases the brands available in dollar stores whenever possible. Another friend says Cuban soap makes him itch, and when he has dollars, he will sometimes purchase soap in the dollar stores. In reality, Cuban toothpaste and soap are quite serviceable but not as appealing as the commercial brands. Thus, those *habaneros* who can afford to purchase commercial toiletries from the dollar stores believe their lives are a little more pleasing as a result.

A range of choices exists for *Cubanos* to acquire clothing. There are stores that sell recycled items, and many *Cubanos* barter and trade with one another. In addition, an indeterminate number of *habaneros* obtain clothes from tourists and from friends abroad. The monthly mean for clothing expenditures is about ninety-one pesos; however, 73 percent of the households say they do not spend any pesos on clothes. Concurrently, about forty-eight households said they expended about US$13 monthly on the purchase of clothes. Field observations suggest that, while most *Cubanos* do not have many clothes, they are well dressed and well groomed. A study of the hundreds of digital photos taken while conducting fieldwork in all parts of the city clearly supports this viewpoint. It is also worth noting that Cuba is a tropical island, where people are often casually and minimally dressed due to the warm climate. Yet, the clothing worn is most often clean and in good condition. Through peso purchases, bartering and reciprocity, gifts, and purchases made in dollars, *habaneros* present themselves as a well-dressed and well-groomed people.

### Household Needs

Household needs refer to expenditures to maintain and improve the living environment. Most cleaning items are probably purchased with the *libreta*, although 70 percent of the households say they have no expenses in this category. Typically, Cuban homes are very neat and clean, with residents constantly cleaning floors, washing dishes, and laundering and hanging out clothing. Most Cubans do not have dryers, so full clothes lines pervade the urban landscape of Havana. Thus, while little expense is noted here, Cubans do use plenty of soap, detergents, and other cleaners. *Habaneros* apparently acquire most of these cleaning items through the *libreta* or through trading or bartering. Only about ninety-two households, of all those surveyed, said they expended about US$5 monthly on cleaning supplies.

Few householders spend money on either household repairs or home improvements. *Habaneros* probably view expenditures in these areas as occasional rather than consistent monthly expenses. Moreover, given their limited incomes, wherever possible residents use their creativity and flexibility to either repair their own homes or try to get the work done through bartering or reciprocal services. Expenditures in dollars are most noticeable in home improvements and housing repairs. These are again occasional expenditures based on a combination of needs and wants. About 19 percent of the households—twenty-seven households—spent an average of $83 dollars on housing repairs, and 17 percent expended an average of $44 dollars on improvements. Given the deplorable nature of housing in many Havana neighborhoods, having the resources to improve housing conditions provides a greater sense of well-being as well as raising the living standard. Perhaps it is here, along with food purchases, that access to dollars has the greatest impact on the quality of life.

In this study no emphasis was placed on occasional purchases. Nevertheless, anecdotal data and field observations suggest that families with dollars invest a significant amount of those resources on occasional purchases, such as furniture, computers, utensils, and fancy stoves, refrigerators, and other appliances. For example, a number of the households surveyed indicated that they have had their refrigerator or furniture since the Revolution triumphed. In addition, many Cubans, especially those in the most vulnerable neighborhoods, live in housing units that reflect a Spartan existence. Therefore, home improvements and the occasional purchase of consumer items show the real distinction between the lives of those with access to dollars and discretionary income and those living on the economic margin.

Last, virtually all households pay dues to the mass organizations in their community. Although the amount is small and organizations base dues on the ability of households to pay, membership in mass organizations, attendance at meetings, and the payment of dues all suggest that residents, despite their ongoing struggle to make ends meet, are still engaged in the life of their community. This observation is important because it demonstrates that economic hardship and consumerism have not generated anomie and civic disengagement. Moreover, the cohesion and solidarity of neighborhoods at the formal organizational level sustain and reinforce interaction among residents at the social level. As one *habanero* reflected, "The crisis brings us closer together because it forces us to rely on one another."

## Wants

Expenditures that are designed to improve one's quality of life, where items are purchased to provide enjoyment, pleasure, and relaxation, are "wants." This type of spending provides insight into the level of discretionary income in a particular household. This category includes such items as alcohol, cigarettes, recreational expenses, and telephone, items that while often desirable are not necessary to daily life. The most important of these expenditures is the telephone. From 1988 to 1990, when Mona Rosendahl completed the fieldwork for her book *Inside the Revolution*, *Cubanos* considered owning a telephone a luxury. In the present survey, 41 percent of the respondents owned telephones, costing an average of nineteen pesos monthly. In Cuba, communication networks are such that telephone ownership is not a necessity. Public telephones are strategically located throughout neighborhoods, and those with telephones often share this resource with their neighbors. Telephone ownership, then, is one indicator that households are generating discretionary income. It is also important to note that dollars are not expended in this category.

What stands out about the remaining expenditures is the percentage of residents who spent no pesos in this area. For example, 84 percent of the respondents stated they did not expend pesos on alcohol, 58 percent spent no pesos on cigarettes or cigars, and 69 percent said they had no recreational expenses in pesos. However, there were dollar expenditures noted in the category of "wants." About 13 percent of the households spent an average of US$3 dollars monthly on alcohol, 16 percent of households expended US$4 dollars monthly on tobacco, and 23 percent of households spent US$9 monthly on recreation. Thus, a small portion of households noted they expended, on average, about US$16 dollars a month exclusively on enjoyment. It is possible that, given the health issues involved in smoking and drinking, the low expenditures in these areas reflect the success of the government's health promotion campaigns. It is also possible that those surveyed understated their use due to social desirability factors.

Cubans are involved in many recreational activities that do not require money, so the fact that only 31 percent of households stated they spent money on recreation is plausible. For example, playing dominos and playing chess are very popular pastimes. "Walking the city," relaxing on the Malecón, and spending time with friends and family talking and playing cards are favorite activities among *habaneros*. Young people create numerous street games and are also involved in traditional sports activities such as stickball, volleyball, and soccer. Rollerblading is omnipresent, and so too is fishing, inner tubing, swimming, and spending time on the beach. In addition, there are many organized activities available in neighborhoods for all groups, including elders. The state also provides many inexpensive entertainment venues; theater, opera, and ballet performances cost only a few pesos a ticket.

## Solidarity, Reciprocity, and Community Support

We emphasize here the concepts of solidarity, reciprocity, and community support, which greatly influence household income, consumption, and expenditure patterns, in order to gain accurate insight into the ways households survive and sustain themselves. Reciprocity refers to work exchanges and gift giving, while community support denotes the willingness of family, friends, and neighbors to help one another in times of need. Because of the embeddedness of Cuban households in communities rich in social capital, where solidarity and neighborliness anchor social relations, residents learn that survival depends on their ability to cooperate and work together. Consequently, gift giving, making loans, sharing scarce resources, and engaging in reciprocal activities are characteristic features of everyday life and culture in *el barrio*.

Reciprocity is a key element in this social equation. Mona Rosendahl says that some forms of reciprocity in Cuba are almost completely social, and the monetary value of articles, goods, and services subsumes a subordinate role to the development and maintenance of social relations. At times, she notes, there are no gifts involved in transactions, just "symbolic capital" that strengthens one's reputation as a "good person" within the context of an established relationship. In other forms of reciprocity scarce goods or services are exchanged and both parties profit. In some instances this type of reciprocity takes the form of bartering. That is, neighbors or friends will trade commodities or exchange a commodity for services rendered. When asked about their reciprocal relationships with neighbors (sharing food, telephone, babysitting, exchanging clothes, soap and the like), about 77 percent of the sample households responded affirmatively.[36]

Community support is also an important part of the scenario of neighborhood life and reciprocity reinforces this. In a world where hard times are characteristic of daily life, even with the government's system of social supports, *habaneros* have learned that they must be able to depend on family, friends, and neighbors for help. When asked about the level of community support they could expect during times of need, residents demonstrated the strength of their social networks. For example, in a time of need 86 percent of the householders said they could expect support from their relatives, 97 percent of householders said their friends would help, and 89 percent said they could also depend on their neighbors. Thus, *Cubanos* believe that they live in a supportive environment, in which during hard times not only does government attempt to supply needed goods and services, but also help from family, friends, and neighbors is forthcoming.

Social relations, therefore, are not only extremely important in *el barrio* for emotional and social outlets but for survival and making ends meet. Thus, social relationships represent an informal safety net that reciprocal action, cooperation, and solidarity sustain and strengthen over time. The mass organizations, as well as informal groups like the *junta de vecinos*, further stabilize neighborhoods by furthering the development of trust and social bonding. In *el barrio*, neighbors helping neighbors is a credo that provides the infrastructure as well as the social foundation of a people-centered society.

## *Hay que Inventar*

*Inventar* (to invent) and *resolver* (to solve) are the final instruments of social capital *habaneros* use to make ends meet. Cubans are a very creative people, and hardships have forced them to use their inventiveness to solve problems and bolster the quality of their lives. As one *habanero* said, "The shortage of materials creates a place where you are always discovering things for the first time, and the lack of material makes people create utopia." Numerous examples of this inventiveness exist. Many *habaneros* find ways to hook up their apartments to the city power grid to avoid the cost of electricity; some individuals learn how to hook up their televisions to the satellite to get "free" cable television; others offer to link their neighbors to the satellite for a fee. There are individuals who turn their bicycles into motorbikes or unique bici-taxis, while still others learn how to create makeshift television antennas out of aluminum trays. Indeed, the ability of *Cubanos* to keep hundreds of 1950s-era U.S. cars running nearly fifty years after the Revolution, in a country where spare parts are a rarity, is a testament to their power of inventiveness.

It is no exaggeration to say that *Cubanos* have transformed recycling into an art form and forms of self-employment. They throw away nothing; residents fix and recycle virtually everything. For example, a visitor from the United States who was staying with friends in Cuba was about to throw away a pair of broken hair curlers. Her friend responded incredulously, "What are you doing?" She replied: "I'm throwing these things away. They don't work." Taking the hair curlers, the friend said, "I can get these fixed!" Two days later her friend proudly showed her the curlers and demonstrated their regeneration. Incredulous, the visitor from the U.S. exclaimed, "They are working better than ever!"

In another example students at a neighborhood elementary school re-created a prototype of a hospital operating room exclusively from recycled materials. Children also create ingenuous street games and build scooters from discarded roller skates. From the refilling of cigarette lighters to the repair of eyeglasses, refrigerators, and automobiles, to the creation of doorbells and other gadgets, Cubans refurbish and create items to enrich their lives, solve problems, and make money. The notions of *inventar* and *resolver* also extend to economic activities within the informal economy. Archibald Ritter and Jorge Pérez-López have written extensively on survival strategies and illegalities in Cuba. In his travelogue, Ben Corbett even referred to these activities in the informal economy as a form of outlaw culture.[37] While these activities might be illegal, *Cubanos* consider them part of the world of "*inventar*" and "*resolver*." Rather than outlaw culture, these are efforts to get by, not reflective of a counterculture or nascent form of rebellion.

Both the *rebeldes* and the *habaneros* know that *hay que inventar* (you have to invent) became a necessary part of the Cuban landscape due to the economic crisis spawned by the abrupt collapse of the Soviet Union. To survive, both the government and the people had to embrace unexpected and previously objectionable policies and practices. For example, Fidel Castro noted that, while the *rebeldes* disliked tourism, they recognized that it had become an economic necessity. Likewise, many people do not like operating outside the law or engaging in illegal activities, but they do what they must to survive. In an ironic sense, the tolerance of a certain level of "illegal" activities allows the government to maintain its revolutionary philosophy while simultaneously making it possible for *habaneros* to use their inventiveness to get by.

## Can Cuba Use Capitalism to Save Socialism?

The abrupt and unexpected collapse of the Soviet Union caused the *rebeldes* to alter dramatically the world in which *Cubanos* worked, lived, and sought to make ends meet. Confronted with only three choices—bad, very bad, and catastrophic—the *rebeldes* selected "bad" and moved forward to reinvent Cuban society. In this remodeled world they reluctantly determined that they could use capitalism to save socialism. In this changed contextual setting *Cubanos* had to find new and creative ways to supplement their incomes and enhance the quality of their lives. *Vida no es fácil* and *hay que inventar* became common refrains that reflected the resiliency, adaptability, and creativity of the Cuban people.

In this new setting the nature and character of everyday life and culture in *el barrio* mitigated the most harmful effects of the economic crisis and formed a neighborhood setting that facilitated the ability of *habaneros* to survive and even thrive. Within this context the *rebeldes* adopted a "bend, but don't break" approach to governance while continuing to develop a genuine partnership with the people. For the *clases populares*, life in this reinvented Cuba meant learning how to negotiate the complicated terrain of a nation that used two different currencies. The attempt to separate *turismo* and marketplace activities was a futile one and created a situation in which ordinary *habaneros* had to carry out transactions in both dollars and pesos. In a world strongly influenced by *turismo*, the dollar increasingly became the determinant of improvements in living standards and quality of life, and consumerism ideology interpreted what improvements in living standards and quality of life meant.

An examination of the consumption and expenditure patterns of households provides insights into the ways *habaneros* typically invested their resources. About 95 percent of those surveyed said their households generated pesos wages, so the peso system is the one most available to *Cubanos*. In the dual economic system it appears that the most basic and essential expenditures (food, housing, electricity, water, transportation, and organizational dues) are affordable, and *habaneros* can manage them within the peso market. It also appears that *habaneros* can manage their other basic expenses (clothing, hair treatment, toiletries, and so on) with their peso wages. By embedding the most vital and essential consumer items within the highly subsidized peso market, the *rebeldes* shielded *habaneros* from the most destructive effects of their dollarized economy. While government subsidies are no longer as ample as they were during the Soviet era, they are adequate to keep getting by from being the dominant theme in *el barrio*. Subsidies, which make possible free education and health care, along with low-cost housing, electricity, water, and the like, bolster purchasing power and thus allow *habaneros* more resources to expend on food and other highly desirable items.

Many households, 69 percent, said they also received revenues from moonlighting. As noted earlier, many household rely on multiple revenue sources, including dollars, to augment their incomes. The discretionary income that results from these activities allows these households to purchase more exotic consumer items, which *Cubanos* believe improve their living standard and quality of life. These are the households that can buy foods that make them "feel good"; they can make occasional purchases, such as sofas, televisions, and artwork, that make their homes more comfortable and inviting. Household members can occasionally eat out at a "nice" Cuban restaurant, go to a discothèque, or go to an upscale bar, maybe even vacation at a resort, or at least have a beer whenever desired. Households with access to dollars and discretionary income are the engines that drive consumerism in Cuba's dollarized economy. Moreover, *habaneros* across the income, occupation, and racial spectrum are no longer consumed with survival.

In Havana, viewed through the data mined here, there are very few *habaneros* that do not have enough resources to get by. Life is still difficult, and most *Cubanos* do moonlight, but their focus is not necessarily on survival but on improvement of their standard of living and quality of life. They think about traveling—seeing other parts of the Cuba, the Caribbean, and the United States. They dream about owning an automobile, cellular telephone, or color television, not about where their next meal will come from.

## A Reinvented Cuba?

In many respects *El Período Especial*, as originally defined by Fidel Castro, no longer exists. Rather, Cuba has entered a new stage in the development of its people-centered society. Cuba has evolved from a needs-based to a wants-based society. Everyday life and culture in *el barrio* are no longer about survival and just getting by. Now, *Cubanos* want to improve their living standard and quality of life. At the same time, Cuba has not entered a post–*vida no es fácil* period. Life is still difficult for many *Cubanos* who live a Spartan existence. However, people are not dying from malnutrition and starvation; homeless people and gangs of street children, turned into scavengers, are not characteristic features of the urban landscape. Neither are violence, crime, desperation, and hopelessness characteristic features of neighborhood life.

In reinvented Cuba consumer desires, not survival needs, are the driving force behind everyday life and culture. In *The Cuban Way* Jatar-Hausmann tells the powerful story of a young *jinetera* (prostitute) that illustrates the impact that *turismo* and consumerism are having on Cuban society. Blanquita is a young psychologist who moonlights because her peso salary cannot pay for the nice clothes she wants for herself or the clothes and food she wants for her son. As a prostitute, she can easily make $100 in one night. One day her neighbor, Jorge, who is a doctor, accused her of enjoying life as a prostitute. He said, "Blanquita, it is one thing to go out and earn some money moonlighting as a prostitute, but to enjoy it? That's something else. You should be ashamed of yourself." She fired back, "I never said I didn't enjoy it. Besides, I wouldn't do it if I didn't like it."

Blanquita did like going out, talking to people from other countries, and getting a taste of what "normal" life could be, or living a life she sees in the movies. She engaged in *jineterismo* because she believed her life was boring and miserable. "I want to live and have some fun. I am sick and tired of Fidel, of El Che, and of all the revolutionary heroes. I want to dance, have a good meal, some drinks, and sex in a nice hotel. What's wrong with that? Isn't that what people do outside? I want to feel alive!" "Look at yourself," she said to Jorge, "a loyal party member, a brilliant heart surgeon, a veteran defending the Nicaraguan socialist government. Who are you today in Cuba? You don't even make enough money to fix your damn Russian refrigerator." Blanquita's story probably reflects the attitudes of many *habaneros* in Cuba and reveals much about everyday life and culture in reinvented Cuba. Blanquita is no *luchadora* (struggler). The motivating forces in her life are not survival and making ends meet. Consumerism and a materialistic notion of the good life are what motivate her.[38]

However, Cuba does not have the economic resources to meet these expectations for all *Cubanos*. A consumer-based society demands a sophisticated credit system to function. Even with its high wages, the United States could not have the type of consumer base it does without an elaborate credit system in which people are able to live beyond their economic means. Cuba is essentially a cash-and-carry society in which the government keeps consumer credit to a minimum, and this is not likely to change. Moreover, Cuba is a small, developing nation with limited natural resources.

Nonetheless, consumer aspirations and a materialist notion of the good life are the driving forces in the lives of many *Cubanos*. Unmet consumer aspirations now constitute a form of structural dissatisfaction in Cuba. Paradoxically, "structural dissatisfaction" reflects the very success of the *rebeldes* in counteracting the most harmful effects of *El Período Especial*. At the same time, their use of capitalism to save socialism has created challenges and obstacles to the sustainable development of a people-centered society. Cuba is not now, and will not be in the foreseeable future, a consumer-based society. This means the *rebeldes* must successfully manage the discontent, frustration, and anger that will continually emanate from this structural dissatisfaction.

Yet, the desire for consumer goods and a more comfortable life do not have to produce a consumer-crazed society in which who one is and what one is are determined by what one owns. Neither does structural dissatisfaction necessarily become the type of unrest, frustration, and anger that leads to a desire for regime change and the resulting transition to a market economy. If properly managed, consumerism and a people-centered society can co-exist. A Cuban friend put it this way: "I'm a champagne socialist. I believe in the Revolution, but I also want to have some nice things and live comfortably." This is the *rebeldes'* challenge: to find a way to make this dream come true for the vast majority of *Cubanos*.

# 5

# THE SAN ISIDRO NEIGHBORHOOD

## A Case Study

In Chapters 3 and 4 we presented a general view of how the *rebeldes'* social-function model turned Havana neighborhoods into stable, highly organized communities with abundant social capital that play a significant role in helping *habaneros* make ends meet. In this chapter we provide a case study of how these attributes of neighborhood life and culture lowered the residents' risk of negative social outcomes while simultaneously increasing their resiliency, social well-being, and ability to make ends meet. Through an intimate exploration of the San Isidro community in Habana Vieja, we gain deeper insight into how Havana neighborhoods worked.

### The San Isidro Community

San Isidro occupies the southern corner of Habana Vieja, which is a UNESCO World Heritage Site as well as Havana's most important tourist destination. With a population of 95,383 occupying an area of about 1.7 square miles, Habana Vieja is also the second-most-congested *municipio* (municipality) in the city.[1] Founded in 1763, along the waterfront, near the present-day central railroad station, San Isidro is historically a working-class neighborhood. It is one of the seven *consejos populares* that form the *municipio* Habana Vieja. Named for Saint Isidro, a laborer and protector of market gardens and sown fields, San Isidro was originally home to the Compeche Indians, freed blacks, and tobacco, dock, and railroad workers, and their presence led to the development of a modest working-class neighborhood.

San Isidro is historically significant because it is the birthplace of José Martí, the legendary leader of the Cuban Revolution. By Council Agreement No. 74, on December 4, 1922, Calle Paula was renamed

149

Calle Leonor Pérez in honor of Martí's mother. It is also the home of Ciro Rodríguez Furneau, one of the founders of the Trio Matamoros, one of the most popular early Cuban bands. The renowned Afro-Cuban singer Beny Moré played with the band from 1945 to 1947. Also located in the neighborhood is La Iglesia de la Merced, one of the most important examples of baroque church architecture in eighteenth-century Havana, the National Archives, and the Estación Central de Ferrocarri (Central Train Station) designed by U.S. architect Kenneth Murchison in 1910.

These important historical sites notwithstanding, San Isidro is still not considered an important tourist site. Still, the neighborhood benefits greatly from the tourist industry because a portion of the revenues derived from tourism is used in the redevelopment of San Isidro. However, San Isidro is a vulnerable neighborhood, and in 1994, the GDIC selected it as a site for the establishment of a workshop for integrated neighborhood transformation. Because of congestion, poor housing, pollution, and the socioeconomic vulnerability of its residents, the Municipal Assembly selected San Isidro as an experimental laboratory for a community regeneration project.[2]

## The Neighborhood Setting

San Isidro is a compact, walking community composed of twenty-two residential blocks occupying about 0.1 square miles. Merced forms the northern boundary; Calle Egido forms the eastern boundary; and Desamparados the southern and western boundaries. San Isidro is a typical eighteenth-century neighborhood with building facades that communicate directly with the narrow streets. This nexus between dwellings and streets creates an intimate environment that transforms the street into a living room, an extension of the home and a comfortable setting that encourages social interaction (see Photo 5–1).

People talking, music and children playing everywhere, and an endless array of activity animate and energize these streets. The community's congestion contributes to the intensity of street life. In San Isidro, approximately 11,385 residents live in about 1,384 dwelling units. This translates into roughly eight persons in each dwelling unit, a density rate much higher than the 3.6-person household size in Malecón-San Isidro reported by Mario Coyula in 2004. San Isidro is a young community, with about 60 percent of the population under thirty-two years of age; approximately 20 percent of this group is under eighteen.

**Photo 5–1.    A Typical Street Scene in San Isidro**

Neighborhood conditions are very poor. In 1996 about 70 percent of the dwelling units were deteriorating, and the community lacked open space for recreational and cultural activities. Although San Isidro was the site of a major housing-regeneration effort, limited financial resources slowed the process. Thus, while housing conditions improved, field visits to the area in 2004 suggested that conditions were still inadequate. San Isidro also has one of the highest levels of air pollution in Habana Vieja. Given the neighborhood's location near the railroad terminal, the docks, and two major thoroughfares, this is not surprising.

## The Social-Function Model
## of Neighborhood Development

The social-function model of neighborhood development stresses not only the location of critical social institutions and organizations in neighborhoods, but also emphasizes the development of positive social relations at three levels:

1. encouraging social interaction among residents;
2. forging positive interactive relationships between residents and organizations and institutions serving the community;
3. developing strong interactive links between the neighborhood and the government.[3]

The fundamental idea is to enhance the social functioning of the neighborhood.[4] A social land-use survey of San Isidro was conducted in order to understand better how community land-use and institutional design heightened the social functioning of San Isidro. To facilitate the process, the neighborhood was divided into seven sectors, and a block-by-block survey was done. The sectors were selected based on the location of "through streets," which ran from Merced, the northern boundary of San Isidro, to Desamparados on the south. The sector map made it possible to determine not only the location of various social organizations, institutions, and land uses, but also to examine their distribution in geographic space.

The land-use survey showed that a range of institutions and places with social functions were scattered throughout the neighborhood. These institutions and organizations included social-service organizations, family doctor and nurse offices, primary schools, kindergartens, markets, eateries, culture centers, parks, playgrounds, community vegetable gardens, recreational centers, and public telephones. Telephones were included as part of the social function of neighborhoods due to their importance in intra-urban communication. Because private telephones are still a luxury item for many households, in vulnerable communities such as San Isidro residents need public telephones to facilitate their ability to communicate with people and service agencies outside the neighborhood.

The social land-use survey showed that not only do numerous social organizations, institutions, and places exist, but they are strategically located throughout the community. Some institutions and organizations, like *bodegas* (corner stores) or family doctor and nurse offices, service primarily those households closest to them, while others, such as the Jesus Sergio Montané Oropesa Gymnasium, provide services for the entire community. Still others, like the National Archives and the Office of Fishermen Affairs, primarily provide citywide services. The organizational matrix revealed that San Isidro had neighborhood services for seniors, children, and youth, along with support services for families and households. The family doctor and nurse teams, the primary schools, the food-distribution system, and recreational facilities underpinned the neighborhood social structure.

## The Family Doctor and Nurse Teams

Our survey identified four family doctor and nurse offices conveniently located in the most populous sections of the neighborhood. According to the Program for Human Development at the Local Level, in 2000 there were seventeen family doctor and nurse teams in San Isidro. When the family doctor-nurse program began in the 1980s, the government built offices for the teams, located in the neighborhoods where they worked. The buildings contained a clinic on the first floor and living quarters for the doctor and nurse on the second and third floors (see Photo 5–2). The goal was to embed the teams within the communities in which they worked. When the economic crisis hit, to increase the number of teams operating in neighborhoods without constructing new buildings, the government turned many existing family doctor-nurse offices into facilities shared by more than one doctor-nurse team.[5] This practice transformed many doctor-nurse offices into "mini–primary care" clinics staffed by a minimum of two doctors and two nurses. Typically, the new *médicos* who shared the office had less experience than did the doctor in residence. They were recent graduates or residents, still learning their specialization.

**Photo 5–2. Family Doctor and Nurse Office at 212 Picota Street**

The distribution pattern among the family doctor-nurse offices suggests that their locations facilitate easy access by neighborhood residents. Moreover, the seventeen doctor-nurse teams translate into a doctor-nurse ratio of approximately one team to every 680 San Isidro residents. Since the launching of the family doctor-nurse program in 1984, these teams have cared for 120 to 150 families or about 600 to 700 people. Lastly, residents value family doctors and consider them to be very important community members. These medical teams also service the primary schools, visit the *casa de abuelos* (senior centers), and give health talks at the Leonor Pérez Cultural Center. Doctors and nurses are an integral part of the community and residents see them in meetings, at the market, and in other neighborhood places.

## The Primary Schools

When UNESCO gave math and language tests to third- and fourth-graders in thirteen Latin American countries, researchers were stunned to find that pupils in Cuba's lowest-income schools outperformed most upper-middle class students in the rest of the region. This test data confirmed years of anecdotal evidence asserting that Cuba's primary schools were the best in Latin America and possibly better than schools in distressed neighborhoods in the United States. Educators Martin Carnoy and Jeffery Marshall argue that the nurturing neighborhood context and a social environment dedicated to high achievement explain why children excel in Cuban schools. Primary schools in San Isidro confirm the Carnoy and Marshall thesis. These schools, like the doctor and nurse offices, are conveniently scattered throughout the neighborhood. This makes it possible for most children to walk to school and facilitates the ability of their parents to interact with teachers and principals (see Photo 5–3).

**Photo 5–3.    Primary Students Walking to Sergio Luis Ferriol Primary School**

Most Cuban parents value education and get involved in their child's schooling. Gladys Alzerez, who is also a CDR president, has a child enrolled in the Sergio Luis Ferriol primary school. She regularly attends teacher meetings, helps her child with homework, and works with other parents to improve conditions at the school. Although Alzerez and other parents strongly support their children's schools and believe that teachers are committed, they are nevertheless concerned about the competence and youth of new teachers. Some San Isidro parents feel that many new teachers are too young and poorly trained. This, they feel, undermines the quality of their children's education.

The government recently acknowledged that Cuba is suffering from an exodus of teachers, which is threatening its public-education system. Educational Minister Luis Ignacio Gomez believes that the loss of teachers is due to low wages and teacher dissatisfaction with the low recognition received for their work. The issue, however, is more complex. Occupational dislocations and standard of living differentials caused by the tourist industry may be having an impact. Workers in the public sector generally receive lower salaries than those who work in tourism or in the informal sector, those who labor in the black market, and those who are self-employed. Workers in these industries are also often able to receive a portion of their earnings in U.S. dollars.[6] Moreover, workers in the tourist industry are frequently able to forge friendships with tourists, which allow them access to dollars, remittances, and other resources. Within this context it is not surprising that many experienced teachers leave their jobs in primary education to find work in the higher paying tourist industry.

To counter this exodus of experienced teachers and to improve the teacher-student ratio, the government established the Emergency Teacher Program in 2002. Under this program the government trains students in education and then sends them into primary and secondary schools. The government pays the "emergency" teachers, but their salaries are less than those of teachers who have completed a regular teacher-education program. This investment did lead to the hiring of more teachers. For example, between 2001 and 2003 the number of primary-school teachers in Cuba jumped from 79,341 to 92,991, an increase of 17 percent. However, due to the inexperience of many of these new teachers, the overall quality of instruction nevertheless declined, according to some residents.

The quality of teachers notwithstanding, the activities of other community institutions and the involvement of community residents counteracted, to a certain degree, the inexperience of the new teachers in San Isidro. For example, the Leonor Pérez Cultural Center, which opened in March 1999, has a rich after-school and summer program for primary students. The center is the outcome of a community participatory process motivated by parental concern for the children. Working parents wanted an after-school program that provided their children with quality educational experiences, as well as a summer program that involved the children in structured activities when school was out. Concurrently, the historian of the city wanted to create a San Isidro history center where residents could learn about their community's past. A blending of the two ideas led to the establishment of the Leonor Pérez Cultural Center.

The purpose of the center is to provide culture and education for residents of all ages. It works with the neighborhood's four primary schools and coordinates after-school activities with the school curriculum so that the students' academic experiences can be reinforced. The center teaches students social skills, including responsibility and respect for others. It is also available to adults and has a small lending library with books on national and local history. Augmenting these activities are concerts, which blend music and dance with discussions held by the family doctor and others on health, environmental concerns, and other neighborhood issues.

Gelo's Garden provides another example of the ways in which neighborhood residents become involved in the schooling process (see Photo 5–4). Gelo, who lived near the Sergio Luis Ferriol primary school, is a retired farmer who moved to San Isidro in 1962. In the 1990s a vacant lot behind Gelo's house became a dumping ground for trash and thus a neighborhood health hazard. In 1994 a delegate from the San Isidro *consejos populares* asked Gelo if he would turn the lot into a community garden. Gelo agreed, and this project became a huge success. Not only did the planting of the garden eliminate the health hazard, but now fruits, herbs, and vegetables are available for all community residents.

Later, Gelo decided to link the gardening process to the educational experience of students at Sergio Luis Ferriol. Working with the school, the CDR, the *consejos populares*, and the Ministry of Agriculture, Gelo developed a teaching workshop for children and adults. Every day, between 2:00 and 4:00 p.m., Gelo taught students about planting and the medicinal value of herbs. He also taught the students the importance of teamwork and responsibility.

**Photo 5–4.   Children Working in Gelo's Garden**

## Community Food Security

Community food security, a vital component of the social-function model of neighborhood development, ensures that residents have access to a safe, nutritionally adequate diet through a food system based on equity and social justice. This is based on the Revolution's belief that people should not live in hunger or fear of starvation. Unlike most countries in Latin America and the United States, Cuba embedded its system of food security in the neighborhood-development process.

### *Mercado Agropecuarios*

The Special Period greatly challenged the Cuban system of neighborhood food security. The severity of the economic crisis, combined with the growing despair and social unrest among the people, forced the *rebeldes* reluctantly to embrace a market mechanism to solve the problem of agriculture production and food distribution.[7] At the Fourth Party Congress in 1991, the *clases populares* called for a return to the free peasant markets *(mercados libres campesinos)* that Castro had dismantled in 1986. In the summer of 1994 widespread social discontent shattered governmental resistance to the *mercado agropecuario* idea. The intensity of discontent and anger among the popular classes sobered the regime and caused it to change its policy on *agromercados*.

In an interview published in *Granma* on September 17, 1994, Raúl Castro announced the opening of *mercado agropecuarios* (agriculture markets). Explaining the policy shift, he said: "The country's main political, military and ideological problem today is to feed itself. . . . In order to alleviate the situation, [we] expect to open farmers' markets soon." On October 1, 1994, the government permitted the establishment of the market-based *mercado agropecuarios*, and subsequently approximately 130 *mercados agropecuarios* opened throughout Cuba.

Producers could now sell their surplus yield once they fulfilled their monthly quotas to the state procurement system *(acopio)*. Unlike the peasant free markets that preceded them, the *mercados agropecuarios* could employ intermediaries to sell the farmer's products. Supply and demand set prices at the new markets, and the government regulated and taxed their operations. Although high prices at the *agromercados* made the struggle to make ends more difficult among the *clases populares*, they still enthusiastically greeted the markets (see Photo 5–5). In San Isidro, a large *mercado agropecuario* located on Calle

Egido services the community. This *agromercado* carries a wide range of fruits, vegetables, rice, beans, and meat. An extension of this market is located on Calle Picota, not far away.

**Photo 5–5.    *Mercado Agropecuario* on Calle Egido**

In addition to the *mercados agropecuarios*, a *mercado agropecuario estatal* (state-owned farmers' market) is also located in the San Isidro neighborhood. Although the products at the state-owned market are cheaper than those sold at the free agricultural markets, residents prefer the latter to the former due to greater choices and their perception that the goods are superior. Augmenting the agricultural markets are two "dollar" *mercados*, both located on Egido. These "dollar" *mercados* sell mostly canned goods and other personal and household items. Unlike the *mercados agropecuarios*, the "dollar" *mercados* did not grow out of popular demand. Rather, when the government legalized the dollar and permitted families to receive remittances from abroad, it needed to create a mechanism to capture these dollars. This led to the establishment of the "dollar" *mercados*, which do not accept Cuban national money. To entice residents to shop in these stores, they carry goods that are not available elsewhere, although the goods are sold at higher prices.

### The Bodegas and Cafeterias

A rationing system undergirds the food-security system in Cuba. Law No. 1015 launched food rationing on March 12, 1962, when the Ministry of Internal Trade distributed one rationing booklet to every household. A household could be composed of one or more individuals, and there could be more than one household per dwelling. The *libreta* made it possible for residents to purchase a variety of items at highly subsidized prices, a fraction of the cost of those items found in the market-based *mercado agropecuarios* or "dollar" *mercados*.[8] The *rebeldes* set up this system to ensure that every *Cubano*, regardless of social or economic status, had a minimum intake of nutritional food. Each household is entitled to purchase a specific quantity of rationed items depending upon the number of consumers in the household.

*Bodegas* or corner stores are the main outlets that sell these rationed products in San Isidro and other neighborhoods (see Photo 5–6). Some *barrios* also have outlets called *placitas* or *puestos*, which sell fruits and vegetables. About eleven *bodegas* were scattered across the San Isidro neighborhood. There is a *bodega* on every block. Each store has a specific market area, and residents must purchase their rationed goods in the *bodega* that services their locale. They cannot make purchases at other *bodegas* unless they obtain a change of address from the Office of the Register of Consumers.

**Photo 5–6.   A Typical *Bodega***

The rationed products sold at the *bodegas* constantly change. As production of some fruits and/or vegetables increases, the government removes them from the rationing system and they are freely sold *(por la libre)*. When they became scarce again, they are returned to the ration booklet. Eggs are perhaps the best example of items that frequently move in and out of the *libreta*. In addition, there are chronic shortages at the *bodegas*, and at times residents cannot sustain themselves on food items available only there. During the Special Period the government reduced the amount of food and other items available for purchase with the *libreta*. Today, the *libreta* will cover food supplies for families for only about two weeks. Consequently, residents need to supplement subsidized purchases with items obtained from the *mercados.*

The food-security system in San Isidro also includes neighborhood eateries: six cafeterias, formal restaurants, and establishments that sell food from corner windows in private homes. At the Comedor Belén residents can purchase breakfast and lunch at reduced prices. This service is particularly important for seniors, whose diets must include some essential foodstuffs. Moreover, La Iglesia de Merced on Calle Cuba serves breakfast and lunch for neighborhood residents. Many residents also have access to subsidized lunches at their work places, and primary-school students are offered lunch at school.

## Culture and Recreation

The Cuban government believes that culture, recreation, and physical activity are critical to the wholesome development of children and young adults. This theme undergirded the *Code on Children and Youth* adopted by the National Assembly of People's Power, June 28–30, 1978. For example, Title V11, Article 88, of the *Code* states: "Physical culture and sports, as integral parts of the life of young people, contribute to forming healthy, strong children and youth capable of efficiently meeting their educational, job and military duties; and develop in them tenacity, combativity, fraternity, collectivity and a sense of discipline. Children and youth are obliged to engage in physical education included in educational programs and should practice sports."

The *rebeldes* made the establishment of facilities suitable for engaging residents in cultural, sports, and recreational activities an integral part of their neighborhood-development strategy. Against this backdrop, residents of San Isidro worked with the Taller San Isidro, *consejos populares,* and CDR to develop and support cultural and recreational facilities in the community. A variety of cultural institutions are scattered throughout the community, such as the Iglesia de Merced, the house where José Martí was born, which is also the location of a school and library, and the Leonor Pérez Cultural Center. The community also converted a vacant lot into a concert area where young people could perform. Meanwhile, residents, working in collaboration with the Taller San Isidro, formulated plans for the development of an outdoor patio on the grounds of the National Archives, which would create stronger links between that institution and the neighborhood.

The creation of recreational space for residents was a top neighborhood priority. The neighborhood also established a cluster of recreational activities in the eastern corner of San Isidro, near the intersection of Calle Cuba and Desamparados. These facilities are the Rafael Trejo Boxing Gym, the Jesus Sergio Montané Oropesa Community Gymnasium, and a dance studio located across the street from the gym. These facilities serve the entire San Isidro community. Two recreational outlets were set up for seniors on Calle Egido, and the Casa de Abuelos offers a range of recreational activities for older residents.

The building of San Isidro's social and recreational infrastructure is a community driven process, and a brief examination of the development of the Jesus Sergio Montané Oropesa Community Gymnasium provides insight into it. This gymnasium grew out of concerns expressed by the young people in the neighborhood. One of the most popular places for youth to play was a vacant lot on the corner of San Isidro and Habana, in the southern part of the community. Here, they played basketball, soccer, baseball, and engaged in a number of other activities. However, a ceiba tree was located on the site, and this created a problem. In Santeria, the ceiba is a holy tree inhabited by powerful spirits. Given its religious significance, older residents decided to turn the lot into a meditative park, which they believed was a more fitting use of the area.[9] This decision did not set well with the young people, and they complained that older residents were taking away their play space.

In response, the Taller de San Isidro, in partnership with the *consejos populares*, CDRs, and children's organizations, searched within the community for a new recreational area. They settled on a site occupied by an abandoned warehouse, situated on the southeastern corner of Calle Cuba, for the development of a community recreational center. With the support of an NGO from the Viareggio, in Tuscany, Italy, the residents were able to convert the warehouse into a state-of-the-art gym.[10] After three years of renovation the facility opened in 1999. Residents now use it for a range of activities: gymnastics, martial arts, aerobics, basketball, soccer, and weight lifting. The manager of the gymnasium says the facility has had a positive impact on neighborhood youth.

## Intra-Urban Transportation

Understanding everyday life and culture in San Isidro, as well as in other similar neighborhoods, is enhanced by exploring how residents travel within their community, as well as how they journey throughout the metropolitan region. The economic catastrophe spawned a serious urban-transportation crisis in Cuba. A combination of resourcefulness, resiliency, and solidarity has enabled *Cubanos* to meet the challenge of navigating a sprawling metropolis with a crippled transportation system.

Havana, like most Latin American cities, had been dependent on bus transportation when the Soviet Union collapsed. Shortages of fuel oil and spare parts dramatically reduced bus service and greatly limited automobile usage, especially during the early years of the Special Period. Decreases in bus service and motorized travel led to a dramatic increase in the number of walking trips. In 2002, for example, the average length of walking journeys was a little over three miles, and more than half of these journeys took longer than forty minutes.[11]

Walking became the main form of transportation within neighborhoods and between closely situated communities. For example, in the survey data obtained during the *El Barrio* household surveys, about 62 percent of the respondents said walking was their primary mode of transportation. However, because of the travel time of walking journeys, bicycle riding became another option during the Special Period. Overnight, Cuba became a nation of bicycle riders. By the mid 1990s there were about 700,000 bicycles in Havana alone, mostly purchased from the Chinese.

*Habaneros* used bicycles not only for travel around the neighborhood but also as a way to commute to work. During the early years of *El Período Especial*, bus service was often unpredictable, with overcrowding and erratic schedules. This created serious problems in making the journey to work. Consequently, many workers rode bicycles to work. It took longer, but in those days the bicycle was more predictable. For example, Enrique Ríos said that his employer loaned him a company-owned bicycle to get to work. Although the journey took him more than an hour, he was able to arrive on time. When someone stole his bike and he had to ride the bus, its unpredictability often caused him to be late for work.[12] He then decided to leave this job to get one closer to home.

The use of bicycles peaked around 1994 and has steadily declined since then. The primary reasons for the decline are improvements in bus service and the growing use of other forms of motorized vehicles, especially a wide range of motorbikes. By 2000 the bus had reclaimed its position as the most important mode of transportation among *habaneros*. In the sample presented here, 68 percent of the respondents claimed that when walking was not an option, the bus was their most important means of transportation. For San Isidro residents, bus stops are conveniently located. Residents can catch buses on the corner of Desamparados or at the Central Train Station, or in the area of the

Capitolio. While the bicycle is still popular in San Isidro, the bici-taxi, which arrived on the scene in the mid 1990s, has become the most popular form of intra-neighborhood transportation in San Isidro and elsewhere.

The bicycle and bici-taxis, along with walking, are primarily intra-neighborhood forms of transportation. For more lengthy journeys residents rely on the bus or the automobile taxi. Very few *habaneros* own automobiles, and those who do are faced with the ongoing challenge of keeping them running due to the lack of basic supplies, including spare parts, fluids, and tires, as well as the cost of gasoline. Thus, many *habaneros* use their automobiles as taxis, both legal and illegal, and these vehicles play a critical role in providing intra-urban transport for many *Cubanos*. Hitchhiking is also a widespread method of traveling in Havana. This practice is encouraged by the government, which requires certain government vehicles to stop and give lifts to people when they have space available. The point is that *Cubanos* can get to any part of the region inexpensively.

Lastly, in *San Isidro*, and elsewhere, the quest to solve the transportation crisis also began to reshape land use and economic development in the neighborhood. The government allowed some vacant lots to be turned into garages where automobiles, motorbikes, bici-taxis, and other vehicles could be stored overnight. In addition, a few auto and bicycle repair shops appeared.

## The Social Foundation of Neighborhood Development

A rich storehouse of social capital anchors the San Isidro neighborhood. Walking through the streets of the community, omnipresent CDR signs, which identify the organization's zonal offices, are a constant reminder of the complex maze of formal and informal social organizations that exist in this community. Stability, solidarity, participation, and reciprocity are the social forces that connect people, link the residents to neighborhood service institutions, and join the neighborhood to the government. In Cuba collective social capital is not independent of the government. The *rebeldes* embrace a governance model that encourages self-help and community participation. For example, high levels of participation in organizations such as the CDR, FMC, the *junta de vecinos*, and religious organizations, especially Santeria, bind the residents together and provide a structure within which the principles of reciprocity and mutual help are easily and readily conducted.

To strengthen the neighborhoods further, especially the most vulnerable ones, the government has developed a system of workshops for integrated neighborhood transformation. The workshops give these vulnerable neighborhoods a full-time, multi-disciplinary professional staff to plan and guide the community-development process in a participatory manner. The importance of such institutions in vulnerable communities cannot be overestimated. The value of the Taller de San Isidro can be seen in the leading role it played in establishing the Leonor Pérez Cultural Center, the Jesus Sergio Montané Oropesa Community Gymnasium, the numerous mini-parks, and other such neighborhood institutions.

The social-function model of neighborhood development calls for social organizations and institutions to work together to solve neighborhood problems. This means the family doctor and nurse not only work with patients in their office, but also in the primary schools, the *casa de abuelos,* and cultural institutions. They interact within the community organizations and institutions, and they interact more informally with residents on the streets and in the markets. The same is true with other professionals. This high level of interaction occurs because most of the doctors, nurses, and teachers that work in San Isidro also live in the community.

The schools are also porous institutions that make parents feel welcome and willingly collaborate with residents on educational projects. The experience of Gelo with the Sergio Luis Ferriol primary school is typical. Gelo's garden also illustrates how community activities in San Isidro create synergies due to collaborative efforts across organizational sectorial lines. The creation and development of Gelo's garden involved Gelo, the school, the CDR, the *consejos populares,* and the Ministry of Agriculture, along with the enthusiastic participation of the children.

The San Isidro experience also demonstrates that neighborhood residents are not timid about voicing their desires or concerns. For example, parental concern led to the development of the Leonor Pérez Cultural Center and its after-school program. Parents have also been critical of the Emergency Teachers Program. Although it is a complex problem with no easy solutions, neighborhood criticism most likely led to the government's recent acknowledgment of the problem. Popular discontent among the *clases populares* also caused the *rebeldes* to set up the *mercado agropecuarios,* despite their great reluctance. The concern of the youth with the elimination of their recreational area led to the establishment of the Jesus Sergio Montané Oropesa Community Gymnasium. The governance model has created important channels of communication between neighborhood residents and the government. Such interaction means that the government always knows about the concerns of the residents. That two-way channel of communication enables the government to support various spontaneous initiatives, such as the urban agricultural movement, which emerged during the 1990s.

The placement of service organizations and institutions that improve and bolster the social functioning of neighborhoods is the hallmark of the Cuban model of neighborhood development. The existence of food-distribution outlets ensures that residents can easily access the healthy food products that are available, while the strategic placement of family doctor and nurse offices facilitates the delivery of health service. Likewise, the placement of primary schools in a safe and nurturing environment enhances students' academic achievement. At the same time, the deployment of thousands of young social workers in neighborhoods like San Isidro has eased the quest to grapple effectively with local social problems, including the unrest among youth.

The complex socioeconomic problems spawned by the collapse of the Soviet Union made using the neighborhood as a framework for problem solving and developing a logical approach to community building. Moreover, by engaging residents in the process of solving their own problems, the *rebeldes* were able both to restore hope and to legitimize the Revolution. The social-function method of neighborhood development, combined with the dense network of associations and the values of solidarity and reciprocity, helps to explain how *Cubanos* made ends meet and survived during the crisis and how they continue to sustain themselves.

# Epilogue

# WHERE DOES CUBA GO FROM HERE?

## The Post-Castro Era

The abrupt collapse of the Soviet Union and the East European Communist Bloc delivered a devastating blow to the Cuban economy. The unexpected loss of trading partners led to a precipitous socioeconomic decline that left Cuba with minimal options, which could only be characterized as bad, very bad, and catastrophic. Fidel Castro had warned the Cuban people that they must be prepared for an era of hardship. There was, however, a silver lining to this dark cloud of economic and social despair. For the first time in its history, Cuba was genuinely free.

The island was not a Spanish colony, a U.S. dependency, or a semi-satellite of the Soviet Union. Problems and hardships notwithstanding, Cuba answered to no master or superior power, and it was now free to pursue its own destiny and develop its own independent political-economic model. Thus, in reality the Special Period was not a moment of temporary hardship, which would eventually be followed by economic recovery. Instead, this era represented the dawning of a new age in Cuban history, a time when the revolutionary leadership was finally free to pursue its own destiny and to develop its own model of political economy. From this perspective the Special Period was not so much about economic recovery as it was about reinvention, and the policies implemented during this period were actually the building blocks of a new society.

Cuba still stood alone in a world market dominated by capitalism. The country would now have to find new trading partners and develop a new political-economic template that would somehow embrace elements of the capitalist model, including joint ventures with foreign corporations and the development of some small enterprises. It also meant that state-owned corporations would have to use managerial principles characteristic of capitalist firms.[1] The great challenge facing Cuba, then, was how to incorporate these new capitalist elements into its economy without abandoning its people-centered approach to governance and socioeconomic development.

Cuba pursued a threefold strategy to meet this challenge. First and foremost, the *rebeldes* maintained their emphasis on developing the social function of neighborhoods and maintaining welfare provisions. Therefore, throughout the economic crisis all of the major health and educational programs continued to be free and available to the public, and the *rebeldes* strengthened the family doctor and nurse program and the primary schools. Housing and utility costs remained low, and the food subsidies and rationing of basic items continued, albeit at a lower level. Cultural, sports, and recreational activities persisted despite cutbacks in funding. Workers displaced because of economic restructuring continued to receive their wages and were offered state-funded jobs and retraining programs. Despite scarcities and social deprivation, crime rates remained far below Latin American and U.S. levels.[2] Thus, because of stable, highly organized neighborhoods combined with people-oriented government policies, ordinary *Cubanos* were shielded from the harshest effects of the economic crisis. The government's approach reinforced the people's trust and kept anger and frustration from degenerating into widespread social unrest and demands for regime change.

Second, the *rebeldes* bet on international tourism to replace sugar as the engine to drive the economy. The bet paid off, with tourism generating the hard currency necessary to import essential commodities, especially petroleum and manufactured products, medical supplies, and food. Simultaneously, to diversify its economy, Cuba created joint ventures to develop and export nickel, rum, tobacco, and citrus products, and made significant investments in new advanced schools of computer science and in bio-technology to stimulate research and development in pharmaceutical exports. These activities provided Cuba with the resources needed to stimulate the island's economic recovery, without having to abandon the nation's people-centered focus.

Third, despite the U.S. boycott, Cuba developed diplomatic and economic relations with numerous countries across the world, and during the opening decade of the twenty-first century it strengthened its relations with many of them, especially in Latin America. The association with Venezuela has been particularly important.[3] With this South American neighbor, Cuba has developed long-term, large-scale trade and investment agreements that have involved Cuban medical teams and medical facilities in exchange for petroleum products. Since 2004, anchored by this friendship, Cuba strengthened its relationship with many other countries throughout the Americas, including Brazil, Bolivia, Mexico, Barbados, Jamaica, Haiti, Ecuador, Argentina, and Nicaragua. The growing alliances with these countries has translated not only into increased resources but also into market opportunities for the export of Cuban goods and services. The left-ward drift of countries in Latin America—from far-right wing to moderate-right neo-liberal regimes—will continue to create favorable external conditions for Cuba.

By 2001 Cuba had even broken the U.S. trade embargo by import-ing food and medicine from the United States, albeit on unfavorable, one-sided terms. Concurrently, Cuba cemented its relationship with Canada and most European countries, especially Spain and Russia, along with Asian, Middle Eastern, and African nations, such as North Korea, Viet Nam, China, Iran, Yemen, Ethiopia, Ghana, Angola, Ni-geria, Mozambique, Botswana, and the Republic of Cape Verde. The bottom line is that after more than forty years of intense effort, the United States still has not been able to isolate and destabilize Cuba. Policies such as the Cuba Democratic Act in 1992 and the Helms-Bur-ton law in 1996, for example, increased hardship and difficulties, but they did not lead to regime change and U.S.-style democratization.

The secret to Cuba's great success in overcoming the obstacles to its survival is the emphasis it has consistently placed on the strength-ening of its neighborhoods, particularly those where the most vul-nerable population groups reside. During the crisis Cuban television announcers often exclaimed, "Not one hospital has been closed; not one teacher has lost a job." That was not hyperbole. Throughout the 1990s the share of Cuba's gross domestic product spent on social pro-grams increased by 34 percent. Throughout the economic crisis the government not only attended to the needs of special populations—children, women, and the disabled—but also used its neighborhood-development strategy to identify specific areas of need and target new at-risk populations. This small-scale, place-based, community-par-ticipatory, social-function model of integrated neighborhood devel-opment shielded the *clases populares* from the most harmful effects of the economic catastrophe.[4]

Most significant, it kept the *clases populares* loyal to the revolution-ary leadership, reinforced the bonds of trust, and strengthened the values of solidarity, reciprocity, equitable wealth distribution, and socioeconomic and racial justice. Yet the very success of the Cuban government in meeting and overcoming the challenges resulting from the collapse of the Soviet Union and the U.S. boycott created a new set of challenges and contradictions.

## Using Capitalism to Save Socialism: The Rise of Consumer Culture and Other Challenges

Cuba based its evolving political economic model on a mixed economy operating within the context of a people-centered society.

Because it was the fastest, easiest, and most logical approach for ending the economic depression and reinventing Cuban society, international tourism anchored the new political economy. While this bold, pragmatic gamble to save socialism paid off, international tourism was far from benign. It solved one problem but generated other daunting problems, the most serious of which was the rise of consumerism.

Tourism placed an indelible imprint on everyday life and culture in Havana. The integration of tourist sites and facilities within residential communities caused international tourism to influence everyday life and culture. The development of luxurious tourist facilities, combined with thousands of tourists roaming through the city spending money on pleasure, imbued *habaneros* with consumerism and material-based notions of the "good life." Through tourism, Cubans evaluated, purchased, and consumed items based on their symbolic content and perceived social meaning. Thus, when *habaneros* want to buy Nikes, or some other recognizable brand, they are more significantly attempting to acquire the lifestyle and experience being advertised. This is indicative of the trend toward a more consumer-based society, one where consumption becomes a means of self-realization and identification. Who one is, is based on what one can buy.

The creation of a tourist infrastructure, combined with the influx of tourists, constituted a frontal assault on Cuban culture. The *rebeldes* recognized the dangers emanating from the tourist industry and hoped their continued emphasis on revolutionary ideals would protect society from this "tourist virus." However, despite intentions to the contrary, the *turista* nevertheless became the new elite in Cuban society, and consumerism became a new Cuban credo. The dollarization of the economy intensified this trend. Prior to the resurgence of international tourism, the retail sector processed transactions only in pesos and sold mostly recycled clothes, inexpensive apparel, and new and used appliances. The store environment was drab and colorless, with no stylish in-store or window displays to encourage buying.

The new retail sector developed during the resurrection of international tourism mimicked the design of retail shops in market-based consumer societies and promoted the values of consumerism. Tourism thus trapped the *rebeldes* in a vicious cycle. They needed to establish market-based retail shops to counteract the black market and to capture dollars. Yet the establishment of this sector helped stimulate the emergence of a culture of consumerism, which countered revolutionary ideology. Although many *habaneros* might simply be window shopping, the desire to own the commodities is real. Thus, regardless of original intent, consumerism and materialism became significant cultural forces in the development of Cuban society during the 1990s.

Many *Cubanos* lack the discretionary income necessary to purchase the goods they want. Nevertheless, they still long for these items. *Cubanos* want more dollars, not because they are needed to make ends meet, but because they want to buy washing machines, furniture, CD and DVD players, computers, stylish clothes, fancy jewelry, perfume, cars, motorbikes, cell phones. They want to eat out in a restaurant, go dancing at the Casa de Musica or some other discothèque, or repair and improve their dwelling units. This is not to suggest that life in Havana and other places in Cuba is not very difficult. Many *Cubanos* work more than one job and engage in a range of bartering and other activities to make ends meet. Nonetheless, *habaneros* do make ends meet. There is no starvation in Cuba, and people do not have to sell body parts to pay debts.[5] Today, in Cuba, life is no longer about making ends meet but about obtaining the resources needed to purchase the things people want. Cuba has morphed from a needs-based to a wants-based society.

The rise of consumerism is a major problem for two interrelated reasons. First, the creation of a revolutionary society necessitated the development of a "new person" motivated by moral rather material aspirations.[6] International tourism, however, spawned a countervailing force to the goals of the Revolution, that is, building a society based on social justice, collectivism, reciprocity, and the equitable distribution of wealth. Consumerism promotes individualism and material incentives and generates ideals of the "good life" based on the acquisition of goods. Thus, consumerism attacks the philosophical foundation of the Revolution.

Second, Cuba is still a poor country with a very primitive system of consumer credit. Cuba does not have the resources to support the type of consumer-based society characteristic of advanced capitalist countries.[7] In the United States, for example, the consumer society could not exist without credit cards and other advanced forms of consumer credit. The *rebeldes* are not likely to support a consumer credit system that opens the door for *Cubanos* to become overburdened with debt. This means that *Cubanos* will be unable to satisfy their growing appetite for consumer items. Thus, the rise of consumerism has created a form of structural discontent that is likely to produce societal tensions for years to come.

At the same time, not all *Cubanos* are enthralled by consumerism. For example, subsets of influential rap music groups are openly hostile to consumerism and market-based ideologies.[8] Moreover, many people do not embrace consumerism but simply want to make purchases that improve the quality of their lives and/or have the resources to go out occasionally. Thus, if the *rebeldes* maintain their focus on improving the social function of neighborhoods, meeting the needs of the *clases populares*, and increasing the availability of a wider range of consumer items, structural discontent will not morph into social unrest and demands for regime change. Even if the income gulf between social groups increases, as it probably will, as long as neighborhoods function at a high social level and people are able to make ends meet, there will be no meaningful social unrest.

## Without Fidel: The Road Ahead

On July 31, 2006, when Fidel provisionally handed over power to his younger brother, Raúl, he bequeathed to the Cuban people a reinvented society anchored by highly stable, well-organized neighborhoods and an economy driven by international tourism. Although Fidel led Cuba out of the gloomy socioeconomic despair of the Special Period, he nonetheless left the country with serious economic problems related to productivity; growing food dependency reflected in increased importation of rice, beans, poultry, pork, beef, and other essentials; nagging problems of transportation; a housing crisis; and pilfering and corruption.[9] On the social side Cuba had shifted from a needs-based to a wants-based society increasingly influenced by consumerism. Thus, as Raúl accepted the mantle of leadership from Fidel, he not only inherited a stable, reinvented society, but also a country with a host of complicated problems.

Against this backdrop Raúl appears to be building on the legacy of Fidel by leading an aggressive reform movement designed to strengthen the internal fabric of Cuban society.[10] There are no signs that Cuba will cast aside the socialist banner and march down the road of capitalist restoration and U.S.-style democracy. This does not mean that Raúl Castro and the new regime do not recognize that Cuba has serious problems with which it must grapple. On the contrary, Cuba does seem to have learned a big lesson from the collapse of the Soviet Union—the internal enemy poses the greatest threat to the survival of Cuba as a people-centered society. Fidel made this point in November 2005 when he warned that Cuban socialism might be destroyed from within. He cited the rampant black market—from pilfered goods to illicit businesses—as the main culprit.[11] With these and other issues in mind, Raúl has urged *Cubanos* to air openly their grievances about waste, governmental inefficiencies, and other societal problems.

This approach is reminiscent of the 1986 Period of Rectification, when there were growing inequalities, corruption, and a corrosion of socialist consciousness at a time when the socialist camp was in a crisis. In a quest to "renovate Cuban socialism," Fidel called upon the masses to participate in the process of exposing the problems the nation faced. Political scientist Jorge Domínguez reminds us that for many years the Cuban government has permitted and even stimulated forms of citizen complaint to expose corruption and mismanagement, allowing local governments to channel these grievances to the central government.[12] Therefore, Raúl is likely to launch a reform movement designed to strengthen Cuban society internally, thereby neutralizing the enemy within. The reform movement will likely occur in three related areas: government and the economy, neighborhood development, and culture.

## Governmental and Economic Reforms

The issues of government corruption, public theft, bureaucratic inefficiency, low economic productivity, pilfering, and the decline of food production are very problematic, and Raúl has been critical of the government's response to them. For example, in a major policy speech on July 26, 2007, he ridiculed the bureaucracy and the dysfunctional agricultural system, and then called for structural changes as well as a debate on how best to bring about improvements. In that same speech Raúl expressed concern about low wages and salaries: "Wages today are clearly insufficient to satisfy all needs and have thus ceased to play a role in ensuring the socialist principle that each should contribute according to their capacity and receive according to their work. This has bred forms of social indiscipline and intolerance, which having taken root proved difficult to eradicate even after the objective causes behind them have been removed."[13]

Toward this end, in December 2007 the government said that it would allow foreign companies to pay Cuban employees with hard currency, a move that legalized widespread "under the table" payments and required workers to declare and pay tax on that income. In the past foreign businesses employed their Cuban staff through government agencies, which were paid in hard currency and, in turn, paid their employees in Cuban pesos. To supplement the low wages, companies often paid their Cuban staff an additional amount under the table.[14] Moreover, on February 24, 2008, Raúl suggested that the government would be grappling with problems of the country's dual monetary system and low wages.[15] On this latter point he will probably push for wage increases for all workers, especially those working in the public sector.

These measures, however, regardless of their success, will not address the more complicated wage issue caused by tourism-related labor distortions. Workers in the tourist industry, regardless of their skill level, are often able to earn wages that far exceed those of highly trained scientists, doctors, and other more skilled workers. Consequently, many workers in high-skill but low-wage sectors are drawn toward work in the tourist industry, and this creates a type of "brain drain" that can become very problematic. The situation needs to be addressed effectively—and soon. However, this is a complex problem with no easy solutions.

Raúl has also identified transportation as a top developmental priority. *Cubanos* often complain about the transportation system, saying that there are not enough decent buses and other vehicles to travel to work, school, and recreational places. In December 2007, the government announced that it will spend more than $2 billion over the next five years to upgrade the transportation system. The upgrades will include adding fifteen hundred buses to the public fleet and more than one thousand taxies to urban streets.[16] Although much more is needed to resolve the transportation problem, these efforts nonetheless allow the government to accrue enormous symbolic capital.[17] Its policies say to the people, "You are very important, and we hear your concerns." Such sentiments sustain the trust established between the government and the people.

## Neighborhood Development

The development of hyper-stable and highly organized neighborhoods that are rich in social capital was the secret to the staying power of Fidel Castro. These communities, anchored by the family doctor and nurse program, primary schools, and other social institutions, earned the government vital public support. The continued improvement and strengthening of the social function of neighborhoods will be critical to the continued survival of the revolutionary government. Raúl Castro seems to understand this. In his first speech as president of Cuba, in February 2008, he said one of the main goals of his administration would be to "meet the basic needs of the population, both material and spiritual, based on the sustained strengthening of the national economy and its productive base."[18]

This is not a trickle-down approach to social development. On the contrary, the *rebeldes* seem intent on traveling simultaneously down the roads of social development and economic development. For example, over the past eight years some 7,200 construction projects were carried out in Cuba in the areas of heath care, education, culture, and sports. Included in this effort were 1,104 schools, residential buildings for teachers, a network of polytechnic education centers, the inaugurating of the University of Information Technology, the refurbishing and remodeling of 250 health-care centers, and the construction and modernization of several hospitals.[19] In 2007 the government built over 50,000 new housing units across the island. According to the government, construction plans for 2008 prioritized the building of houses and the repair of roads, among other items.

The new housing projects are extremely important. Cuba suffers from both a housing shortage and poor housing conditions. These are daunting problems that will not be easily solved. For example, while the new buildings will help with the housing shortage, this effort will not have an impact on the poor condition of existing housing units. At the same time, the symbolic value of these measures is incalculable. They demonstrate that the government cares about the people and is prioritizing their concerns.

Recognizing the demand for increased consumer items among the masses, the government has also authorized the unrestricted sale of computers, cell phones, DVD and video players, and, beginning next year, air conditioners. The availability of these electrical devices will not affect the lives of most *Cubanos*. For example, cell phones are extremely expensive, and only a handful of *Cubanos* will be able to afford computers, and even fewer will be able to afford Internet access. Many of the video and DVD recorders may well fall into the hands of enterprising *Cubanos*, who will use them to record pirated movies and music videos for rental or sale on the black market. Moreover, although *Cubanos* can now stay in tourist hotels, only a very few will be able to afford it. Regardless, these efforts will generate good will and provide evidence that the government is attempting to improve Cubans' access to consumer goods.

Every effort to improve everyday life and culture in neighborhoods, including symbolic measures, strengthens the government by reinforcing its popular base. For instance, the regime knows that people must do many "illegal" things in order to make ends meet. So, it has adopted a tolerant attitude toward many of these legal transgressions. For example, the black market has been a useful tool for the *rebeldes* because it has helped ordinary *Cubanos* grapple successfully with economic dire straits. Ana Julia Jatar-Hausmann provides an insightful example of how bartering and black-market activities facilitated everyday life prior to the Special Period. In need of coffee, a well-educated *habanero* turns to her husband and suggests that he should get in touch with their "red market" contact, Marino. "We are running out of coffee and our next ration isn't due for two weeks. Tell him we have a bottle of rum to trade with the Russians, for coffee. But be firm with him, you know how these Russians are. They think we're all stupid. We want at least three pounds of coffee for that bottle. If not, we can get a better deal somewhere else in the black market." "Red markets" were special stores where the Soviets stationed in Cuba bought goods, and they would, when it suited their purposes, resell certain items to the Cubans. The islanders paid for these goods in pesos or in rum. Typically, the rum came from illegally processed sugarcane in the countryside.[20]

The government knows about these illegal deals. However, by making it possible for the people to buy and sell items that are not easily obtained in state-run facilities, it created critical outlets in times of stress. Today, it is still possible to get almost anything from the black market, including DVD players, movies, clothes, meat, and the like. The availability of goods in the formal and informal markets explains in part why there have been no food or consumer riots in Cuba. Simply put, the black market lends the government a helping hand. For these reasons the *rebeldes* tolerate illegal markets and other forms of "hustling."

This means also that Raúl must be very careful as he moves Cuba toward a more rationalized and efficient economy and governance structure. The disruption or elimination of some of these delicate informal elements of neighborhood life could create severe social dislocations and mass unrest. The blending of formal societal structures and the informal mechanism of neighborhood life is what enables *Cubanos* to survive the city and to make ends meet. This unconventional and inefficient system works; it makes life easier for the masses, while enabling the government to retain popular support. Careless or uninformed tampering with such informal structures could disrupt the balance and produce serious negative outcomes. Thus, as Cuba streamlines and moves toward a more efficient government, it must still cautiously manage the interplay between the informal and formal economy.

## Culture

The forces of consumerism will continue to challenge revolutionary culture. Fidel was intensely aware of the importance of mobilizing the nation's youth in support of national goals and aspirations. Thus the *rebeldes* chose to use young people to attack the problems confronting youth and the society as a whole. With this in mind, in 1999, they launched the Battle of Ideas movement. A central component of the movement was the establishment of a network of emergency training schools *(escuelas emergentes)* in five specific areas: social work, primary teaching, nursing, cultural education, and information technology.[21]

The new campaign grew out of awareness that Cuba's social problems had worsened since 1990 and that they needed immediate attention. Most important, the government believed that the talents of young people were being under-utilized and that youth itself could be an important force in the ideological struggle to win back *Cubanos*, especially the young, to the Revolution. They also realized that this approach would enable them to put thousands of young people to work in meaningful jobs. A brief look at the establishment of the School of Social Work in Havana provides insight into one aspect of this Battle of Ideas movement.

In July 2001 Fidel Castro asked the president of the University Student Federation, Hassan Pérez Casabona, to postpone the usual summer volunteer brigades and start addressing socioeconomic problems in three Havana communities (Cerro, Plaza, and Centro Habana). This led to the establishment of the Brigadas Estudiantiles de Trabajo Social (Brigade of Student Social Workers) and the creation of a School of Social Work in Cojímer. The goal of the school was twofold. The first part was to create groups of young social workers who would return to their communities and engage residents, especially young people, in finding solutions to the problems they faced. The second part was to provide young people with jobs that had upward social mobility. For example, students participating in the social-work program could enroll in any university course and could eventually complete their degree. By mid 2004 there were twenty-one thousand graduates of the Cuban social-work program.

A similar development pattern appeared in *escuelas emergentes* in other target areas. The *rebeldes* were clearly aware of the importance of reinforcing the ideals that drive the Revolution and the necessity of continually reframing and linking these ideals to young people. How successful these efforts are remains to be seen. For example, there are ongoing complaints about the lack of experience of young teachers in the primary schools and young doctors and nurses in the family and nurse clinics. There is also ongoing grumbling about the extent of humanitarian aid offered to other countries, particularly when it is perceived to detract from domestic programs and activities.

These issues notwithstanding, what is important is government recognition of the need to engage in a Battle of Ideas with the people, especially the youth. Concurrently, it recognizes the importance of creating a forum where people can voice their opposition to governmental policies and programs that concern them. This openness appears to be an important feature of the Raúl Castro regime. In an interview Elíades Acosta, head of the Department of Culture of the

Central Committee of the Communist Party of Cuba, explained the government's viewpoint on criticism.

> There's the abuse of institutional practices to limit criticism. We cannot ignore that—for many reasons and for a long time—questions became a nuisance. True, the enemy uses our errors and our criticism. . . . Also, it uses the empty spaces we leave. Criticism can help solve our problems; silences never solve anything. Asked to choose, we opt for criticism. We must abandon the practice of shushing down the problems, which does not help the Revolution but instead protects posts or postures that are harmful to the ethical climate of society.[22]

An ongoing struggle for the hearts and minds of the Cuban people is occurring at two levels. At one level there is the Battle of Ideas, and at the other level there is the emphasis on criticism and the rectification of mistakes. The paramount goal is to involve *Cubanos* in the struggle to reform Cuban society while keeping them wedded to the principles of the Revolution. This method highlights the flexibility of the *rebeldes*. Cuba does not currently and never has approached governance in a dogmatic or rigid manner. It has relied upon and survived through its capacity to adapt and change, to approach problem solving in a very creative manner, and this explains to a significant degree the regime's ability to endure.

## A Final Note

In the conclusion of *Children on the Streets of the Americas*, Roslyn Arlin Mickelson says, "The presence of homeless and street children within sight of the skyscrapers, museums, and luxury apartments of great North and South American cities exposes the contradictions between the concentration of wealth and the intensification of poverty and accompanying globalization."[23] From this vantage point the importance of Cuba's quest to build a people-centered society becomes more apparent. Yet, because of ideological biases, many Cuba watchers have trouble assessing Cuba through an objective lens, or at the very least, acknowledging the biases that frame their view.

In the late nineteeth century an ideological duality emerged between the *clases populares* and *clases económicas* over the type of society that should be built after the revolution against Spain. The popular classes wanted to create a people-centered society based on the principles of solidarity, reciprocity, the equitable distribution of wealth, and socioeconomic justice. The elites had another vision. Therefore, from the late nineteenth century to the present, an internal struggle in Cuba has been waged between these conflicting visions of the nation. Today, *Cubanos* throughout the diaspora, including Miami Cubans, are participants in this ongoing ideological struggle.

This is the "real" fight taking place behind the socialism versus capitalism debate, and it should be acknowledged as such. At issue here is the subtle ideological bias that most often drives Cuban studies. This bias frames and conceptualizes issues, dictates the subject of the research as well as what research questions are posed, and informs the way that evidence is presented and interpreted. Moreover, not only is the ideological bias subtle, but sadly it often represents the unintentional action of scholars who have failed to recognize how their own values shape their research. Yet, while the ideological bias might be subtle, unconscious, and largely unintended, it is unmistakably clear and omnipresent in Cuban studies. By admitting that it is problematic, we can start the important and more useful process of moving beyond neo–Cold War studies of Cuban society.

"Cuba is no paradise," as one young social worker reflected. It is a poor nation with a host of daunting problems, but it is nevertheless pursuing the laudable goal of building a people-centered society situated in a globalized world where poverty, disease, violence, and hopelessness are commonplace. The findings of *Inside El Barrio* indicate that Cuba, with all of its imperfections, is a society striving to meet the most important challenges any nation faces, those outlined in September 2005 by Kofi Annan, former United Nations secretary-general, in his report to the General Assembly entitled *In Larger Freedom*:

> The notion of larger freedom also encapsulates the idea that development, security and human rights go hand in hand. . . . Even if he can vote to choose his rulers, a young man with AIDS who cannot read or write and lives on the brink of starvation is not truly free. Equally, even if she earns enough to live, a woman who lives in the shadow of daily violence and has no say in how her country is run is not truly free.

# Notes

## Prologue

1. Hershberg, *Philadelphia*, 1–29.
2. Sampson, Morenoff, and Gannon-Rowley, "Assessing 'Neighborhood Effects.'"
3. Johnson and Onwuegbuzie, "Mixed Methods Research."
4. Faugier and Sargeant, "Sampling Hard to Reach Populations."

## 1 The Unfinished Revolution

1. Poyo, "Evolution of Cuban Separatist Thought," 494.
2. Helg, *Our Rightful Share*, 78n124, 269.
3. Ibid., 59.
4. Scott, *The Moral Economy of the Peasant*, 31–32.
5. Howard, *Changing History*, 131–32.
6. Langley, *The Cuban Policy of the United States*, 1–19.
7. Jenks, *Our Cuban Colony*, 7–17.
8. U.S. Department of State, *Part 1: Papers Relating to the Foreign Relations of the United States 1895*, 29.
9. Smith, "William McKinley: Special Message to the Congress of the United States, 109–11.
10. Foner, *The Spanish-Cuban-American War*, 258–59.
11. Smith, "Document 12: Joint Resolution of Congress, 111–12.
12. Hitchman, *Leonard Wood and Cuban Independence, 1898–1902*, 12.
13. William McKinley, quoted in ibid., 13.
14. Hagedorn, *Leonard Wood*, 260.
15. Leonard Wood, quoted in L. A. Pérez, *Cuba under the Platt Amendment*, 44.
16. O'Brien, *The Revolutionary Mission*, 207.
17. Leonard Wood, quoted in Healy, *The United States in Cuba*, 179.
18. Porter, *Industrial Cuba*, 204–210; 390–407.
19. L. A. Pérez, *Cuba and the United States*, 104.
20. Leonard Wood, quoted in L. A. Pérez, *Cuba under the Platt Amendment*, 348.
21. Department of War, *Report of the Census of Cuba*, 225–98.
22. Santamarina, "The Cuba Company and the Creation of Informal Business Networks," 62–86, 64.

23. Santamarina, "The Cuba Company and the Expansion of American Business in Cuba," 41–83, 45.

24. "Report of William H. Carlson, Commissioner of Railroads"; *Report of the Military Governor of Cuba on Civil Affairs*, 2, Part 3, 2.

25. Zanetti and Alvarez, *Sugar and Railroads*, 213.

26. National Archives, "Letters Received 1899–1902." These records contain hundreds of revocable permits granted by the Military Government and provide insight into the arguments given to secure them. The records document the many different types of businesses that took advantage of this loophole and show clearly the enormous influence that Van Horne had over railroad development in Cuba.

27. U.S. Library of Congress, Manuscript Division, "Wood Report to McKinley on Conditions in the Santiago Province," container 28 (1900), 3.

## 2 This Time the Revolution Is for Real

1. *Life*, "Liberator's Triumphal March through an Ecstatic Island," 28–32.

2. Draper, *Castroism*, 57–135.

3. Knox, "The Restless Urban Landscape"; Wohl and Strauss, *Symbolic Representation and the Urban Milieu*, 523–32; and Lawrence and Low, "The Built Environment and Spatial Forms."

4. Harvey, *Consciousness and the Urban Experience*, 36–62.

5. Foglesong, *Planning the Capitalist City*, 3–27.

6. Pérez-Stable, *Cuban Revolution*, 3–13.

7. Scarpaci, Segre, and Coyula, *Havana*, 53–54.

8. Scarpaci, "Back to the Future," 196–204.

9. Oliveras and Núñez, "There Will Be Reason to Keep Balance," 2.

10. Cook, "Urrutia," 220–32.

11. Gonzales, *About Schemes, Plans and Master Plans for Havana*, 20–28.

12. Lejeune, Beusterien, and Menocal, "The City as Landscape," 151–85.

13. Bertaud and Renaud, "Cities," 137–51.

14. Acosta and Hardoy, *Urban Reform in Revolutionary Cuba*, 8.

15. In ibid., 61.

16. Coyula and Hamberg, "Understanding Slums," 1–39.

17. Acosta and Hardoy, *Urban Reform*, 63.

18. Kapur and Smith, "Housing Policy," 5.

19. Coyula, Oliveras, and Coyula, *Hacia un Nuevo Tipo de Comunidad en La Habana*, 5–16.

20. Torche and Spiler, "Household Wealth in Latin America," 1–47.

21. "Cuba: Havana Battles Housing Shortage." Online.

22. Michener and Kings, *Six Days in Havana*, 29.

23. Peters, *International Tourism*, 1–16.

24. Colantonio and Potter, *Urban Tourism and Development in the Socialist State*, 21.

25. Scarpaci, "Back to the Future," 196–204.

# 3 Inside *El Barrio*

1. Sampson, Morenoff, and Gannon-Rowley, "Assessing 'Neighborhood Effects,'" 443–78.
2. Coyula, Oliveras, and Coyula, *Hacia un Nuevo Tipo De Comunidad En La Habana*, 5–16.
3. Portes, "Social Capital," 1–24.
4. Cuba Project, *Havana Neighborhoods*.
5. Coyula and Hamburg, "Understanding Slums," 18–20.
6. Cuba Project, *El Barrio Household Surveys*.
7. Helg, *Our Rightful Share*, 3–4.
8. Ochoa and Visbal, "Civil Society and Health System in Cuba."
9. Coyula, Uggen, and Angotti, "The Neighborhood as Workshop."
10. Aguirre, "The Conventionalization of Collective Behavior in Cuba."
11. Aguirre, "Social Control in Cuba."
12. Kruger, "Community-Based Crime Control in Cuba."
13. Taylor, "Discussions on the Committees for the Defense of the Revolution: Interviews and Field Notes."
14. Kruger, "Community-Based Crime Control," 105.
15. Roman, *People's Power*, 1–8, 62–102.
16. Kennedy, Rivera, and Tilly, "Looking at Participatory Planning."
17. Castro, "The Role of Revolutionary Instructors in Cuba," 1–20.
18. Berube, *Education and Poverty*, 89.
19. Carnoy and Marshall, "Cuba's Academic Performance in Comparative Perspective."
20. Coleman, "Social Capital."
21. Cuba Project, "Primary Education Survey."
22. Coyula and Hamberg, "Understanding Slums," 17.
23. Juan Casassus, quoted in Wolff, Schiefelbein, and Schiefelbein, "Primary Education in Latin America."
24. Lewis and Weigert, "Trust as a Social Reality."
25. Feinsilver, *Healing the Masses*, 26–27.
26. Cuba Project, "Family Doctor and Nurse Survey."
27. Forero, "Cuba Perks Up as Venezuelan Foils Embargo," *New York Times*, August 4, 2006. Online.
28. Thompson and Gaviria, *Weathering the Storm*, 1–10.
29. Sims and Vogelmann, "Popular Mobilization and Disaster Management in Cuba."
30. Cuba Project, "Disaster Preparation Survey."
31. Thompson and Gaviria, *Weathering the Storm*, 27.
32. Sims and Vogelmann, "Popular Mobilization and Disaster Management in Cuba," 395–96.

# 4 Using Capitalism to Save Socialism

1. Pearson, "The Political Economy of Social Reproduction," 254.
2. Herrera and Nakatani, "De-Dollarizing Cuba," 84–95.

3. Fidel Castro, quoted in Rohr, "Planning for Sustainable Tourism in Old Havana, Cuba," 66–67.

4. Arthur Schlesinger, Jr., quoted in L. A. Pérez, *Cuba*, 305.

5. Jayawardene, "Revolution to Revolution," 55.

6. Mesa-Lago, "The Cuban Economy Today," 5.

7. Jatar-Hausmann, *The Cuban Way*, 49.

8. Pérez-López and Díaz-Briquets, "Remittances to Cuba," 396–409.

9. De la Fuente, *A Nation for All*, 318–19.

10. Perry, Steagall, and Woods, "Cuba Tourism," 141–49.

11. Colantonio and Potter, *Urban Tourism and Development in the Socialist State*, 161–91.

12. Ministry of Tourism, Resolution No. 10 of 2005.

13. De la Fuente, *A Nation for All*, 319.

14. Ritter, "Survival Strategies and Economic Illegalities in Cuba," 342–59.

15. Locay, *The Future of Cuba's Labor Market*, 3–8.

16. Mesa-Lago, "The Cuban Economy Today," 3–6.

17. Fidel Castro, quoted in Espino, "International Tourism in Cuba."

18. This idea of the "Whitney Houston rule" is based on her hit song, "It's Not Right, But It's OK" (Arista, 1999).

19. See, for example, the images and advertisements in the tourist magazine published by Cubanaran, *SoL y SoN*, no. 3 (2007), 44–45.

20. Hirschman, "The Ideology of Consumption."

21. Colantonio and Potter, *Urban Tourism and Development in the Socialist State*, 161–91.

22. Gordy, "Sales + Economy + Efficiency = Revolution"?

23. Cuba Project, "Household Survey."

24. Mesa-Lago, *Growing Economic and Social Disparities in Cuba*, 3.

25. Ibid., 5

26. Togores González, "Cuba," 23–27.

27. Cuba Project, "Basic Needs Survey."

28. Pérez-López and Díaz-Briquets, "Remittances to Cuba," 400–403.

29. Coyula and Hamberg, "Understanding Slums," 22.

30. Mesa-Lago, *Growing Economic and Social Disparities in Cuba*, 23.

31. Viviana Togores González, quoted in ibid., 25.

32. Mesa-Lago, *Growing Economic and Social Disparities in Cuba*, 31.

33. Coyula and Hamberg, "Understanding Slums," 6–7.

34. Alvarez, "Rationed Products and Something Else," 305–22.

35. Fidel Castro, quoted in Yamaoka, "Cuba's Social Policy after the Disintegration of the Soviet Union," 310.

36. Rosendahl, *Inside the Revolution*, 45–49.

37. Ritter, "Survival Strategies and Economic Illegalities in Cuba"; Pérez-López, *Cuba's Second Economy*; Corbett, *This Is Cuba*.

38. Jatar-Hausmann, *The Cuban Way*.

## 5 The San Isidro Neighborhood

1. Oficina Nacional de Estadísticas, *Estudio Y Datos Sobre La Poblacíon Cubana.*

2. La Cuidad Oficina del Historiador de la Cuidad, *San Isidro, La Nueva Imagen,* 3, 8, 24.

3. Coyula, Oliveras, and Coyula, *Hacia un Nuevo Tipo de Comunidad en La Habana,* 5–16.

4. Historiador de la Ciudad de la Habana, "Programa para el Desarrollo Humano a Nivel Local."

5. Rodriguez et al., "El Trabajo en Equipo en Consultorios Médicos Compartidos," 2.

6. Yamaoka, "Cuba's Social Policy after the Disintegration of the Soviet Union," 320.

7. Espinosa, "Markets Redux," 51.

8. Alvarez, "Overview of Cuba's Food Rationing System," 6.

9. I. L. Miller, "Religious Symbolism."

10. Grey, "The Changing Dynamics of Cuban Civil Society."

11. Enoch et al., "The Effect of Economic Restrictions on Transport Practices in Cuba."

12. Ibid., 67–76.

## Epilogue

1. Leftwich, "Is There a Socialist Path to Socialism?"; Burawoy and Lukacs, "Mythologies of Work."

2. Petras and Eastman-Abaya, "Cuba."

3. Ritter, "Cuba's Economic Reorientation."

4. Uriarte, *Cuba: Social Policy at the Crossroads,* 3.

5. McBroom, "Program to Track Global Traffic in Organs."

6. Martinez-Saenz, "Che Guevara's New Man."

7. Betancourt, "Felipe Pazos, Institutions and Retrospective View," 121–25.

8. Fernandes, "Island Paradise, Revolutionary Utopia or Hustler's Haven?" 359.

9. Agarwal, "Cuba's Path to a Market Economy."

10. Raúl Castro, "Speech as President of the State Council and the Council of Ministers."

11. Fidel Castro, quoted in Smith and Schuett, "Cuba Changes."

12. Domínguez, "The Secrets of Castro's Staying Power," 97–107.

13. Raúl Castro, quoted in Karl, "Work Incentives."

14. Boadle, "Cuba Allows Foreign Firms to Pay in Hard Currency."

15. Acosta, "Cuba."

16. "Minister: More than $2 Billion Will Upgrade Cuba's Transportation System."

17. Bourdieu, *Distinction,* 32.

18. Raúl Castro, "Speech as President of the State Council and the Council of Ministers."

19. "Social Infrastructure Boosted in Cuba."

20. Jatar-Hausmann, *The Cuban Way,* 22–23.

21. Kapcia, "Educational Revolution and Revolutionary Morality in Cuba," 400.

22. Fernández, "If Asked to Choose, We Opt for Criticism."

23. Mickelson, *Children on the Streets of the Americas,* 280.

# Bibliography

Acosta, D. "Cuba: Economic Changes, Not If or When, but How" (2008). Available online.

Acosta, M., and J. E. Hardoy. *Urban Reform in Revolutionary Cuba.* Translated by M. Bochner. ARP Occasional Papers. New Haven, CT: Yale University, 1973.

Agarwal, C. "Cuba's Path to a Market Economy: Washington Consensus, Doi Moi, or Reforma á la Cubana?" Proceedings of the Fourteenth Annual Meeting of the Association for the Study of the Cuban Economy: *Cuba in Transition,* 2004.

Aguirre, B. E. "The Conventionalization of Collective Behavior in Cuba." *The American Journal of Sociology* 90, no. 3 (1984): 541–66.

———. "Social Control in Cuba." *Latin American Politics and Society* 44, no. 2 (2002): 67–98.

Aguirre, B. E., and R. J. Vichot. "The Reliability of Cuba's Educational Statistics." *Comparative Education Review* 42, no. 2 (1998): 118–38.

Aitken, S. C. "Local Evaluations of Neighborhood Change." *Annals of the Association of American Geographers* 80, no. 2 (1990): 247–67.

Alba, R. D., et al. "Neighborhood Change under Conditions of Mass Immigration: The New York City Region, 1970–1990." *International Migration Review* 29, no. 3 (1995): 625–56.

Allen, E., ed. *José Martí: Selected Writings.* London: Penguin, 2002.

Almanoz, A. "The Garden City in Early Twentieth-Century Latin America." *Urban History* 31, no. 3 (2004): 437–52.

Alvarez, J. "Overview of Cuba's Food Rationing System." *Extension Data Information Source* (EDIS) FE482 (2004): 1–6.

———. "Rationed Products and Something Else: Food Availability and Distribution in 2000 Cuba." Proceedings of the Eleventh Annual Meeting of the Association for the Study of the Cuban Economy: *Cuba in Transition,* 2001.

Annan, Kofi. *In Larger Freedom: Toward Development, Security and Human Rights for All: Report of the Secretary-General.* New York: United Nations, 2005.

Appleyard, D. "Livable Streets: Protected Neighborhoods?" *Annals of the American Academy of Political and Social Science* 451 (1980): 106–17.

Arnould, E. J., and C. J. Thompson. "Consumer Culture Theory (CCT): Twenty Years of Research." *The Journal of Consumer Research* 31, no. 4 (2005): 868–82.

Ayala, C. J. "Social and Economic Aspects of Sugar Production in Cuba, 1880–1930." *Latin American Research Review* 30, no. 1 (1995): 95–124.

Bandell, B. "Census Highlights Miami Poverty, Lower Palm Beach Wages" (2005). Available online.

Betancourt, R. R. "Felipe Pazos, Institutions and Retrospective View of 'Problemas Económicos de Cuba en El Período de Transición.'" Proceedings of the Eleventh Annual Meeting of the Association for the Study of the Cuban Economy: *Cuba in Transition*, 2001.

Berelowitz, J. A. "Review: Protecting High Culture in Los Angeles: MOCA and the Ideology of Urban Redevelopment." *Oxford Art Journal* 16, no. 1 (1993): 149–57.

Bertaud, A., and B. Renaud. "Socialist Cities without Land Markets." *Journal of Urban Economics* 41, no. 1 (1997): 137–51.

Berube, M. R. *Education and Poverty: Effective Schooling in the United States and Cuba*. Westport, CT: Greenwood Press, 1984.

Boadle, A. "Cuba Allows Foreign Firms to Pay in Hard Currency" (2007). Available online.

Bohl, C. C. "New Urbanism and the City: Potential Applications and Implications for Distressed Inner-City Neighborhoods." *Housing Policy Debate* 11, no. 4 (2000): 761–801.

Bonilla-Silva, E. "We Are All Americans! The Latin Americanization of Racial Stratification in the USA." *Race and Society* 5, no. 1 (2002): 3–16.

Borchert, J. *Alley Life in Washington: Family, Community, Religion, and Folklife in the City, 1850–1970*. Urbana: University of Illinois Press, 1980.

Borgmann, A. "The Moral Complexion of Consumption." *The Journal of Consumer Research* 26, no. 4 (2000): 418–22.

Bourdieu, P. *Distinction: A Social Critique of the Judgment of Taste*. Cambridge, MA: Harvard University Press, 1984.

Bray, D. W., and M. W. Bray. "Introduction: The Cuban Revolution and World Change." *Latin American Perspectives* 29, no. 3 (2002): 3–17.

Bretos, M. A. "Imaging Cuba under the American Flag: Charles Edward Doty in Havana, 1899–1902." *The Journal of Decorative and Propaganda Arts* 22 (1996): 82–103.

Briquets, S. D. "Demographic and Related Determinants of Recent Cuban Emigration." *International Migration Review* 17, no. 1 (1983): 95–119.

Brundenius, C. *Economic Growth, Basic Needs, and Income Distribution in Revolutionary Cuba*. Lund, Sweden: Lund University, Research Policy Institute, 1981.

Brundenius, C., and M. Lundahl. *Development Strategies and Basic Needs in Latin America: Challenges for the 1980s*. Boulder, CO: Westview Press, 1982.

Bumpass, L., and H. H. Lu. "Trends in Cohabitation and Implications for Children's Family Contexts in the United States." *Population Studies* 54, no. 1 (2000): 29–41.

Bunck, J. M. *Fidel Castro and the Quest for a Revolutionary Culture in Cuba*. University Park: Pennsylvania State University Press, 1994.

Burawoy, M., and J. Lukacs. "Mythologies of Work: A Comparison of Firms in State Socialism and Advanced Capitalism." *American Sociological Review* 50, no. 6 (1985): 723–37.

Burchardt, H. J. "Contours of the Future: The New Social Dynamics in Cuba." *Latin American Perspectives* 29, no. 3 (2002): 57–74.

Burgess, E. W. *The Urban Community*. Chicago: University of Chicago Press, 1925.

Buscaglia-Salgado, José F. *Undoing Empire: Race and Nation in the Mulatto Caribbean*. Minneapolis: University of Minnesota Press, 2003.

Butterworth, D. *The People of Buena Ventura: Relocation of Slum Dwellers in Postrevolutionary Cuba*. Urbana: University of Illinois Press, 1980.

Corzo, M. A. G. "Housing Cooperatives: Possible Roles in Havana's Residential Sector." Proceedings of the Fifteenth Annual Meeting of the Association for the Study of Cuban Economy: *Cuba in Transition*, 2005.

Carley, R. *Cuba: 400 Years of Architectural Heritage*. New York: Whitney Library of Design, 2000.

Carnoy, M., J. Samoff. *Education and Social Transition in the Third World*. Princeton, NJ: Princeton University Press, 1990.

Carnoy, M. A., and J. Marshall. "Cuba's Academic Performance in Comparative Perspective." *Comparative Education Review* 49 (2005): 230–61.

Carr, B. "Identity, Class, and Nation: Black Immigrant Workers, Cuban Communism, and the Sugar Insurgency, 1925–1934." *The Hispanic American Historical Review* 78, no. 1 (1998): 83–116.

Casanovas, J. *Bread or Bullets! Urban Labor and Spanish Colonialism in Cuba, 1850–1898*. Pittsburgh: University of Pittsburgh Press, 1998.

Castro, Fidel. "The Role of Revolutionary Instructors in Cuba: School of Revolutionary Instruction." June 30, 1962. Castro Speech Data Base, Latin American Network Information Center.

———. "Castro Holds News Conference on Tourism." June 7, 1993. *Castro Speech Data Base*, Latin America Network Information Center.

Castro, Raúl. "Speech as President of the State Council and the Council of Ministers, at Closing Session of the National Assembly of People's Power, Havana," February 2008. Available online.

Cebreco, A. Discussion with Henry Louis Taylor, Jr. *Interviews and Field Notes*. Buffalo: Center for Urban Studies, University at Buffalo, July 2006.

Chambers, E., ed. *Tourism and Culture*. Albany: State University of New York Press, 1997.

Chin, J. J. "Doctor-Patient Relationship: A Covenant of Trust." *Singapore Medical Journal* 42, no. 12 (2001): 579–81.

Clark, K. B. *Dark Ghetto: Dilemmas of Social Power*. 2d ed. Middletown, CT: Wesleyan University Press, 1965.

Colantonio, A. "Tourism in Havana during the Special Period: Impacts, Residents' Perceptions, and Planning Issues." Proceedings of the Fourteenth Annual Meeting of the Association for the Study of the Cuban Economy: *Cuba in Transition*, 2004.

Colantonio, A., and R. B. Potter. *Urban Tourism and Development in the Socialist State: Havana during the 'Special Period.'* Aldershot, England: Ashgate, 2006.

Cole, K. "Cuba: The Process of Socialist Development." *Latin American Perspectives* 29, no. 3 (2002): 40–56.

Coleman, J. S. "Social Capital in the Creation of Human Capital." *The American Journal of Sociology* 94 (1988): S95–120, S109–16.

Cook, M. "Urrutia." *Phylon* (1940–1956) 4, no. 3 (1943).

Corbett, B. *This Is Cuba: An Outlaw Culture Survives.* Cambridge, MA: Westview Press, 2002.

Coyula, M., J. F. Uggen, T. Angotti. "The Neighborhood as Workshop." *Latin American Perspectives* 23, no. 4 (1996): 90–103.

Coyula, M., and J. Hamberg. "Understanding Slums: The Case of Havana, Cuba." In *Understanding Slums: Case Studies for the Global Report 2003.* London: UN Habitat, 2003.

Coyula, M., R. Oliveras, and M. Coyula. *Hacia un Nuevo Tipo de Comunidad en La Habana: Los Talleres De Transformacion Integral Del Barrio.* Havana: GDIC, 2002.

Crane, J. "The Epidemic Theory of Ghettos and Neighborhood Effects on Dropping Out and Teenage Childbearing." *The American Journal of Sociology* 96, no. 5 (1991): 1226–59.

Cravey, A. J. "The Politics of Reproduction: Households in the Mexican Industrial Transition." *Economic Geography* 73, no. 2 (1997): 166–86.

Cuba Project. "Basic Needs Survey: SPSS Online Database." Buffalo: El Barrio Household Survey Center for Urban Studies, University at Buffalo, 2007.

———. "Disaster Preparation Survey: SPSS Online Database." El Barrio Household Survey. Buffalo: Center for Urban Studies, University at Buffalo, 2007.

———, *El Barrio Household Surveys.* Buffalo: Center for Urban Studies, University at Buffalo, 2007.

———. "Family Doctor and Nurse Survey: SPSS Online Database." El Barrio Household Survey. Buffalo: Center for Urban Studies, University at Buffalo, 2007.

———. *Havana Neighborhoods: Field Notes and Photographs.* Buffalo: Center for Urban Studies, University at Buffalo, 2007.

———. "Primary Education Survey: SPSS Online Database." El Barrio Household Survey. Buffalo: Center for Urban Studies, University at Buffalo, 2007.

Dahrendorf, R. *Life Chances: Approaches to Social and Political Theory.* Chicago: University of Chicago Press, 1979.

de la Fuente, A. *A Nation for All: Race, Inequality, and Politics in Twentieth Century Cuba.* Chapel Hill: University of North Carolina Press, 1994.

———. *A Nation for All: Race, Inequality, and Politics in Twentieth-Century Cuba.* Chapel Hill: University of North Carolina Press, 2001.

Department of War. *Report of the Census of Cuba.* Washington DC: Government Printing Office, 1900.

Dewey, R. "The Rural-Urban Continuum: Real but Relatively Unimportant." *The American Journal of Sociology* 66, no. 1 (1960): 60–66.

Dharmaratne, P. "The Politics of Dependent Capitalism." *Social Scientist* 10, no. 12 (1982): 40–46.

Díaz-Briquets, S., and J. F. Pérez-López. "The Special Period and the Environment." Proceedings of the Fifth Annual Meeting of the Association for the Study of the Cuban Economy: *Cuba in Transition*, 1995.

Díaz, M. R. B. "La Comunidad de Atarés." Havana: Grupo para el Desarrollo Integral de la Capital, 2000.

Dilla, H., and P. Oxhorn. "The Virtues and Misfortunes of Civil Society in Cuba." *Latin American Perspectives* 29, no. 4 (2002): 11–30.

Domínguez, J. I. "The Secrets of Castro's Staying Power." *Foreign Affairs* (1993): 97–107.

———. "U.S. Cuban Relations: From the Cold War to the Colder War." *Journal of Interamerican Studies and World Affairs* 39, no. 3 (1997): 49–75.

Draper, T. *Castroism: Theory and Practice.* New York: Frederick A. Praeger, 1965.

Dresang, L. T., L. M. Brebrick, D. Shallue, and L. A. Sullivan-Vedder. "Family Medicine in Cuba: Community-Oriented Primary Care and Complementary and Alternative Medicine." *The Journal of the American Board of Family Practice* 18, no. 4 (2005): 297–303.

Du Bois, W. E. B. *The Souls of Black Folks.* Chicago: A. C. McClurge and Company, 1903.

Duvall, R. D., and J. R. Freeman. "The State and Dependent Capitalism." *International Studies Quarterly* 25, no. 1 (1981): 99–118.

Eakin, M. C. *Tropical Capitalism: The Industrialization of Belo Horizonte, Brazil.* New York: Palgrave, 2002.

Eckstein, S. *Back from the Future: Cuba under Castro.* Princeton, NJ: Princeton University Press, 1994.

———. "Capitalist Constraints on Cuban Socialist Development." *Comparative Politics* 12, no. 3 (1980): 253–74.

Edge, K., J. Scarpaci, and H. Woofter. "Mapping and Designing Havana: Republican, Socialist and Global Spaces." *Cities* 23, no. 2 (2006): 85–98.

Enoch, M., J. P. Warren, H. V. Rios, and E. H. Menoyo. "The Effect of Economic Restrictions on Transport Practices in Cuba." *Transport Policy* 11, no. 1 (2004): 67–76.

Epstein, R. M., et al. "Patient-Centered Communication and Diagnostic Testing." *Annals of Family Medicine* 3, no. 5 (2005): 415–21.

Espino, M. D. "Cuban Tourism during the Special Period." Proceedings of the Eleventh Annual Meeting of the Association for the Study of the Cuban Economy: *Cuba in Transition*, 2000.

———. "International Tourism in Cuba: An Economic Development Strategy?" Proceedings of the First Annual Meeting of the Association for the Study of the Cuban Economy: *Cuba in Transition*, 1991.

Espinosa, J. C. "Markets Redux: The Politics of Farmers' Markets in Cuba." Proceedings of the Fifth Annual Meeting of the Association for the Study of the Cuban Economy: *Cuba in Transition*, 1995.

Eyles, J., and W. Peace. "Signs and Symbols in Hamilton: An Iconology of Steeltown." *Geografiska Annaler,* Series B, *Human Geography* 72, no. 2/3 (1990): 73–88.

Faugier, J., and Mary Sargeant. "Sampling Hard to Reach Populations." *Journal of Advanced Nursing* 26 (1996): 790–97.

Favro, D. "Meaning and Experience: Urban History from Antiquity to the Early Modern Period." *The Journal of the Society of Architectural Historians* 58, no. 3 (1999): 364–73.

Feinsilver, J. M. "Cuban Medical Diplomacy: When the Left has Got it Right." *Council on Hemispheric Affairs*, 2006. Available online.

———. *Healing the Masses: Cuban Health Politics at Home and Abroad.* Berkeley and Los Angeles: University of California Press, 1993.

Fernandes, S. *Cuba Represent! Cuban Arts, State Power, and the Making of New Revolutionary Cultures.* Durham, NC: Duke University Press, 2006.

———. "Island Paradise, Revoutionary Utopia or Hustler's Haven? Consumerism and Socialism in Contemporary Cuban Rap." *Journal of Latin American Cultural Studies* 12, no. 3 (2003): 359–75.

Fernández, D. J. *Cuba and the Politics of Passion.* Austin: University of Texas Press, 2000.

Fernández, I. "If Asked to Choose, We Opt for Criticism: An Interview with Elíades Acosta (Head, Department of Culture, Communist Party of Cuba)." *Progreso* (April 2008). Available online.

Ferrer, A. *Insurgent Cuba: Race, Nation, and Revolution, 1868–1898.* Chapel Hill: University of North Carolina Press, 1999.

Foglesong, R. E. *Planning the Capitalist City: The Colonial Era to the 1920s.* Princeton, NJ: Princeton University Press, 1986.

Foner, P. S. *Antonio Maceo: The Bronze Titan of Cuba's Struggle for Independence.* New York: Monthly Review Press, 1977.

———. *A History of Cuba and Its Relations with the United States.* New York: International Publishers, 1962.

———, ed. *Our America: Writings on Latin America and the Struggle for Cuban Independence.* Trans. Elinor Randall. New York: Monthly Review Press, 1977.

———. *The Spanish-Cuban-American War and the Birth of American Imperialism, 1895–1902.* New York: Monthly Review Press, 1972.

Forero, Juan. "Cuba Perks Up as Venezuelan Foils Embargo." *New York Times.* August 4, 2006. Available online.

Fornias, C. V., N. G. Menocal, and E. Shaw. "Havana between Two Centuries." *The Journal of Decorative and Propaganda Arts* 22 (1996): 12–35.

Foscue, E. J. "The Central Highway of Cuba." *Economic Geography* 9, no. 4 (1933): 406–12.

Foster, M. "City Planners and Urban Transportation: The American Response, 1900–1940." *Journal of Urban History* 5, no. 2 (1979): 365–96.

Gasperini, L. "The Cuban Educational System: Lessons and Dilemmas." *Country Studies: Education Reform and Management Publication Series* 1, no. 5 (2000): 1–36.

Gillette, H., Jr. "The Military Occupation of Cuba, 1899–1902: Workshop for American Progressivism." *American Quarterly* 25, no. 4 (1973): 410–25.

Gómez, R. O., ed. *Con Las Fortalezas del Barrio.* Havana: Grupo para el Desarrollo Integral de la Capital, 2001.

Gonzales, M. *About Schemes, Plans, and Master Plans for Havana.* Havana: Grupo para el Desarrollo Integral de la Capital, 1995.

Gordy, K. "Sales + Economy + Efficiency = Revolution? Dollarization, Consumer Capitalism, and Popular Responses in Special Period Cuba." *Public Culture* 18, no. 2 (2006): 383–412.

Grajales, M. Discussion with Henry Louis Taylor, Jr. *Interviews and Field Notes.* Buffalo: Center for Urban Studies, University at Buffalo, July 2006.

Gray, J. *Sin Embargo: Nevertheless*. Watertown, MD: Documentary Educational Resources, 2004. 48 minutes.

Grey, A. I. "The Changing Dynamics of Cuban Civil Society: Traditional Priorities, New Approaches." Discussion Paper IPS-DPUL-0401. *Journal of Political Studies* 3 (2004): 1–12.

Guevara, C. "Socialism and Man" (March 1965). Available online.

Gunson, P. "Venezuela Struggles with Doctor Shortage." *Miami Herald*. February 12, 2007. Available online.

Halebsky, S., and J. M. Kirk, eds. *Cuba in Transition: Crisis and Transformation*. Boulder, CO: Westview Press, 1992.

Hagedorn, H. *Leonard Wood, a Biography*. Vol. 1. New York: Harper and Brothers, 1931.

Halperin, M. *Return to Havana: The Decline of Cuban Society under Castro*. Nashville, TN: Vanderbilt University Press, 1994.

Hamberg, J. *The Dynamics of Cuban Housing Policy*. New York: Columbia University, 1994.

Hansing, K. "Changes from Below: New Space, New Attitudes and Actions in Contemporary Cuba." *Hemisphere* 17 (2006): 4–6.

Harner, J. "Place Meaning and Neoliberalism in Sonoran Copper-Mining Towns." *Geographical Review* 86, no. 1 (1996): 115–16.

Harvey, D. *Consciousness and the Urban Experience: Studies in the History and Theory of Capitalist Urbanization*. Baltimore: Johns Hopkins University Press, 1985.

Hayden, D. *The Power of Place: Urban Landscapes as Public History*. Cambridge, MA: The MIT Press, 1997.

Healy, D. *The United States in Cuba, 1896–1902: Generals, Politicians, and the Search for Policy*. Madison: University of Wisconsin Press, 1963.

Healey, P., and S. M. Barrett. "Structure and Agency in Land and Property Development Processes: Some Ideas for Research." *Urban Studies* 27, no. 1 (1990): 89–104.

Helg, A. *Our Rightful Share: The Afro-Cuban Struggle for Equality, 1886–1912*. Chapel Hill: University of North Carolina Press, 1995.

———. "Race and Black Mobilization in Colonial and Early Independent Cuba: A Comparative Perspective." *Ethnohistory* 44, no. 1 (1997): 53–74.

Hennessy, C. A. M. "The Roots of Cuban Nationalism." *International Affairs* 39, no. 3 (1963): 345–59.

Henthorne, T. L., and M. M. Miller. "Cuban Tourism in the Caribbean Context: A Regional Impact Assessment." *Journal of Travel Research* 42, no. 1 (2003): 84–93.

Hernandez, R., H. Dilla, J. D. Abbassi, and J. Diaz. "Political Culture and Popular Participation in Cuba." *Latin American Perspectives* 18, no. 2 (1991): 38–54.

Herrera, R., and P. Nakatani. "De-Dollarizing Cuba." *International Journal of Political Economy* 34, no. 4 (2004–5): 84–95.

Hershberg, T., ed. *Philadelphia: Work, Space, Family, and Group Experience in the Nineteenth Century, Essays toward an Interdisciplinary History of the City*. Oxford: Oxford University Press, 1981.

Himadri, R., and S. Majumdar. "Of Diamonds and Desires: Understanding Conspicuous Consumption from a Contemporary Marketing Perspective." *Academy of Marketing Science Review* 11, no. 8 (2006): 1–18.

Hirschman, E. C. "The Ideology of Consumption: A Structural-Syntactical Analysis of 'Dallas' and 'Dynasty.'" *The Journal of Consumer Research* 15, no. 3 (1988): 344–59.

Historiador de la Ciudad de la Habana. "Programa para el Dasarrollo Humano a Nivel Local: La Habana Vieja, Pinar Del Río." *Granma.* 1998.

Hitchman, J. H. "The American Touch in Imperial Administration: Leonard Wood in Cuba, 1898–1902." *The Americas* 24, no. 4 (1968): 394–403.

———. *Leonard Wood and Cuban Independence, 1898–1902.* The Hague: Nijhoff, 1971.

———. "Unfinished Business: Public Works in Cuba, 1898–1902." *The Americas* 31, no. 3 (1975): 335–59.

Hood, R. J. "Cuban Health System Offers an Uncommon Opportunity." *Journal of the National Medical Association* 92, no. 12 (2000): 547–49.

Howard, P. A. *Changing History: Afro-Cuban Cabildos and Societies of Color in the Nineteenth Century.* Baton Rouge: Louisiana State University Press, 1998.

Ibarra, J. *Prologue to Revolution: Cuba, 1898–1958.* Boulder, CO: L. Rienner Publishers, 1998.

Imbroscio, D. L. *Reconstructing City Politics: Alternative Economic Development and Urban Regimes.* Thousand Oaks, Calif., Sage Publications, 1997.

———. "Shaming the Inside Game: A Critique of the Liberal Expansionist Approach to Addressing Urban Problems." *Urban Affairs Review* 42, no. 2 (2006): 224–48.

Imbroscio, D. L., T. Williamson, and G. Alperovitz. "Local Policy Responses to Globalization: Place-Based Ownership Models of Economic Enterprise." *Policy Studies Journal* 31, no. 1 (2003): 31–52.

Institute for Statistics. *Latin America and the Caribbean: Regional Report Series.* UNESCO, January 10, 2007.

Jackiewicz, E. L. "Bowling for Dollars: Economic Conflicts and Challenges in Contemporary Cuba." *Yearbook of the Association of Pacific Coast Geographers* 64 (2002): 98–111.

Jatar-Hausmann, A. J. *The Cuban Way: Capitalism, Communism, and Confrontation.* West Hartford, CT: Kumarian Press, 1999.

———. "What Cuba Can Teach Russia." *Foreign Policy* 113 (1998): 87–103.

Jayawardena, C. "Revolution to Revolution: Why Is Tourism Booming in Cuba?" *International Journal of Contemporary Hospitality Management* 15, no. 1 (2003): 52–58.

Jenks, L. H. *Our Cuban Colony, a Study in Sugar.* New York: Vanguard Press, 1928.

Johnson, R. B., and A. J. Onwuegbuzie. "Mixed Methods Research: A Research Paradigm Whose Time Has Come." *Educational Researcher* 33, no. 7 (2004): 14–26.

Jorgensen, M. *Preliminary Inventories: Records of the Military Government of Cuba.* Washington DC: National Archives, General Services Administration, 1962.

Judd, D. R. (1999). "Constructing the Tourist Bubble." In *The Tourist City*, ed. D. R. Judd and S. S. Fainstein, 35–53. New Haven, CT: Yale University Press. 1999.

Jung, J. K. (2007). "Computer-Aided Qualitative GIS (CAQ-GIS) for Critical Researchers: An Integration of Quantitative and Qualitative Research in the Geography of Communities." Buffalo: Department of Geography, University at Buffalo, 2007.

Kapcia, A. "Educational Revolution and Revolutionary Morality in Cuba: The 'New Man', Youth, and the New 'Battle of Ideas.'" *Journal of Moral Education* 34, no. 4 (2005): 399–412.

Kaplan, H. R., and C. Tausky "The Meaning of Work among the Hard-Core Unemployed." *The Pacific Sociological Review* 17, no. 2 (1974): 185–98.

Kapur, D., and J. McHale. "Migration's New Payoff." *Foreign Policy* 139 (2003): 48–57.

Kapur, T., and A. Smith. "Housing Policy in Castro's Cuba." Boston, Joint Center for Housing Studies, Graduate School of Design, Kennedy School of Government, Harvard University, 2002.

Karande, V., and K. Karande. "The Effect of Retail Store Environment on Retailer Performance." *Journal of Business Research* 49, no. 2 (2000): 167–81.

Karl, T. "Work Incentives in Cuba." *Latin American Perspectives* 2, no. 4 (1975): 21–41.

Kay, C. "Community Development in Cuba: The Case of San Isidro." Buffalo: Department of Urban and Regional Planning, University at Buffalo, 2004.

Keiffer, A., and S. K. Wagner. "Promoting Place through Architectural Heritage: Restoration and Preservation of Twentieth Century Architectural Design in Miramar, Habana, Cuba." Proceedings of the Eighth Annual Meeting of the Association for the Study of the Cuban Economy: *Cuba in Transition*, 1998.

Kennedy, M., L. Rivera, and C. Tilly. "Looking at Participatory Planning in Cuba through an Art Deco Window." *Planners Network* (2003). Available online.

Kirk, J. M., and P. McKenna. "Review: Trying to Address the Cuban Paradox." *Latin American Research Review*, 34, no. 2 (1999): 214–26.

Knox, P. L. "The Restless Urban Landscape: Economic and Sociocultural Change and the Transformation of Metropolitan Washington, DC." *Annals of the Association of American Geographers* 81, no. 2 (1991): 181–209.

———. "Spatial Variations in Level of Living in England and Wales in 1961." *Transactions of the Institute of British Geographers* 62 (1974): 1–24.

Konvitz, J. W. *The Urban Millennium: The City-Building Process from the Early Middle Ages to the Present*. Carbondale: Southern Illinois University Press, 1985.

Kruger, M. H. "Community-Based Crime Control in Cuba." *Contemporary Justice Review* 10, no. 1 (2007): 101–14.

Kumar, V., and K. Karande, "The Effect of Retail Store Environment on Retailer Performance." *Journal of Business Research* 49, no. 2 (2000): 167–81.

La Rosa Corzo, G. *Runaway Slave Settlements in Cuba: Resistance and Repression*. Chapel Hill: University of North Carolina Press, 2003.

Lakshmanan, I. A. R. "Help for Venezuela Strains Cuban Health Care." *International Herald Tribune* (2005). Available online.

Lamperilla, Y. Discussion with Henry Louis Taylor, Jr. *Interviews and Field Notes*. Buffalo: Center for Urban Studies, University at Buffalo, July 2006.

Langley, L. D. *The Cuban Policy of the United States: A Brief History*. New York: John Wiley and Sons, 1968.

Lara, J. B., ed. *Cuba in the 1990s*. Havana: Instituto Cubana Del Libro, 1999.

Lawrence, D. L., and S. M. Low. "The Built Environment and Spatial Form." *Annual Review of Anthropology* 19 (1990): 453–505.

Leaf, M. "Inner City Redevelopment in China: Implications for the City of Beijing." *Cities* 12, no. 3 (1995): 149–62.

Leftwich, A. "Is There a Socialist Path to Socialism?" *Third World Quarterly* 13, no. 1 (1992): 27–42.

Lejeune, J. F., J. Beusterien, and N. G. Menocal. "The City as Landscape: Jean Claude Nicolas Forestier and the Great Urban Works of Havana, 1925–1930." *The Journal of Decorative and Propaganda Arts* 22 (1996): 150–85.

Levine, R. M. "Semiotics for the Historian: Photographers as Cultural Messengers." *Reviews in American History* 13, no. 3 (1985): 380–85.

Lewis, J. D. and A. Weigert. "Trust as a Social Reality." *Social Forces* 63, no. 4 (1985): 967–85.

Lewis, O. *La Vida: A Puerto Rican Family in the Culture of Poverty—San Juan and New York*. New York: Random House, 1966.

———. *A Study of Slum Culture; Backgrounds for La Vida*. New York: Random House, 1968.

Lewis, O., R. M. Lewis, and S. M. Rigdon. *Four Women: Living the Revolution: An Oral History of Contemporary Cuba*. Urbana: University of Illinois Press, 1977.

Programa de Desarrollo Humano Local. "Caracterización Y Prioridades Del Municipio De La Habana Vieja: Líneas Directrices, Para La 111 Faze Del Programa De Desarrollo Humano Local." L. H. V. Asamblea Municipal Podar Popular, PDHL de Cuba, Oficina del Historiador. Havana: Programa de Desarrollo Humano Local, 2000.

*Life,* "Liberator's Triumphal March Through an Ecstatic Island." January 19, 1959, 28–32.

Locay, L. *The Future of Cuba's Labor Market: Prospects and Recommendations*. Miami, FL: Institute for Cuban and Cuban-American Studies, University of Miami, 2004.

———. "Schooling vs. Human Capital: How Prepared Is Cuba's Labor Force to Function in a Market Economy?" Proceedings of the Thirteenth Annual Meeting of the Association for the Study of the Cuban Economy: *Cuba in Transition*, 2003.

Lopez, Kevin A. *Entre Luz Y Sol: A Documentary about the Social Effects of Tourism in Cuba*. Buffalo: Department of Media Studies, University at Buffalo, 2005. 30 minutes.

Lopez-Maceo, M. Discussion with Henry Louis Taylor, Jr. *Interviews and Field Notes*. Buffalo: Center for Urban Studies, University at Buffalo, July 2004.

Lowndes, V., and Chris Skelcher. "The Dynamics of Multi-Organizational Partnerships: An Analysis of Changing Modes of Governance." *Public Administration* 76, no. 2 (1998): 313–33.

Lutjens, S. L. "Education and the Cuban Revolution: A Selected Bibliography." *Comparative Education Review* 42, no. 2 (1998): 197–224.

La Oficina Para el Rehabilitación del Malecón. *El Malecón de la Habana: Un Proceso de Transfomación y de Cooperación*. Havana: 1998.

Marquis, C. "Cuba Leads Latin America in Primary Education, Study Finds." *New York Times*. December 14, 2001. Available online.

Martinez-Saenz, M. "Che Guevara's New Man: Embodying a Communitarian Attitude." *Latin American Perspectives* 31, no. 6 (2004): 15–30.

Mathey, K. "Recent Trends in Cuban Housing Policies and the Revival of the Microbrigade Movement." *Bulletin of Latin American Research* 8, no. 1 (1989): 67–81.

Mazarr, M. J. "Prospects for Revolution in Post-Castro Cuba." *Journal of Interamerican Studies and World Affairs* 31, no. 4 (1989): 61–90.

McBroom, P. "Program to Track Global Traffic in Organs." *Public Affairs* (November 1999). Available online.

McCracken, G. "Culture and Consumption: A Theoretical Account of the Structure and Movement of the Cultural Meaning of Consumer Goods." *The Journal of Consumer Research* 13, no. 1 (1986): 71–84.

McKinley, J. C. "A Health System's 'Miracles' Come with Hidden Costs." *New York Times*. November 20, 2007. Available online.

McShane, C. "Transforming the Use of Urban Space: A Look at the Revolution in Street Pavements, 1880–1924." *Journal of Urban History* 5, no. 2 (1979): 279–307.

Mesa-Lago, Carmelo. *Availability and Reliability of Statistics in Socialist Cuba*. Pittsburgh: Center for Latin American Studies, 1970.

———. "The Cuban Economy Today: Salvation or Damnation?" The Institute for Cuban and Cuban-American Studies, University of Miami, 2005.

———. *Growing Economic and Social Disparities in Cuba: Impact and Recommendations for Change*. Miami: Institute for Cuban and Cuban-American Studies, University of Miami, 2002.

———, ed. *Revolutionary Change in Cuba*. Pittsburgh: University of Pittsburgh Press, 1971.

Mesch, G. S., and O. Manor. "Social Ties, Environmental Perception, and Local Attachment." *Environment and Behavior* 30, no. 4 (1998): 504–19.

Michener, James A., and John Kings. *Six Days in Havana*. Toronto: McClelland and Steward, 1989.

Mickelson, Roslyn Arlin. *Children on the Streets of the Americas: Homelessness, Education and Globalization in the United States, Brazil and Cuba*. London: Routledge, 2000.

Miller, D. "Consumption and Commodities." *Annual Review of Anthropology* 24 (October 1995): 141–161.

Miller, D. B. (1976). "A Partial Test of Oscar Lewis's Culture of Poverty in Rural America." *Current Anthropology* 17, no. 4 (1995): 720–23.

Miller, I. L. "Religious Symbolism in Cuban Political Performance." *The Drama Review* 44, no. 2 (2000): 30–55.

"Minister: More than $2 billion will Upgrade Cuba's Transportation System Over 5 Years" (December 15, 2007). Available online.

Ministry of Tourism. Resolution No. 10 of 2005. Republic of Cuba. Available online.

Moore, C. *Castro, the Blacks, and Africa*. Berkeley and Los Angeles: University of California Press, 1988.

Moreno Fraginals, M. *The Sugar Mill: The Socioeconomic Complex of Sugar in Cuba 1760–1860*. New York: Monthly Review Press, 1976.

Moreno Fraginals, M., F. Moya Pons, and S. L. Engerman, eds. *Between Slavery and Free Labor: The Spanish-Speaking Caribbean in the Nineteenth Century*. Johns Hopkins Studies in Atlantic History and Culture. Baltimore, MD: Johns Hopkins University Press, 1985.

Morley, M. H., and C. McGillion. *Unfinished Business: America and Cuba after the Cold War, 1989–2001*. Cambridge, NY: Cambridge University Press, 2002.

Morrison, A. "The Tramways of Cuba." 2002. Available online.

Moses, C. *Real life in Castro's Cuba*. Wilmington, DE: Scholarly Resources, 2000.

Mullan, F. "Affirmative Action, Cuban Style." *New England Journal of Medicine* 351, no. 26 (2004): 2680–82.

Murguia, E., and R. Saenz. "An Analysis of the Latin Americanization of Race in the United States: A Reconnaissance of Color Stratification among Mexicans." *Race and Society* 5, no. 1 (2002): 85–101.

Naison, M. "Outlaw Culture and Black Neighborhoods." *Reconstruction* 4, no. 4 (1992): 128–31.

National Archives, Record Group 140. *Records of the Military Government of Cuba (1898–1903)*. "Letters Received 1899–1902." Boxes 91, 153, 166, 174, 195, 196, 197, 247, and 707. Silver Springs, MD.

National Archives, Record Group 140. *Records of the Military Government of Cuba (1898–1903)*. "Records of the Late Military Government of Cuba: Letters Sent, 1902–1903." Boxes 16, 17, and 18. Silver Springs, MD.

National Assembly of People's Power. *Code on Children and Youth*. Havana: José Martí Publishing House, 1984.

Nazzari, M. "The "Woman Question" In Cuba: An Analysis of Material Constraints on Its Solution." *Signs* 9, no. 2 (1983): 246–63.

Neighborhood Planner. Discussion with Taller de San Isidro: Summer Study Abroad Class, *Interview and Field Notes*. June 2003. Havana, Cuba Project: Center for Urban Studies, University at Buffalo.

Newman, P. C. *Cuba before Castro: An Economic Appraisal*. Ridgewood, NJ: Foreign Studies Institute, 1965.

Noever, P. *The Havana Project: Architecture Again*. Munich: Prestel, 1996.

Núñez Fernandez, R. "Land Planning and Development in Havana City: Two Study Cases: The New Investment Context Regarding Land." Grupo Para el Desarrollo Integral de la Capital, Havana, 1995.

O'Brien, T. F. *The Revolutionary Mission: American Business in Latin America, 1900–1945*. Cambridge: Cambridge University Press, 1996.

Ochoa, F. R., and L. A. Visbal. "Civil Society and Health System in Cuba." A Study Commissioned by the Health Systems Knowledge Network (March 2007). Available online.

Offner, J. L. *An Unwanted War: The Diplomacy of the United States and Spain Over Cuba, 1895–1898.* Chapel Hill: University of North Carolina Press, 1992.

Oficina del Historian de la Cuidad. *San Isidro, La Nueva Imagen: Proyecto Social Revitalizacíon Integral de un Barrio Habanero.* Havana: 1998.

Oficina Nacional de Estadísticas. *Estudio Y Datos Sobre La Poblacíon Cubana,* Pubication No. 35. Rebública de Cuba, Centro de Estudios de Poblción y Desarrollo, 2005.

Oliveras, R., and R. Núñez. "There Will Be Reason to Keep Balance, Urban Segregation in Havana: Policies, Instruments and Results (Working Paper)." International Seminar on Segregation in the City. Lincoln Institute of Land Policy (2001): 1–25.

Oppenheimer, A. *Castro's Final Hours: The Secret Story behind the Coming Downfall of Communist Cuba.* Carmichael, CA: Touchstone Books, 1993.

Oppenheimer, A., and A. J. Jatar-Hausmann. "Cuba's Comeback." *Foreign Policy* 114 (1999): 140–42.

"Over 50,000 Houses Built in Cuba." December 24, 2007. Available online.

Otero, G., and J. O'Bryan. "Cuba in Transition? The Civil Sphere's Challenge to the Castro Regime." *Latin American Politics and Society* 44, no. 4 (2002): 29–57.

Paquette, R. L. *Sugar Is Made with Blood: The Conspiracy of La Escalera and the Conflict between Empires over Slavery in Cuba.* Middletown, CT: Wesleyan University Press, 1988.

Paulston, R. G. "Cultural Revitalization and Educational Change in Cuba." *Comparative Education Review* 16, no. 3 (1972): 474–85.

Pearson, R. "The Political Economy of Social Reproduction: The Case of Cuba in the 1990s." *New Political Economy* 3, no. 2 (1998): 241–59.

Pérez, L. A., Jr. *Cuba: Between Reform and Revolution.* New York: Oxford University Press, 1988, 2006.

———. "Cuba between Empires, 1898–1899." *The Pacific Historical Review* 48, no. 4 (1979): 473–500.

———. "Cuba Materials in the Bureau of Insular Affairs Library." *Latin American Research Review* 13, no. 1 (1978): 182–88.

———. *Cuba under the Platt Amendment, 1902–1934.* Pittsburgh, University of Pittsburgh Press, 1986.

———. *Cuba and the United States: Ties of Singular Intimacy.* 2nd edition. Athens: University of Georgia Press, 1997.

———. *Essays on Cuban History: Historiography and Research.* Gainesville: University Press of Florida, 1995.

———. *Lords of the Mountain Social Banditry and Peasant Protest in Cuba, 1878–1918.* Pittsburgh, University of Pittsburgh Press, 1989.

———. *On Becoming Cuban: Identity, Nationality, and Culture.* Chapel Hill: University of North Carolina Press, 1999.

———. "Politics, Peasants, and People of Color: The 1912 'Race War' in Cuba Reconsidered." *The Hispanic American Historical Review* 66, no. 3 (1986): 509–39.

———. "Vagrants, Beggars, and Bandits: Social Origins of Cuban Separatism, 1878–1895." *The American Historical Review* 90, no. 5 (1985): 1092–1121.

———. *The War of 1898: The United States and Cuba in History and Historiography.* Chapel Hill: University of North Carolina Press, 1998.

Pérez, M. *Local Policy Approach with Community Participation for Environmental Improvement.* Grupo Para el Desarrollo Integral de la Capital. Havana: 1996.

Pérez-López, J. *Cuba's Second Economy: From Behind the Scenes to Center Stage.* New Brunswick: Transaction Publishers, 1995.

Pérez-López, J., and S. Díaz-Briquets. "Remittances to Cuba: A Survey of Methods and Estimates." Proceedings of the Fifteenth Annual Meeting of the Association for the Study of the Cuban Economy: *Cuba in Transition,* 2005.

Pérez-López, J. F. "The Cuban Economy in an Unending Special Period," Proceedings of the Twelfth Annual Meeting of the Association for the Study of the Cuban Economy, *Cuba in Transition,* 2002.

———. *The Economics of Cuban Sugar.* Pittsburgh, University of Pittsburgh Press, 1991.

———. "Review: Two Decades of Cuban Socialism: The Economic Context." *Latin American Research Review* 18, no. 3 (1983): 227–42.

Pérez-Stable, M. *The Cuban Revolution: Origins, Course, and Legacy.* New York: Oxford University Press, 1993.

Perry, M. D. "Los Raperos: Rap, Race, and Social Transformation in Contemporary Cuba." Department of Anthropology. Austin: University of Texas, 2004.

Perry, J., J. Steagall, and L. Woods. "Cuba Tourism, Economic Growth, and the Welfare of the Cuban Worker." Proceedings of the Seventh Annual Meeting of the Association for the Study of the Cuban Economy: *Cuba in Transition,* 1997.

Peters, D. H., Anu Garg, Gerry Bloom, Damian G. Walker, William R. Brieger, and M. Hafizur Rahman. "Poverty and Access to Health Care in Developing Countries." *Annals of the New York Academy of Sciences 1196* 10 (2007): 1–34.

Peters, P. *Rescuing Old Havana.* Arlington, VA: Lexington Institute, 2001.

———. *International Tourism: The New Engine of the Cuban Economy.* Arlington, VA: Lexington Institute, 2002.

Petras, J., and R. Eastman-Abaya. "Cuba: Continuing Revolution and Contemporary Contradictions." *Dissident Voices* (Internet Weekly), August 13, 2007: 1–14. Available online.

Porter, R. P. *Industrial Cuba Being a Study of Present Commercial and Industrial Conditions with Suggestions as to the Opportunities Presented in the Island for American Capital, Enterprise and Labour.* New York: Putnam, 1988.

Portes, A. (1998). "Social Capital: Its Origins and Applications in Modern Sociology." *Annual Review of Sociology* 24: 1–24.

Potter, R. B., and D. Conway, eds. *Self-Help Housing, the Poor, and the State in the Caribbean.* Knoxville: University of Tennessee Press, 1997.

Poyo, G. E. "Evolution of Cuban Separatist Thought in the Emigre Communities of the United States, 1848–1895." *The Hispanic American Historical Review* 66, no. 3 (1986): 485–507.

Prestamo, F. J., N. G. Menocal, and E. Shaw. "The Architecture of American Sugar Mills: The United Fruit Company." *The Journal of Decorative and Propaganda Arts* 22 (1996): 62–81.

Prey, T. S. Discussion with Henry Louis Taylor, Jr. *Interviews and Field Notes.* Buffalo: Center for Urban Studies, University at Buffalo, 2007.

Rabinowitz, P. "Voyeurism and Class Consciousness: James Agee and Walker Evans, Let Us Now Praise Famous Men." *Cultural Critique* 21 (1992): 143–70.

Retamar, R. F., and J. Beverley. "The Enormity of Cuba." *Boundary* 2, 23, no. 3 (1996): 165–90.

Rieder, R., and C. Ashby. "Preliminary Inventory of the Records of the Provisional Government of Cuba (1906–1909): Record Group 199." Washington DC: National Archives, 1962.

Ritter, A. R. M. "Cuba's Economic Reorientation." In *Cuba: In Transition? Pathways to Renewal, Long-Term Development, and Global Reintegration*, ed. M. A. Font, 3–25. New York: Bildner Center for Western Hemisphere Studies, City University of New York, 2006.

———. *The Economic Development of Revolutionary Cuba: Strategy and Performance.* New York: Praeger, 1974.

———. "Entrepreneurship, Microenterprise, and Public Policy in Cuba: Promotion, Containment, or Asphyxiation?" *Journal of Interamerican Studies and World Affairs* 40, no. 2 (1998): 63–94.

A. R. M. Ritter, and N. Rowe. "Cuba: From "Dollarization to Euroization or Peso Reconsolidation?" *Latin American Politics and Society* 44, no. 2 (2002): 99–123.

———. "Survival Strategies and Economic Illegalities in Cuba." Proceedings of the Fifteenth Annual Meeting of the Association for the Study of the Cuban Economic: *Cuba in Transition*, 2005.

Robinson, A. G. *Cuba and the Intervention.* New York: Longmans, Green, 1905.

Rodriguez, S. A., A. J. Díaz Soccarás, A. M. Ibarra Salal, P. de Vos, M. Alonso, P. Van der Stuyft, and M. H. B. Borbea. "El Trabajo en Equipo en Consultorios Médicos Compartidos: Opción a Desarrollar en la Atención Primaria." *Revista Cubana de Higiene y Epidemiología* 44, no. 1 (2006): 1–9.

Rohr, E. "Planning for Sustainable Tourism in Old Havana, Cuba." Ottawa, Ontario: Carlton University, 1997.

Roman, P. *People's Power: Cuba's Experience with Representative Government.* Boulder, CO: Westview Press, 1999.

Root, E. *The Military and Colonial Policies of the United States: Addresses and Reports.* Cambridge, MA: Harvard University Press, 1916.

Rosegrant, M. W., and S. A. Cline. "Global Food Insecurity: Challenges and Policies." *Science* 302, no. 5652 (2003): 1917–19.

Rosenberg, E. S. *Spreading the American Dream: American Economic and Cultural Expansion, 1890–1945.* New York: Hill and Wang, 1982.

Rosendahl, Mona. *Inside the Revolution: Everyday Life in Socialist Cuba.* Ithaca, NY: Cornell University Press, 1997.

Roucek, J. S. "Pro-Communist Revolution in Cuban Education." *Journal of Inter-American Studies* 6, no. 3 (1964): 323–35.

Roux Diez, A. V. "Investigating Neighborhood and Area Effects on Health." *American Journal of Public Health* 91, no. 11 (2001): 1783–89.

Ruscoe, G. C. "Moral Education in Revolutionary Society." *Theory into Practice* 14, no. 4 (1975): 258–63.

Sampson, R. J., Jeffrey D. Morenoff, and Thomas Gannon-Rowley. "Assessing 'Neighborhood Effects': Social Processes and New Directions in Research." *Annual Review of Sociology* 28 (2002): 443–78.

Santamarina, J. C. "The Cuba Company and the Creation of Informal Business Networks: Historiography and Archival Sources." *Cuban Studies* 35 (2004): 62–86.

———. "The Cuba Company and the Expansion of American Business in Cuba, 1898–1915." *The Business History Review* 74, no. 1 (2000): 41–83.

Sawyer, M. Q. *Racial Politics in Post-Revolutionary Cuba.* Cambridge: Cambridge University Press, 2006.

Scarpaci, J. L. "Back to the Future: The Sociopolitical Dynamics of Miramar's Real Estate Market." In *Cuba in Transition—Volume 6.* Washington DC: Association for the Study of the Cuban Economy, 1996.

———. "On the Transformation of Socialist Cities." *Urban Geography* 21, no. 8 (2000): 659–69.

Scarpaci, J. L., R. Segre, and M. Coyula. *Havana: Two Faces of the Antillean Metropolis.* Chapel Hill: University of North Carolina Press, 2002.

Schoonover, T. D. *Uncle Sam's War of 1898 and the Origins of Globalization.* Lexington: University Press of Kentucky, 2003.

Schugurensky, D. "UNESCO Report Ranks Cuban Students First in International Math and Reading Tests." *History of Education: Selected Moments in the 20th Century* (1998). Available online.

Schulz, D. E. "Can Castro Survive?" *Journal of Interamerican Studies and World Affairs* 35, no. 1 (1993): 89–117.

Scott, James C. *The Moral Economy of the Peasant: Rebellion and Subsistence in Southeast Asia.* New Haven, CT: Yale University Press, 1976.

Scott, R. J. "Race, Labor, and Citizenship in Cuba: A View from the Sugar District of Cienfuegos, 1886–1909." *The Hispanic American Historical Review* 78, no. 4 (1998): 687–728.

———. *Slave Emancipation in Cuba: The Transition to Free Labor, 1860–1999.* Princeton, NJ: Princeton University Press, 1985.

Sims, H., and K. Vogelmann. "Popular Mobilization and Disaster Management in Cuba." *Public Administration Development* 22 (2002): 389–400.

Small, M. L., and K. Newman. "Urban Poverty after the Truly Disadvantaged: The Rediscovery of the Family, the Neighborhood, and Culture." *Annual Review of Sociology* 27 (2001): 23–45.

Smith, J. "The 'Splendid Little War' of 1898: A Reappraisal." *History* 80, no. 258 (1995): 22–37.

Smith, L. M., and A. Padula. *Sex and Revolution: Women in Socialist Cuba.* New York: Oxford University Press, 1996.

Smith, R. F. "Document 12: Joint Resolution of Congress." In *What Happened in Cuba? A Documentary History.* New York: Twayne Publishers, 1963.

———. "William McKinley: Special Message to the Congress of the United States, April 11, 1898." In *What Happened in Cuba? A Documentary History.* New York: Twayne Publishers, 1963.

Smith, W., and J. Schuett. "Cuba Changes, U.S. Policy Stagnates." *Counterpunch* (2007). Available online.

"Social Infrastructure Boosted in Cuba" (January 2008). Available online.

Sternberg, E. *The Economy of Icons: How Business Manufactures Meaning.* Westport, CT: Praeger, 1999.

Stewart, F. "Basic Needs Strategies, Human Rights, and the Right to Development." *Human Rights Quarterly* 11, no. 3 (1989): 347–74.

Stratton, J. "Youth Subcultures and Their Cultural Contexts." *Journal of Sociology* 21, no. 2 (1985): 194–218.

Strug, D. "Community-Oriented Social Work in Cuba: Government Response to Emerging Social Problems." *Social Work Education* 25, no. 7 (2006): 749–62.

Tarr, J. A. "The Separate vs. Combined Sewer Problem: A Case Study in Urban Technology Design Choice." *Journal of Urban History* 5, no. 2 (1979): 308–39.

Taylor, H. L., Jr. Discussions on the Committees for the Defense of the Revolution. *Interviews and Field Notes.* Buffalo, NY: Cuba Project, Center for Urban Studies, University at Buffalo, 2000–2007.

———. Discussion with Evan Green on Education in San Isidro. *Interviews and Field Notes.* Buffalo, NY: Cuba Project, Center for Urban Studies, University at Buffalo, July 2003.

———. Havana Neighborhoods. *Photographs and Field Notes.* Buffalo, NY: Cuba Project, Center for Urban Studies, University at Buffalo, 2004.

———. Retailing and Consumerism. Reports and Photographs. *Interviews and Field Notes.* Buffalo, NY: Cuba Project, Center for Urban Studies, University at Buffalo, 2006.

———. *The San Isidro Project: Field Notes and Photographs.* Buffalo: Cuba Project, Center for Urban Studies, University at Buffalo, 2007.

———. "The Use of Maps in the Study of the Black Ghetto Formation Process: Cincinnati, 1802–1910," *Historical Methods* 17, no. 1 (1984): 44–58.

Thom, D. H., Mark A. Hall, and L. Gregory Pawlson. "Measuring Patients' Trust in Physicians When Assessing Quality of Care." *Health Affairs* 23, no. 4 (2004): 124–32.

Thompson, M., with I. Gaviria. *Weathering the Storm: Lessons in Risk Reduction from Cuba.* Boston: Oxfam America, 2004.

Torche, F., and S. Spiler. "Household Wealth in Latin America." Research Paper No. 2006/114. Tokyo: United Nations University, World Institute for Development, 2006.

Toro-Morn, M. I., A. R. Roschelle, and E. Facio. "Gender, Work, and Family in Cuba: The Challenges of the Special Period." *Journal of Developing Societies* 18, no. 2–3 (2002): 32–58.

United States Congress. *Congressional Records,* 55th Congress, 2nd Session. Washington DC: Library of Congress, 1888.

United States Department of the State. *Part 1: Papers relating to the Foreign Relations of the United States, 1895.* Washington DC: Government Printing Office, 1896.

United States Library of Congress, Manuscript Division. *The Papers of Leonard Wood.* Washington DC. Containers 3, 28, 29, 30, 32, 33, and 239.

University of Buffalo Summer Study Abroad Class. "Neighborhood Life in San Isidro." *Comprehending the Socialist City.* Buffalo: Cuba Project, Center for Urban Studies, University at Buffalo, 2004.

Uriarte, M. *Cuba, Social Policy at the Crossroads: Maintaining Priorities, Transforming Practice.* Boston: Oxfam America, 2002.

Vela, A. Discussion with Henry Louis Taylor, Jr. *Interviews and Field Notes.* Buffalo: Center for Urban Studies, University at Buffalo, 2005.

Wald, K. *Children of Che: Childcare and Education in Cuba.* Palo Alto, CA: Ramparts Press, 1978.

Wang, X. "Assessing Public Participation in U.S. Cities." *Public Performance and Management Review* 24, no. 4 (2001): 322–36.

West, A., and J. Hughes. "An Evaluation of Hotel Design Practice." *The Service Industries Journal* 11, no. 3 (1991): 362–80.

Wilson, B. M. *Race and Place in Birmingham: The Civil Rights and Neighborhood Movements.* London: Rowman and Littlefield, 2000.

Wisan, J. E. *The Cuban Crisis as Reflected in the New York Press (1895–1898).* New York: Columbia University Press, 1934.

Wohl, R. R., and A. L. Strauss. *Symbolic Representation and the Urban Milieu.* Chicago: University of Chicago Press, 1958.

Wolff, L., E. Schiefelbein, and P. Schiefelbein. "Primary Education in Latin America: The Unfinished Agenda. Sustainable Development Department." Technical Paper Series. Washington DC: Education Unit, Inter-American Development Bank, 2002.

Wood, L. "The Military Government of Cuba." *Annals of the American Academy of Political and Social Science* 21 (1903): 1–30.

World Health Organization. *Core Health Indicators for the Americas.* The WHOSIS DATABASE. Geneva: WHO, 2007.

World Tourist Organization. *Tourism Highlights.* Madrid: UN World Tourist Organization, 2007.

Wu, F., and A. G. Yeh. "Changing Spatial Distribution and Determinants of Land Development in Chinese Cities in the Transition from a Centrally Planned Economy to a Socialist Market Economy: A Case Study of Guangzhou." *Urban Studies* 34, no. 11 (1997): 1851–80.

Yamaoka, K. "Cuba's Social Policy after the Disintegration of the Soviet Union: Social Development as Legitimacy of the Regime and Its Economic Effectiveness." *The Developing Economies* 42, no. 2 (2004): 305–33.

Zanetti L. O., and A. G. Alvarez. *Sugar and Railroads: A Cuban History, 1837–1959.* Chapel Hill: University of North Carolina Press, 1998.

Zuelueta Cardenas, O. Discussion with Henry Louis Taylor, Jr. *Interviews and Field Notes.* Buffalo: Center for Urban Studies, University at Buffalo, 2004.

———. Discussion with Henry Louis Taylor, Jr. *Interviews and Field Notes.* Buffalo: Center for Urban Studies, University at Buffalo, July 2005.

# Index

# About the Author

Henry Louis Taylor, Jr., an internationally known scholar, is a full professor in the Department of Urban and Regional Planning, coordinator of the Community Development and Urban Management Specialization, and founding director of the University at Buffalo Center for Urban Studies (CENTER), a research, neighborhood-planning, and community-developing institute that focuses on developing distressed urban communities. Taylor is the editor of three books and a monograph and has written more than eighty articles, book reviews, commentaries, and technical reports on urban and regional planning. He has appeared on ABC's *Nightline,* and he has been quoted in numerous national publications, including the *New York Times, USAToday,* and *Time Magazine.* He has received numerous awards for his research and neighborhood planning, and in 2005 he was the recipient of the Distinguished Leadership Professional Planner Award from the American Planning Association, New York Upstate Chapter.

# green press
## INITIATIVE

Kumarian Press is committed to preserving ancient forests and natural resources. We elected to print this title on 30% post consumer recycled paper, processed chlorine free. As a result, for this printing, we have saved:

6 Trees (40' tall and 6-8" diameter)
2,097 Gallons of Wastewater
4 million BTU's of Total Energy
269 Pounds of Solid Waste
505 Pounds of Greenhouse Gases

Kumarian Press made this paper choice because our printer, Thomson-Shore, Inc., is a member of Green Press Initiative, a nonprofit program dedicated to supporting authors, publishers, and suppliers in their efforts to reduce their use of fiber obtained from endangered forests.

For more information, visit www.greenpressinitiative.org

Environmental impact estimates were made using the Environmental Defense Paper Calculator. For more information visit: www.papercalculator.org.

*Kumarian Press, located in Sterling, Virginia, is a forward-looking, scholarly press that promotes active international engagement and an awareness of global connectedness.*